# HOW OLD ARE YOU?

## Age Consciousness in
## American Culture

*Howard P. Chudacoff*

PRINCETON UNIVERSITY PRESS
PRINCETON, NEW JERSEY

Library of Congress Cataloging-in-Publication Data

Chudacoff, Howard P.
How old are you? : age consciousness in American culture / Howard
P. Chudacoff.
p.  cm.
Includes index.
ISBN 0-691-04768-5 (alk. paper)
1. Age groups—United States—History—19th century. 2. Age
groups—United States—History—20th century. 3. United States—
Social conditions—1865-1918. 4. United States—Social
conditions—1918-1932.  I. Title.
HM131.C7325  1989
305.2—dc19                                                          89-31014
                                                                         CIP

# HOW OLD ARE YOU?

To Nancy

# CONTENTS

ACKNOWLEDGMENTS ix

INTRODUCTION 3

CHAPTER 1. BLURRED AGE DISTINCTIONS: AMERICAN SOCIETY BEFORE 1850 9

CHAPTER 2. ORIGINS OF AGE GRADING: EDUCATION AND MEDICINE 29

CHAPTER 3. AGE NORMS AND SCHEDULING: THE 1890s 49

CHAPTER 4. INTENSIFICATION OF AGE NORMS: 1900–1920 65

CHAPTER 5. EMERGENCE OF A PEER SOCIETY 92

CHAPTER 6. ACT YOUR AGE: THE CULTURE OF AGE, 1900–1935 117

CHAPTER 7. AGE CONSCIOUSNESS IN AMERICAN POPULAR MUSIC 138

CHAPTER 8. CONTINUITIES AND CHANGES IN THE RECENT PAST 157

CONCLUSION 183

NOTES 191

INDEX 229

# ACKNOWLEDGMENTS

The materials that formed the research base for this book were, by their nature, scattered. I could not start with a list of, say, six archives and have confidence that if I explored the collections of those archives I would have examined the basic sources needed for the book. Rather, almost every source, primary and secondary, that could be used for the study of American social history was of some relevance to the topic of age in American culture. Thus, the sources were everywhere, and many individuals, too numerous to list, suggested places to find useful information and helped me uncover it.

I would like, however, to recognize and thank some people who were especially helpful. Assisting in research, which in part was funded by a Ford Foundation Endowment Grant to the Brown University Population Studies and Training Center, were Clare Fox, Gretchen Adams, Barbara Nunn, and Barbara Baer. Several librarians also provided valuable assistance, particularly Janet Draper and Ethel Lee, of the Rockefeller Library at Brown University; Jennifer Lee and Rosemary Cullen, of the John Hay Library at Brown; and the staff of the Kinsey Institute for Research in Sex, Gender, and Reproduction at Indiana University. I owe a special debt of gratitude to the Archives of the Hallmark Card Company, especially to Sally Hopkins and Sharon Uhler. Jacqueline McGlade, of the Smithsonian Institutions, provided valuable assistance in the form of both photo research and comments on book content.

Though I alone am responsible for all errors of fact and interpretation, several colleagues aided me with comments, criticisms, and suggestions. Most of all, I wish to thank James T. Patterson, whose careful, constructive reading of the manuscript at various points in the project strengthened the work immeasurably. Glen H. Elder, Jr., opened my eyes to life-course analysis and contributed to the theoretical underpinnings of the book. John Modell, Maris A. Vinovskis, and Tamara K. Hareven also helped with their insights, and John L. Thomas, Theodore Sizer, Richard Meckel, and the faculty and student members of the Brown University History Workshop offered useful comments along the way. The staff at Princeton University Press have been very supportive, especially Gail Ullman, who encouraged me from the beginning and provided welcome inspiration as the project progressed, and Janet Stern, whose sharp editorial pencil often created clarity from muddied prose. Finally, I wish to thank my wife, Nancy Fisher Chudacoff, whose editorial assistance and constant support have motivated me at every age.

# HOW OLD ARE YOU?

# INTRODUCTION

"How old are you?" This is one of the most frequently asked questions in contemporary American society. It is directed explicitly at children, either by adults who deem it the easiest way to begin intergenerational conversation or by peers curious about how they compare with each other. And the question arises implicitly whenever unacquainted adults encounter each other. Indeed, age and sex are the first classifications that come to mind when we initially see or meet someone. Impressions such as "elderly man," "woman of about thirty," or "middle-aged male" cross our consciousness as we try to gauge a person's essence.

American speech—and thus culture—abounds in expressions of age. Some terms and phrases are simple descriptions with implicit values attached: "terrible twos," "sweet sixteen," "over thirty," "golden-ager." Others may convey more explicit norms: "cradle-robber," "life begins at forty." Every age carries with it expectations, roles, status. Contemporary Americans automatically link specific ages to specific conditions, such as "in school," "married," "prime of life," and "retired." Moreover, each age and each status imply norms that society establishes as appropriate.[1] Thus, at age ten, a person *should be* in school; at thirty-two, the person *should be* married; at seventy-five, the person *should be* retired. Negative norms pertain as well. An individual is *too young* to be married at sixteen; a woman of forty-seven is *too old* to have children; someone who retires at age fifty-eight does so *early*. Certain ages, such as twenty-one, thirty, forty, and sixty-five, have assumed special symbolic significance, blending various biological, social, and legal qualities into the same year. Undeniably, American society of the late twentieth century is exceedingly conscious of age and its meaning in daily life.

Was it always that way? Has age always been a strong organizing principle in American institutions and attitudes? If not, how did Americans become so aware of age, and how did norms come to be attached to individual ages and age groups? If the commonly asked question "How old are you?" symbolizes our curiosity about age, the common admonition "Act your age" summarizes the rationale for the questions, references, and value judgments that underlie the statement. How that rationale evolved is the subject of this book.

3

EVERY person has an age; it is a direct, objective measure of the duration that someone has lived. Though we sometimes try to alter or distort age, it is an inescapable attribute of life; ultimately we cannot change or manipulate it as we can change our weight, hair color, or even sex. But in the past century or so, age has come to represent more than a chronological, biological phenomenon. It has acquired social meaning, affecting attitudes, behavior, and the ways in which individuals relate to each other. To be sure, in pre-modern and primitive societies, stage of life often determined a person's roles and social standing. Rites of passage, whether they involved the donning of new types of clothing or trials of physical skill, accompanied certain levels of maturity, qualifying the individual for new kinds of social participation through entry into—or exit from—military, political, or family responsibilities, for example.

But in modern times, especially in Western Europe and North America, the mere completion of a span of years, represented by numerical age, has replaced the rituals and symbols of the past as a means of defining an individual's status. Not only have we attached scientifically defined biological and psychological characteristics to specific ages, but also we have established roles and rewards in such a way that an individual experiences a kind of social mobility, receiving greater or lesser rewards, as he or she passes from one chronological age to another.[2] At age twenty-one a person becomes eligible for certain prerogatives denied at younger ages, and at age sixty-five a person can lose prerogatives that previously had been granted him or her. There are numerous other instances of age-related mobility that are less obvious but nonetheless common. Age has become a substitute for, and even a predictor of, characteristics that society expects to be related to age, and we treat persons of one age or age group differently from the way we treat those of another age or age group.

Just as every person has an age, every society is divided into a system of age groupings. In simple societies, there may be only two or three age strata: children, adults, and, perhaps, elders. More complex societies contain more narrowly defined strata, such as infants, toddlers, teenagers, young adults, middle-agers, the "young old," the "old old," and so on.[3] In some instances, a stratum or cohort may be defined by a single age: all eighteen-year-olds, for example. Moreover, as a person ages and moves from one stage to the next in a complex, stratified age structure, he or she experiences more variation in roles and rewards. The society has different expectations and rewards for teenagers than it does for "preteens," who in turn receive different treatment from "preschoolers" or "toddlers." The same is true for the "young old" as compared with middle-agers or the "old old."

I contend in the following chapters that the age stratification of American society began to become more complex in the latter half of the nineteenth century, and that the age consciousness and age grading that resulted intensified in the first three decades of the twentieth century. This process created much of the social and institutional organization that prevailed through the middle of the twentieth century and remains predominant, with some modifications, today. Over the entire period, consciousness of age has permeated theories and practical applications in the fields of education, medicine, and psychology, and has spread to the realm of popular culture. Throughout American society, age has been adopted as an organizing principle that reflects people's need for ordering and understanding modern life.

Awareness of age and the age grading of activities and institutions were part of a larger process of segmentation within American society during the late nineteenth and early twentieth centuries. These periods marked an era in which science, industry, and communications influenced people's lives in revolutionary ways. New emphases on efficiency and productivity stressed numerical measurement as a means of imposing order and predictability on human life and the environment. Scientists, engineers, and corporate managers strove for precision and control through the application of specialization and expertise. These same endeavors were applied to human institutions and activities— schools, medical care, social organizations, and leisure. The impetus for rationality and measurement also included the establishment of orderly categories to facilitate precise understanding and analysis. Age became a prominent criterion in this process of classification.

Behind the transformations of factories, offices, and schools were even larger changes in human values and relationships. As a result of urbanization and technological feats, the scale and variety of human contacts expanded. Railroads, telegraph, telephones, newspapers, magazines, streetcars, automobiles, radio, advertising—all revised conceptions of time and space. Dependence on the clock and notions of "on time" entered every facet of daily life. In addition, Americans adopted a culture of consumerism. The United States had always been a country that abounded in resources and opportunities, but in the late nineteenth and early twentieth centuries Americans for the first time believed that abundance was a real possibility for everyone. Their vocabulary and habits reflected a new emphasis on needs, buying, selling, recreation, and satisfaction.[4]

These changes related to age consciousness and age grading in two ways. First, the revolution in communications and media made possible the dissemination of new values concerning age to a broader audience than was possible in previous eras. More people were exposed to and absorbed the age norms that were being fashioned by physicians, educators, psychologists, and other experts in the realms of health, education, recreation, work, and family life. The media thus reinforced attempts to order society and segment it in uniform ways. At the same time, the media enabled consumers to increase their exposure to the lives and thoughts of other people, prompting them into comparisons and identifications with a greater number and range of people.

As relentless as it was, the spread of age consciousness and age grading in the United States did not always meet with willing acceptance. Countless fibers of the social fabric resisted attempts to weave them into the pattern of age norms and age organization. As the nineteenth century closed, commentators voiced concern over the increasing numbers of career-minded men and, especially, women who seemed to be delaying marriage beyond the "appropriate" age. Vestigial "island communities," relatively untouched by social and economic change, maintained schools that did not adopt age-graded organization and family systems that defied bureaucratic methods of classifying and ordering society. Members of racial and ethnic minorities purposely avoided the reach of white, middle-class institutions such as the Boy and Girl Scouts, the YMCA and YWCA, settlement houses, and civic and educational associations that were structured according to age criteria. Many working-class people retained traditional intergenerational contacts in their family and social activities, and they refused to observe age-related legal restrictions, such as child labor and compulsory school attendance laws, in order to sustain their family economy. Large numbers of shops, factories, and offices were age-integrated rather than age-segregated. Even some promoters of the newer leisure-time activities, such as vaudeville, movies, and spectator sports, tried to appeal to patrons of all ages rather than to a distinct group. There was, then, widespread resistance to efforts by elites to impose age grading, and the organizations and associations of people in other than age-graded groups and institutions signaled that American society was still, and would continue to be, divided by other social characteristics, such as class, race, ethnicity, and gender.

Nevertheless, age became, and has remained, a dominant feature of American social organization, and it increasingly was absorbed into society's attitudes, concerns, anxieties, and language. Writers of books and magazine articles mentioned age and age groups with a specificity uncommon before about 1880. In their social analysis, advice, and fiction, these writers reflected a strong awareness of age norms—what they thought constituted appropriate behavior and attainments for people of particular ages. This consciousness could be recognized in various forms of popular culture, such as the songs people sang and heard on the stage and radio. The birthday celebration, that seemingly frivolous ritual so universal among Americans today that we seldom look beyond its almost obligatory observance, became an important new feature and reflection of the age awareness that was developing. Age, so it seemed, was not only something that everyone possessed but also an attribute that influenced one's life during every waking hour.

The processes that were generating social change—bureaucratic organization, new scientific and medical theories, rationalization of production, consumerism, falling birthrates, rising life expectancy, and migration—made differences between age groups more significant than differences within age groups. This consequence particularly affected youths, but it extended to older people as well when they transferred into adulthood the habits and associations they had developed as children, adolescents, and young adults. Reformers and policymakers in the late nineteenth century often created formal institutions as an antidote to the alleged breakdown of the family, which they believed was buckling under the pressures of social change. Schools, clubs, and playgrounds removed young people from the age-integrated family setting and structured their lives according to peer associations. These peer groups not only served the reformers' goals of education and character-building but also acted as important socializing agents, imparting values and habits to their members and helping to mediate between their members and the larger society.

THE two major themes that underlie this study are (1) the processes by which American society became age-conscious and age-graded and (2) the interrelationships between those processes and broader social change. The causative links in these processes and interrelationships are perhaps more blurred than in other forms of historical analysis. Though there seldom are single, obvious reasons for the outcome of a particular war or the election of a particular candidate, direct lines of cause and effect usually can be identified: a certain battle or access to supplies and personnel in the first case; a certain speech or the state of the economy in the second. In contrast, the issue of age in American history, while involving change over time, consists of patterns and trends that move with plodding slowness, bumping and teetering until finally fixed on a clear path. Direction is not set by a discrete event such as a battle or a speech.

Most of the following analysis of age highlights the predominant, or at least the most visible, segment of modern American culture: the urban, white middle class. Occasional references, comparisons, and contrasts are made to rural, nonwhite, immigrant, and working-class Americans; but to include detailed examinations of all the sociocultural, socioeconomic, and gender variations would have extended the research and writing beyond reasonable and manageable limits. I do not mean to ascribe exclusive significance to the material that the following chapters contain; rather, I have tried to identify the most prevalent and general developments, leaving variations and alternatives to later or others' research. Moreover, I believe that the development of age norms and age-based organizations was so pervasive, so powerful, that it affected almost every individual and group in the United States. Thus, although social variations matter, the phenomena of age were deeply ingrained throughout the entire society.

# · 1 ·

## BLURRED AGE DISTINCTIONS:
## AMERICAN SOCIETY BEFORE 1850

New Englanders have always had a reputation for their dry wit, a homespun mixture of irony, sarcasm, whimsy, and philosophy that is uttered with dour countenance and twinkling eyes. The cryptic homilies and retorts characterizing this old form of American humor often contain revealing cultural commentaries. Such is the case with a popular mid-nineteenth-century witticism. A "down east" fellow, it seems, was asked his age. The codger scratched his chin for a moment and replied, "Wal, I don't know exactly, but I have had the seven year itch three times."[1]

The inability of this mythical Yankee to reckon his age with any exactness was probably not uncommon before 1850, because age did not play an important role in the structure and organization of American society. As in most cultures, age, when it was known, had simple functions. It measured how long a person had lived and what a person's physical strength and knowledge should be. But as a basis for categorizing people in the society at large, age held considerably less importance than it would assume in the twentieth century. To some extent, one's age did affect access to power and rewards within the community, but the formal or informal norms that age carried for entering or leaving particular stages and responsibilities of life were not nearly as strong as they would be later. That is, knowing an individual's age did not automatically provide insight into that person's roles or social standing. Thus, age was more a biological phenomenon than a social attribute.[2]

To be sure, before 1850 Americans had certain concepts about stages of life—youth, adulthood, old age—and about behaviors appropriate to such stages, but demarcations between stages were neither distinct nor universally recognized. The term *youth*, for example, could apply to practically anyone between ages seven and thirty. The word *boy* had mixed implications, referring as it did to a very young male, an unmarried male, and a male servant of practically any age. Although vestiges of the confusion between age status and social status remain today, with *boy* and *girl* retaining demeaning connotations, meanings were even more blurred in both Europe and America before the mid-nineteenth century.[3] Though age-related norms and prescriptions were not totally absent—most communities, for example, frowned upon a marriage between a young man and an elderly woman—cultural values associated with age were imprecise. High death rates among children (from disease) and young adults (from war and childbirth as well as disease) prevented many individuals from completing a full life cycle. Thus, age-graded stages of life, such as Shakespeare's "seven ages of man," were more often theoretical than experienced.[4] Those age restrictions that did exist seldom were applied. Many states did not have or enforce laws requiring parental consent for individuals marrying at young ages, and those organizations, such as militia companies and literary societies, that set minimum ages for membership often ignored their own requirements.[5]

Like other agrarian societies in the Western world, the United States before the mid-nineteenth century was not a place where age played a vital part in people's everyday lives and associations. The country's institutions were not structured according to age-defined divisions, and its cultural norms did not strongly prescribe age-related behavior. The evidence for this lack of age grading and age consciousness is diverse. Nevertheless, it is possible to learn how early Americans perceived, or failed to perceive, age by examining three general contexts: family life; the larger community; and cultural values.[6] The evidence assembled here is not intended to be comprehensive or definitive. Rather, it is meant to suggest the extent to which early Americans neglected age considerations in the organization of their everyday lives.

## INTEGRATION OF AGE GROUPS IN THE EARLY AMERICAN FAMILY

In the rural American home before the mid-nineteenth century, different generations worked together and depended on each other virtually every day. Often geographically removed from broad social contacts, families tended to function as self-contained economic units. In the fields and in the home, roles were differentiated more by sex than by age, though there could be considerable switching, even between men's and women's functions.[7] And in urban, pre-industrial households as well, the family home economy tended to blend together age groups. Many productive and commercial undertakings, such as boot- and shoemaking and operating small retail shops, involved joint efforts by all family members and their journeymen, apprentices, and helpers.[8]

To pre-industrial Americans, the concept of family itself had broad implications that both flowed from and reinforced age and generational integration. Though the vast majority of kin groupings tended to be nuclear in structure—including only parents and children and not extended kin such as grandparents and adult siblings—the term *family* most commonly referred to all people who lived together under a common household head, and who engaged in some common economic activity.[9] Thus, the family was more than a reproductive unit; it was synonymous with "household" and could include slaves, servants, laborers, apprentices, and journeymen, as well as blood relatives. Such units were large, containing on average about six people, compared with an average of around five people per unit by the late nineteenth century and even fewer today.[10]

Though no single case is fully typical, the family of Sarah and Andrew Williamson, who lived in Middlesex County, Virginia, in the late seventeenth century, can illuminate much about age relations in early American families.[11] Sarah and Andrew moved to the county from England in 1663, when both probably were in their late twenties or early thirties. They already had three sons, and a fourth was on the way. The Williamsons first rented land, then purchased their own farm about a mile from the county courthouse. By 1679 Sarah had borne at least eight more children; a total of twelve had survived, and probably one or more had died in infancy. (The fifth through twelfth children were born in eleven years after a six-year gap between the fourth and fifth, suggesting that non-surviving births might have occurred during this hiatus.) Such a large family was not unusual in that era; around 36 percent of all families had nine or more children, and because so many families were so large, over half of all children were members of very large families. Birthrates in colonial America were high compared with those of other Western societies of that era and compared with recent trends. In the eighteenth century annual birthrates averaged about 50 per 100,000 people; the number recently has hovered around 15 per 100,000.[12] Sarah Williamson's fecundity enabled her to bear children from the late 1650s until her last birth in 1679, over twenty years. It also meant that Sarah and Andrew would still have been raising young children in the 1680s and early 1690s.

High birthrates resulted in significant patterns of family organization. Family size combined with the structure of work to blur distinctions based on age. With so many births occurring, the composition of a family like that of the Williamsons was constantly changing for possibly as long as forty years, first expanding as new children were born and gradually contracting as older children left home. In completed families, the classification "child" could include individuals across an age range from infancy to the twenties. Thus, when Margaret, the youngest Williamson child, was born in 1679, she had three siblings

11

still under five years of age but also three others who were over seventeen. Birth order had particular implications for children. Those born first or second could grow up with parents who were young and vigorous, while those born last would know only parents who were old and perhaps worn from two decades of child raising. Sarah Williamson was past fifty-five before her youngest child was ten, and Andrew died when his youngest was three.

Birth order also affected children's relationships to siblings. Firstborns often acted as surrogate parents, tending younger children when their actual parents were absent, unable to, or distracted by other responsibilities. Lastborns, on the other hand, related to several parental or quasi-parental figures, whose ages varied considerably.[13] A broad range of ages among siblings, moreover, tended to fill age gaps that otherwise would have separated the family into sharply defined generations. In 1680, when the Williamsons had borne all their children, their household could have contained twelve children aged one through twenty-two, parents in their forties, and possibly servants and laborers in their twenties and thirties. Such an assembly not only had a more complex structure than, but also involved vastly different relationships from, a modern family of two children aged ten and twelve and parents in their mid-thirties, with no others living in the household.[14] Thus, a great many early American families did not segment into neatly defined generations. The oldest children might have married and had children themselves before their parents had completed their own families, and the youngest children could have had aunts and uncles close to their own age, as well as much older siblings whose status resembled or actually represented parenthood.

Notions of childhood as a special, age-bounded life stage were much less developed than they were to become later. As in Western Europe, American society before the mid-nineteenth century was more adult-centered than it later became; children were subordinate to their parents' concerns and needs. There was little acknowledgment that children were in a special stage of life and had unique needs and capacities. Colonial American children were dressed as their parents dressed. In New England, for example, little boys, like their fathers, wore doublets, leather breeches, leather belts, and knit caps; little girls, like their mothers, wore chemise bodices, linen petticoats, and cotton skirts.[15] Though infants and very young children were deemed weak in a moral sense, with wills that needed to be tamed, by age seven children were considered capable of gradually assuming adult responsibilities. Children's own physical development and their parents' expectations, more than external influences such as schools or peer-based organizations, determined their progress toward adulthood. No age norms governed how or when children were educated. In late-seventeenth-century Maryland, for example, Thomas Dickinson directed that his son be sent to school only at age sixteen, Robert Coles sent his five children to school at various ages between five and twelve, and William Hawton ordered that his godson be sent to school for just two years starting at age seven or eight.[16]

The process of maturation, however, could last for more than two decades, as youths in their teens and early twenties—especially males—lived in a state of semi-dependence, partially assuming responsibility for their own support but not quite free from parental control. Many sons were forced to remain at home until they were almost thirty, waiting for their father to grant or bequeath land to them so they could establish their own household. Daughters usually lived at home until they married, though many were sent out to be live-in servants in other households, where they fell under the supervision of a second set of authority figures. Thus, a household often contained adult offspring, further confounding age structures and relationships.[17]

If frequent births and children's semi-dependence distended the premodern American family, death harshly disrupted it, but with results that tended to suppress age consciousness and age grading. Disease, accidents, nature, and human conflict snuffed out life at all ages more regularly than today. High infant death rates mitigated the effects of high birthrates; large percentages of American children did not survive the first year or so of life. Infant mortality was highest in the South and among blacks and Native Americans, but even in relatively healthy New England there were around 150 infant deaths for every 1,000 live births in the eighteenth century.[18] Noah Webster found that of 3,378 deaths in his New York Episcopal congregation between 1786 and 1796, 1,440, or 42 percent, were children under two years of age.[19] Life expectancy at birth was only about forty to forty-five years. Once an individual survived the dangers of infancy and childhood to age twenty, the chances of living to age sixty were fairly good.[20] Yet elderly people were not very common in most communities; as late as 1850, only 4 percent of the American population was age sixty or older, and death of a parent or spouse continued to be a primary cause of family dissolution.

The almost capricious intrusion of death upon the family created uncertainties that in turn required adaptations among family members. Death was not age-related. When it occurred, adults and children had to adjust in ways not usually experienced by late-twentieth-cen-

13

tury Americans, who expect infants to survive, who link death closely to advanced age, and who turn to outside agencies when death impairs emotional or economic stability. The fragility of early American family life fostered interdependence among all age groups in the household. In 1770, over half the population was younger than age twenty, and in spite of infant mortality, one third of the population was under age ten. As a result, a minority of the total population fell within the age range of sixteen to sixty, presumably the most productive, independent years of life. Consequently, for every individual in his or her "productive" years, there were 1.1 persons under sixteen or over sixty who likely would have had to depend on the producing class for some sort of support.[21] By 1820, the ratio of dependents to producers had risen to 1.5, and by 1850 it was still relatively high at 1.2. (In 1950, by contrast, the ratio was only about 0.7, reflecting the drastic decline in fertility over the previous century.)[22] With so many children and, to a much lesser extent, old people dependent upon non-elderly adults in early America, the death of an adult family member thrust the remaining members into new roles, responsibilities, and functions that superseded age norms and expectations. Thus, a twelve-year-old girl whose mother had died might have had to assume parental functions for younger siblings and housewife functions for her widowed father. Moreover, the crowded quarters in which families lived not only precluded privacy but also dulled any sense of oneself as distinct—including age-distinct—from others.[23] There was little possibility of having an "adult room" or a private bedroom decorated with artifacts common to a particular age group, such as a teenager or eight-year-old.

The wide range of ages and shifting composition of the early American household created a complex stratification with variations in members' power and access to rewards. The system was not always harmonious or conducive to trust. A father often bequeathed property to his children only on the condition that they take care of their mother after his death, a practice reflecting the need for coercion to supplement filial love and obligation.[24] Nevertheless, a strong, intertwined family constituted the major bulwark against the uncertainties of life. Few individuals lived alone, and intergenerational association generally prevailed over peer-group socialization.

## WEAK AGE NORMS IN THE COMMUNITY

Like the family, the organization and institutions of American rural and pre-industrial urban communities blended age groups to a much greater extent than would be the case from the mid-nineteenth century onward. Churches and other community groups were constituted on the bases of family, locality, and common interest, and their activities were not age-graded. Peer associations inevitably formed within these groups, but such aggregations tended to be fleeting, and age-based subcultures received no formal sanction from society at large. Though groups such as the New England Puritans did recognize distinctions between childhood and adulthood, they did not believe the intellectual and emotional differences to be great.[25]

The major exceptions to the predominance of intergenerational association were early factory towns such as Lowell, Massachusetts, where there arose in the 1820s and 1830s a peer-based society consisting of thousands of young women who lived, worked, and learned together. Their joint activities and common experiences isolated Lowell mill workers from other age groups to a much greater extent than was common among young women in other communities, and they fostered a cohesiveness that could be translated into actions such as labor protest.[26] But such cohesiveness was exceptional. In most places, there was no universal schooling that would encourage the development of youth peer groups, and there was no prolonged education that would serve to postpone children's entry into the world of adult work. Occupations as well as the work setting lacked sharp age grading.

Before the inception of age-graded schools in the 1850s and 1860s, the process of educating youths followed diverse and unsystematic paths. On farms, girls and boys acquired vital knowledge and skills from other family members. Older persons explained, demonstrated, and commanded; younger persons watched, listened, asked, and practiced. Most teaching took place within the context of everyday life, not in classes that grouped together unrelated children and professional instructors.[27] The Puritans, for example, believed every person should be able to read the Bible, but they relied upon parents to teach their children how to read.[28]

By the late eighteenth century, organized schooling had spread throughout North America (though less extensively in the South than in the North and Midwest), but, according to historian Lawrence Cremin, it took a wide variety of forms, ranging "from semiformal classes that met in farmhouse kitchens and frontier churches, to the charity schools of New York and Philadelphia, to the town-sponsored ventures of New England, to the quasi-public academies that sprang up in every region of the country." There was no uniform age of entry into, or departure from, these schools, and it was not uncommon to see very young children in the same classroom with teenagers. And since there was no regularity in the ages at which pupils began school or how often they attended, age was a poor predictor of a child's level of study.[29] The most common institution, the one-room schoolhouse, contained children of widely varying ages, supervised by one teacher whose chief task was to keep everyone occupied. Sometimes groups of children recited or drilled together; at other times children worked alone or learned from a sibling or another student. According to Cremin, the usual inexperience of the teacher, plus the lack of discipline among the pupils, exacerbated the system's disorganization. The school yard reflected the same degree of age integration that was evident inside the school: the various games and other play activities included children of widely diverse ages.[30]

The few colleges that existed in the United States during the National Period, 1790 to 1850, structured many of their activities in age-integrated fashion. Though most institutions offered a four-year curriculum and divided students into distinct classes of freshmen, sophomores, juniors, and seniors, the age range within any one class and within the student body as a whole was much broader than that which would characterize colleges in the late nineteenth century. The presence of fourteen-year-old boys at colleges such as Harvard and Yale was not unusual; neither was the attendance of men in their mid-twenties. At the same time, the ages of the tutors, faculty, and administrators overlapped with those of the older students. Joseph Caldwell, who presided over the University of North Carolina at Chapel Hill, was only twenty-four when he assumed the presidency in 1804. Students and faculty participated in many joint activities outside the classroom. Chapel services, residences, and dining halls combined age and status groups in ways that were to become foreign to twentieth-century college life. Students did organize their own activities within groups such as literary societies, fraternities, and sports teams, but the assortment of ages within these organizations blunted strict peer socialization; and, at least before 1850, campus-wide events were more common as extracurricular activities than smaller group events.[31]

Beyond the education process, participation of youths in adult-like associations brought them into other spheres of age-integrated membership. As Joseph Kett has noted, many adults were willing to accept "precocity" among youths, a toleration that would diminish in the modern era. In the early 1800s, for example, children and teenagers participated in religious revivals to the same extent as adults did. Reform and fraternal organizations often had no age requirements, so that membership encompassed a broad spectrum of ages. Kett cited a Delaware abolition society that formed in 1800 and included individuals ranging in age from the teens to the fifties. Temperance societies,

Bible societies, and debate clubs were open to youths and adults of widely different ages.[32] Though early juvenile temperance societies sometimes set age limits, usually twelve to eighteen, the chief goal of both juvenile and adult temperance societies was to induce members to take the pledge not to drink—a goal that assumed that children had the same temptations and faculties as adults.[33] Also, organizations that later coalesced into the YMCA indiscriminately grouped young males without regard to age. Thus, in the 1820s, when David Naismith of Glasgow, Scotland, became the coordinator of seventy young men's Christian societies in the United Kingdom, France, and the United States, he found that membership consisted of individuals ranging in age from fourteen to thirty-five.[34]

Community activities, especially in rural villages and towns, also blended together individuals of different ages and generations more than would be characteristic of later years. In the Nanticoke Valley of upstate New York, quilting parties, which exemplified social life throughout the nineteenth century, were integrated by both gender and age.[35] "Young folks" were an identifiable group at these parties, but they were not segregated or given tasks different from those of older adults. Likewise, all members of the community regardless of age, participated in "play parties," social gatherings common among American pioneers around 1830. Play parties, consisting of games and songs, did involve different activities for different generations. Young couples danced around a ring, while children and elders clapped and stamped in the background. A young male in the center of the ring would try to "steal" or choose a female partner. Yet all generations and ages participated in the activity, and all sang together, often chanting refrains of the song "Skip to My Lou" (*lou* meaning sweetheart, from *loo*, the Scottish word for love).[36]

Many communities failed to observe laws and customs that established age limits for some activities. For example, few states passed laws prohibiting child labor, but in those states that did have such laws in the early nineteenth century, there were no provisions requiring employers to ascertain proof of age, and most employers ignored such statutes. Also, provisions requiring parental consent for marriages below a certain age went unenforced, and some communities were so indifferent to age that they did not even record age at marriage.[37]

Public provisions for poor relief further reflected the lack of age consciousness in prevailing attitudes before the mid-nineteenth century. Most American communities were more concerned with identifying the "worthy poor" than with defining categories of indigents and treating them distinctly. In the eighteenth century, many towns and villages

17

cared for poverty-stricken citizens by boarding them in local homes. This policy was applied to those deemed worthy of relief, whether they were orphaned, insane, senescent, widowed, or physically handicapped. Young, middle-aged, and elderly indigents all were subject to the same welfare measures. When public, tax-supported asylums began to open in the 1820s and 1830s, they similarly failed to differentiate inmates by age or condition. Poorhouses contained dependents of mixed ages, both sexes, and varying degrees of incapacity. In larger cities, physical abilities made some difference in the form of relief that someone received, but not age. All able-bodied, worthy indigents, except small children, were expected to work and could be confined to a workhouse as long as they remained in good health.[38]

The workplace itself provided another setting in which different age groups mingled. Farm work, which dominated the everyday life of rural families, required joint efforts by all family members. Basic distinctions in tasks were determined by experience and physical capacity, and occasionally by gender, but seldom by age. In artisanal crafts before 1830, rough age divisions—categories based on the acquisition and practice of skills—did exist, but the work environment was not strictly segregated. Generally, workers between the ages of fourteen and twenty-one (though they could be as young as seven) were apprentices, trainees learning a trade. Journeymen, who owned their tools but worked under someone else, usually were in their twenties and thirties. By the time a craftsman reached age forty, he probably had attained the status of master, an independent producer who employed others and owned the materials and the product.[39] Some early manufacturing processes segregated tasks. For example, in the shoemaking industry of Lynn, Massachusetts, in the late eighteenth century, journeymen and masters worked outside the home in "ten-footers," tiny workshops in which they cut leather, tacked soles, and sewed soles to the upper parts of shoes; meanwhile, wives, apprentices, and children worked inside the house, binding the upper parts.[40] Yet in most crafts, such as saddle and harness making, blacksmithing, carpentry, and jewelry making, all producers worked together on the same product with minimal task—or age—differentiation.[41]

Though age integration in the workplace continued into the nineteenth century, shifts in the manufacturing process began to squeeze workers into more sharply defined age and skill categories. In most trades, industrialization effected two basic changes in the nature of the work: a decrease in the complexity of the tasks to which any worker would be assigned, and therefore a decrease in the required number of skills, and the utilization of more machines. The first major consequence of these changes was the destruction of the apprenticeship system, eliminating many teenaged workers from the productive process. As crafts became mechanized, the youngest laborers came to be needed only for the most unskilled tasks—as helpers and messengers—not to serve as a future corps of skilled craftsmen. Moreover, employers in many industries, believing boys to be unreliable workers, replaced them with unskilled, often immigrant, men. The decline of apprenticeship was quite sudden. For example, as Newark, New Jersey, one of the nation's leading manufacturing centers, industrialized between 1850 and 1860, the proportion of white males between ages fifteen and twenty who worked in skilled trades dropped from 65 percent to 41 percent, and the proportion of white males in the same age group who were unemployed or students rose from 7 percent to 27 percent.[42] A similar decline in apprenticeship and expulsion of teenagers from the work force occurred within Lynn's shoe industry.[43]

The process of industrialization also began to force older workers out of some trades. The acquired knowledge and skills that accompanied advanced age were less needed, and the tending of new machines required quick reflexes and peak physical efficiency. Thus, in some industrializing crafts, the ages of workers were compressed into narrower ranges, and distinct categories of unemployed teenagers and elderly men began to emerge.[44]

Still, because the process of industrialization had not advanced very far by 1850 and had affected only a few areas of the country, the setting and nature of most work remained age-integrated and unspecialized. The few state laws that set minimum ages below which children were prohibited from working were vaguely drawn and weakly enforced. No compulsory school attendance laws existed that would erect an age boundary between childhood and the world of education on one side and adulthood and the world of work on the other. At the opposite end of the age spectrum, no provisions for mandatory or pensioned retirement existed that would detach old age from productive adulthood. On farms, men and women worked as long as they were physically capable. In workshops, they toiled as long as their skills and experience were needed or until injury or physical decline incapacitated them. In an era in which most business establishments were small and mass production was in its infancy, self-employment could be found among all age groups, especially older individuals.

It would be fallacious to romanticize the era of age-integrated work. Most people labored chiefly to sustain themselves and their families, a goal not always easy to achieve. Farm and business failures were many, hours were long, and employment depended upon fickle swings of the business cycle. Important transformations that would segment the work force and cause age to become more distinct as a classification than it was before 1850 were yet to occur.

## WHEN AGE WAS INSIGNIFICANT

If considerations of age were blurred in people's family roles and community participation, it is a logical concomitant that social norms similarly failed to reflect consciousness of age. The values expressed by Americans before the mid-nineteenth century seldom included specific age expectations, and the popular culture reinforced the age-integrated nature of society. This culture was not uniform across all regions, classes, races, and ethnic groups; nevertheless, popular writings of the era suggest that when Americans contemplated or prescribed the organization of their society, they seldom included age as a significant distinguishing principle.

The early nineteenth century was a time in which prescriptive literature devoted to conduct and the development of character flowered. Partly as a consequence of the Second Great Awakening, an intensification of evangelical Christianity that swept much of the country in the early 1800s, religious and lay writers published scores of tracts and manuals lighting what they believed to be the path to proper, moral behavior. Some authors tried to replicate or emulate old-world politeness and elitism. Various etiquette manuals directed their prescriptions to men and women aspiring to become part of the upper crust, offering advice on behavior appropriate chiefly in a royal court or in the most fashionable circles. These works recognized differences between stages of life but almost never specified norms and demeanor appropriate to discrete ages or age groups. For example, Charles William Day's *Hints on Etiquette*, originally published in England but available in several editions in the United States, contained no references to age in any of its numerous chapters on dinner seating, marriage, dress, conversation, and general comportment. In fact, the term *age* occurred only once, in the chapter on dinners: "When the members of the party have all assembled in the drawing room, the master or mistress of the house will point out which lady you are to take into the dining room, according to some real or fancied standard of precedence, rank, . . . age, or general importance."[45]

Day's handbook, which was directed at men, was paralleled by the publication *Etiquette for Ladies*, which distinguished between "young ladies" and "aged ladies" but offered no specific age-bounded definitions of those classes. Thus, the author advised that a proper lady's conversation should "always be consistent with her sex and age," and that in dress "the rules suitable to age resemble those which mediocrity of fortune imposes;—for instance, old ladies ought to abstain from gaudy colours, *recherche* designs, . . . and graceful ornaments, as feather, flowers, and jewels." But the book did not suggest explicit ages at which certain conduct was acceptable and other behavior was not.[46] The author also offered no specific age recommendations when advising that at elegant dinners, "young guests are placed at the lower end of the table"; such a prescription does suggest, however, that elite dinner parties could be attended by a variety of young adult and adult age groups.[47] Likewise, *How To Be a Lady*, by popular American etiquette writer Harvey Newcomb, mentioned no age norms in its various pointers on religious piety, public demeanor, table manners, reading material, and style of dress.[48] Newcomb intended this book as a precursor to *The Young Ladies Guide*, but in neither book did he denote the appropriate age range of his readers; rather, he wrote merely that *The Young Ladies Guide* was addressed to those "who have attained some degree of maturity of character, and who are supposed already to have entered upon a religious life," while *How To Be a Lady* was written "for a younger class of females."[49] This absence of age specificity would become uncharacteristic of prescriptive and educational literature by the end of the century.[50]

Norms were also expressed by prescriptive writers for middle-class readers, and these lacked age standards as well. Much of the middle-class advice literature of the early and mid-nineteenth century linked secular virtue with Christian piety. An outpouring of manuals reflected the attempt by clergy and lay leaders to prepare young people for a life of duty, to both God and society. One of the most representative of these writers was Joel Hawes, pastor for nearly fifty years of the First Congregational Church of Hartford, Connecticut, and author of the popular *Lectures to Young Men on the Formation of Character*, first published in 1828. Hawes was particularly concerned with reminding his readers that they were "soon to occupy the houses, and own the property, and fill the offices, and possess the power, and direct the influence that are now in other hands," and that they needed to develop intelligence, upstanding and virtuous character, public spirit, and personal religion to be able to assume those responsibilities.[51] He recognized vague stages of adult life and the dependency of each stage on the one preceding it. Thus, he warned, "He who cares only for himself in youth, will be very niggard in manhood, and a wretched miser in old age."[52]

Hawes's sense of the periods of life and the urgency of developing a virtuous character in youth prompted him to offer a more explicit definition of this stage than was characteristic in the writings of his contemporaries, but his definition also revealed a common aspect of early nineteenth-century age consciousness. In his lecture on the "Dangers of Young Men," Hawes asserted:

> Every period of life has its peculiar temptations and dangers. But were I to specify the period which, of all others, is attended with the greatest peril, and most needs to be watched, I would fix upon that which elapses from fourteen to twenty-one years of age. This, pre-eminently, is the forming, fixing period; the spring season of disposition and habit; and it is during this season, more than any other, that the character assumes its permanent shape and colour, and the young man is wont to take his course for life and for eternity. . . . The time we usually denominate one a *young man*, is the most important and perilous period of his whole existence.[53]

This point of view was absorbed seventy-five years later into G. Stanley Hall's theories of adolescence (see Chapter 4), but several factors show it to be representative of the period in which it was written. Hawes defined "young manhood" as the stage bounded by ages fourteen and twenty-one, a period somewhat broad by modern standards; grouping a fourteen-year-old and a twenty-one-year-old in the same age category today is less acceptable than it was a century and a half ago. More importantly, Hawes's identification of a teenager as a "young man" reflected prevailing norms about the merging of childhood with adulthood. Manhood could begin at age fourteen because there were few if any expectations of prolonged dependency into the late teens, or of the need to protect teenagers from the burdens of adult life.[54] In fact, the anonymous author of the 1852 advice book *The Well-Bred Boy and Girl* fixed the beginning of manhood at age ten, when the young male began to follow adult rules of comportment and assume adult responsibilities for the care of others.[55] Other conduct manuals, such as John A. James's *The Young Man From Home* (1839), Daniel Eddy's *The Young Man's Friend* (1850), and Daniel Wise's *The Young Man's Counsellor* (1850), also defined young manhood, though in less precise terms than Hawes used. These authors usually defined this period as ranging between the ages of fifteen and twenty-five, confirming both the breadth and looseness of age-based parameters.[56]

Many writers of prescriptive manuals for young men and women devoted at least one chapter to marriage. As well as containing lengthy discourses on the religious and social import of matrimony, these chapters gave stern advice about whom to marry and about how to distinguish between flirtation and genuine courtship. Significantly, however, the authors rarely offered axioms specifying the proper age at which a person should marry; rather, only vague notions of age norms were expressed, usually in warnings about marrying too hastily. Timothy Titcomb, for example, counseled that during the "transitional stage" a young woman "should remember that her special business is to fit herself for the duties of life. . . . She should remember that she is too young to know her own mind and that, as a general thing, it is not worth knowing." Thus, he concluded, it is all right for a "young woman" to flirt with a man but not to consider marriage.[57] Titcomb offered similar advice to young men: "Don't get into a feverish longing for marriage. . . . Especially don't imagine that any disappointment in love which takes place before you are twenty-one years old will be of any material damage to you."[58] Likewise, the treatise *Marriage, Physiologically Discussed*, translated from its original French edition and popularized in the United States in the 1840s, argued that marriage was the only cure for the evils of masturbation but at the same time urged young readers to be "more than usually fascinated" with a potential spouse and to give "due consideration" before marrying.[59] Though their authors were conscious of age and cognizant that there were ages when a person was too young to be married and too old not to be married, these and other mid-nineteenth-century manuals lacked the precise age prescriptions—and the implied reproval of those who were out of step with their peers by not following such prescriptions—that characterized marriage advice at the end of the century (see Chapter 3).

When they considered the years of a person's life after marriage, the period of adult "manhood" and "womanhood," colonial and early-nineteenth century Americans made virtually no distinctions based on age, or even life stage. Timothy Titcomb's chapters in his section entitled "Letters to Young Married People" contained no age-related norms, such as when to begin and end childbearing, when to expect physical and psychological changes, when to anticipate maximum family income and expenditures, and the like—norms that, by the late nineteenth century, would be linked to specific ages.[60] *The House I Live In*, a popular layman's guide to physiology written in the mid-nineteenth century, similarly offered no information on age-related biological patterns. The author, prolific advice writer William A. Alcott, organized the treatise in terms of an extended metaphor, likening the human body to a building, in which the skeleton is the frame, skin and muscles the covering, eyes the windows, and internal organs the furniture. In his explanations of how each part works, Alcott omitted reference to growth or any age-related developmental process, except to note in passing that softer bones become hard "after we become older."[61] Alcott's only reference to specific ages was a brief observation that a person between the ages of twenty and seventy, walking forty miles a day, six days a week, would swing each knee 751,200,000 times.[62]

This lack of age and stage consciousness in the way early Americans perceived adulthood is further suggested by historian John Demos in his analysis of the Salem, Massachusetts, witch trials of the late seventeenth century. Tabulating the ages of witches accused and prosecuted in Salem and elsewhere, Demos observed that a preponderance of the women—and a few men as well—were in their forties and fifties, a period identified today as "midlife" or "middle age." But, according to Demos, no one during the period of the witchcraft mania attached overt importance to this fact, because colonial Americans did not recognize midlife as a distinct stage in the life cycle. To be sure, the colonials did reckon age, and if they ascribed any characteristic at all to men and women between the ages of forty and sixty, it was that of fully developed power and capacity. Men in this age group were usually at the peak of their prestige, wealth, and responsibility; women in midlife had their completed families under their care and were at the peak of their authority as mistresses of their households. According to Demos's hypothesis, women and men who held power over others would be those most likely accused of witchcraft in a time of hysteria. Yet it is important to stress, as Demos has, that no one at the time of the witchcraft scare explicitly expressed any consciousness of the ages or life stages of those accused.[63]

The existence of elderly people in early American communities prompted some age-related considerations. The young were expected to respect, and sometimes to venerate, older people, and the literature of groups such as the Puritans claimed that old age was a gift from God.[64] Puritan minister Increase Mather, for example, preached, "If any man is favored with long life, it is God that has lengthened his days." He continued, "The law written in [people's] hearts by nature has directed them to give a peculiar respect and deference to aged men."[65] Colonial Americans thus recognized old age as a distinct life stage, the image of which, as David Hackett Fischer has contended, shifted in the early nineteenth century when social practices and language began affixing negative qualities to the elderly: men and women began dressing to look young rather than old, while terms such as *gaf-*

*fer* and *fogy* assumed negative connotations and reflected contempt for old men.[66]

Yet in other ways, cultural expressions ignored the peculiarities or even the existence of old age. Diaries of colonial ministers and landowners seldom mentioned retirement or reduced activity due to advanced years. Virginia Colony planter William Byrd's diary tells us that shortly before his death at age seventy he was studying Latin, Greek, and Hebrew; dancing every day; and seducing female servants regularly—all without any reference to his age or to impairments in his faculties caused by age.[67] Fiction writers expressed awareness of old age mostly in vague ("lost youth"), metaphorical ("winter season"), or relative terms. For example, a story from a mid-nineteenth-century popular journal includes a passage in which a character describes the difference between old age and younger years by observing: "The old times and new times are pretty much alike. . . . A little more rheumatism, a little more weariness when one goes to bed, and a little more stiffness when one gets up in the morning; that's the most of the difference I can see."[68] Writers such as Henry David Thoreau and Ralph Waldo Emerson made mention of the special qualities of old age, but they, like other writers, never specified the exact age at which or precise ways that the transition to old age occurred.

Finally, reflections in diaries and autobiographies, which often reveal a person's relationship with the culture that surrounds him or her, present little evidence of age norms. Diaries from inhabitants of New York's rural Nanticoke Valley, for example, demonstrate that age norms seldom were used to determine people's participation in family and social activities; young people described their taking on of new social roles as occurring when they were interested in assuming them and when their parents agreed they were ready to do so. Parents, especially mothers, measured their lives not by years but through the experiences of their children and the transitions from one generation to another. Diarists from the Nanticoke Valley discussed the passage of time and the transformation of their lives in terms of events such as the death of a parent, marriage of a child, and birth of a grandchild, rather than in terms of birthdays or other personal reckonings.[69] Because writers of diaries did not intend their musings for public inspection, they may not have had reason to specify children's ages, which they took for granted. Autobiographers, on the other hand, were writing for an audience, yet they also omitted reference to children's and other relatives' ages. For example, in an autobiography originally published in 1848, Rebecca Burlend described in intricate detail her family's migration in 1831 from Yorkshire, England, to Pike County, Illinois. Though her group consisted of herself, her husband, and her five children, Burlend did not deem it important to list her children's ages; she noted casually only that her eldest boy was "*about* nine years old" (emphasis added).[70]

One of the more revealing representations of mid-nineteenth-century attitudes, albeit somewhat elitist, is the diary written by teenaged Agnes Lee, daughter of Robert E. and Mary Custis Lee. Agnes's entries between 1852 and 1858, when she was eleven to eighteen, contain virtually no remarks about age among her many intimate observations. She did not mention her own birthday or reflect upon achieving a new age at all.[71] Such absence of or casual reference to a birthday, common among other nineteenth-century diarists as well, indicates that people did not attach significance to turning a new age or use the occasion of a birthday to take stock of their achievements. When Agnes Lee did take an introspective survey, it was on the occasion of society's new year, not on the anniversary of her own birth. Thus, on January 22, 1854, when Agnes was still thirteen, she wrote: "In one year I have learnt & experienced a great deal. I feel differently too; young as I am I must sit up & talk & walk as a young lady and be constantly greeted with ladies do this & that & think so all as if I was twenty."[72] This observation also mirrors values expressed in contemporary advice manuals: for girls of "right and proper" families, the transition was directly from childhood to ladyhood, with little thought given to the special period later identified as adolescence. Moreover, Agnes and other early diarists such as Anne Morrison Read described numerous family gatherings and visits, involving people of all ages and generations, without referring to age distinctions or separate peer activities at these assemblies.

Though the prescriptive and personal writings of Americans during the Colonial and National Periods show some sensitivity to stages of life and passage of personal time, they reveal that changes in the life course were conceived of in terms of gradual evolution (for example, the movement back and forth between independence, dependence, and semi-dependence and the unhurried assumption of adult roles as children matured), rather than as abrupt shifts marked by discrete ages. The norms and prescriptions that people adhered to, or that were imposed on them, were concerned with imparting a sense of propriety, and age was at most only implied. There was no consensus on the age boundaries of life stages, only vague references to what was appropriate for amorphous periods such as youth, manhood, ladyhood, and old age. And when people took introspective surveys of their lives, they rarely measured their status and accomplishments against some cultural age standard, and their descriptions represented an age-integrated society more than they did an age-segregated society.

THE foregoing analysis in support of the generalization that American society before the latter half of the nineteenth century was characterized by a lack of sharp age awareness, age norms, and age grading is based, to some extent, on negative evidence; that is, the sources show an unconcern with, or omission of reference to, age. True, people did contemplate age on some occasions, and their social organization reflected an implicit age stratification. Moreover, the first 250 years of American history were not static with regard to age; attitudes and customs certainly changed in many ways. By the early nineteenth century, for example, religious liberals such as Horace Bushnell were revising the Puritan belief that God's grace pulled men—meaning adults—toward Him. Rather, said the liberals, all people, including children, experience stages of moral growth and, with the help of religious education, seek God on their own accord. Nevertheless, as the following chapters will indicate, the degree to which age pervaded culture and institutions in these early years was far less significant than what it would become from the 1850s onward.

In the pre-modern social environment that characterized these first two and one-half centuries, shifts in an individual's life course were marked by formal rites of passage on the one hand and informal latitude in role assumption on the other. Formal rites included the donning of long pants or a long skirt, rising from apprentice to journeyman status, and experiencing religious conversion. Though vaguely age-related, these rites carried few if any explicit age norms. Even biological rites, such as first dentition, menarche, and menopause, seldom were associated with age. The process of role assumption, such as beginning to work or becoming a parent, often could be disorderly; as noted above, a change in status from dependent childhood to independent adulthood was not irreversible, because youths occupied a state of semi-dependency. Thus, within many households the status of parent and that of child could be confounded. And though rough age norms were needed to control competition for certain statuses—it was rarely acceptable for an eighteen-year-old male to be a master craftsman or for a fifty-year-old woman to marry a twenty-five-year-old man—such norms existed as traditional conventions rather than as modern institutional means for ordering society.[73]

By the end of the nineteenth century, however, institutionalized transitions were replacing rites of passage and regularizing the process of role assumption. Transitions such as starting and completing school, beginning one's adult work life, establishing a family through marriage and procreation, and entering old age through retirement began to be more strictly defined and more formally sanctioned. The consequence of these developments was a culture and a society that were age-conscious and age-graded to an extent greater than early Americans would have thought possible.

# · 2 ·

## ORIGINS OF AGE GRADING:
## EDUCATION AND MEDICINE

The manifold process that created modern age grading in the United States began with the education and medical care of children. In the Middle Ages, the European ancestors of Americans had little concern for the intellectual, physical, or moral problems of children. Soon after they were weaned, children began to assume their places in adult society. But beginning in the sixteenth and seventeenth centuries and accelerating in the eighteenth and nineteenth centuries, scholars, churchmen, and physicians looked upon the well-being of children as crucial to the establishment of a moral order. As Philippe Ariès, the noted historian of childhood, has written, "Henceforth, it was recognized that the child was not ready for life, and that he had to be subjected to a special treatment, a sort of quarantine, before he was allowed to join the adults."[1]

During the seventeenth and eighteenth centuries, Americans generated a variety of educational institutions. There were religious elementary schools organized by different Protestant sects; private academies, which taught special subjects such as science and foreign languages as well as reading and writing; colleges, which trained young men in the professions of law, medicine, and religion; special societies, which offered lectures and forums for discussion; private tutors, who instructed the offspring of the wealthy; special schools which offered instruction in dancing, fencing, music, and other upper-class pursuits; and Catholic convents for the rich and missions for the poor. Beginning with Massachusetts in 1642, several colonies established schools supported by public funds, usually through taxation. Because they generally attracted only the children of poor families, public schools were tainted by a popular identification of them with charity. Thus, the early American educational system was fragmented and variously organized.

One of this country's major institutional accomplishments in the nineteenth century was the establishment of municipally supported common schools that not only provided comprehensive education for the vast majority of children but did so in an environment that mixed children of different social classes. The story of how American common schools were instituted and how they reinforced the values of the emerging bureaucratic order has been well chronicled.[2] But most historians have only touched on the process by which American education became age-graded, and on the cultural consequences of that organization.

If the early American education establishment encompassed a variety of institutions for the edification of children, the medical establishment organized virtually no institutions to tend to children's health needs. While medical science was making notable advances in the seventeenth and eighteenth centuries, pediatric medicine was lagging behind. Sick children were cared for by mothers and midwives; a doctor was summoned only when family remedies failed.[3] But by the nineteenth century, new clinical studies of diseases prompted physicians to focus more attention on children and to redefine their perceptions of morbidity. The result was a heightened awareness of the age relationships of diseases and a new attitude toward children that American medical personnel helped to transfer to the rest of American society.

## INFLUENCES ON AGE-GRADED EDUCATION

Age-graded education by no means originated in the United States or even in the modern era. The formal education of young males in ancient Greece and Rome usually was divided into three levels that conformed to vague age divisions. Movement from one level to the next occurred as part of a formal rite of passage. Thus, when at about age sixteen a Roman youth exchanged the *toga praetexta* for the *toga virilis*—a ceremony that marked the attainment of manhood and its responsibilities—he also left the school of the *grammaticus*, where he had engaged in the study of grammar and literature, for more specific occupational training.[4]

Greek and Roman schools served as models for European education into the sixteenth century, when methods of instruction became the topic of several influential writers. The most important educational theorist in early modern times was probably the German scholar and religious reformer Philip Melancthon. After visiting the churches and schools in the principality of Thuringia, Melancthon published a *Book of Visitation* in 1528, in which he outlined a system of instruction that divided children into three levels. These divisions were defined less by age than by mastery of certain skills and subjects, such as reading, grammar, and classical literature. Nevertheless, Melancthon's proposal implied a formalized grading system that later educators elaborated upon and incorporated into the school codes of Würtemburg in 1559 and Saxony in 1580. In the 1630s, the Moravian reformer Johan Amos Comenius proposed an educational system that resembled the

Greek and Roman systems and set a solid precedent for reforms of the nineteenth century. In his *Didactia magna*, Comenius delineated three age-graded schools: a vernacular or elementary school for ages six to twelve; a Latin or secondary school for ages twelve to eighteen; and an academia or university for ages eighteen to twenty-four.[5]

Comenius's plan for establishing a hierarchy of grades was not fully implemented until 1819, when the Prussian school system was established. Thereafter, it had considerable influence on educational reformers; especially in America. During the 1830s, several of these educators were dispatched by their state governments to observe Prussian schools. The state of Ohio sent Calvin Stowe, Harriet Beecher's husband, to Prussia in 1836; Massachusetts sent Horace Mann in 1843. Their reports strongly endorsed the Prussian system. Mann, for example, wrote: "The first element of superiority in Prussian schools . . . consists in the proper classification of the scholars. In all places where numbers are sufficiently large to allow it the children are divided according to ages and attainments, and a single teacher has the charge of only a single class."[6] These observations propelled the establishment of common elementary schools in Ohio, Massachusetts, and other states.

A second stream of influential European educational theory flowed out of Switzerland and originated with Jean-Jacques Rousseau's famous novel, *Emile*, which first appeared in 1762. In this description of a boy's ideal education, Rousseau expounded on a new system that fit the process of learning to the natural process of growing up. The book served as a critique of formal ecclesiastical education, which prepared the student for life after death, in its substitution of a theory that emphasized self-realization in the existing "state of Nature." Rousseau, then, added notions of human development to Prussian ideas about graded organization.

Among those most profoundly influenced by Rousseau was the Zurich teacher and humanitarian Johann Heinrich Pestalozzi. From the beginning of his career as a school director in 1769 until his death in 1827, Pestalozzi worked to develop a scheme of education that followed the natural growth of a child's talents and capacities. Expanding upon Rousseau, Pestalozzi asserted that an educator must discover the laws of a child's development and assist nature in molding the whole person. To better conform to the child's organic growth, Pestalozzi believed, education should be graded so that each stage followed logically from the one that preceded it and prepared the child for the stage that followed.[7] Like those of other European educational theorists, Pestalozzi's ideas and experiments attracted the attention of Americans traveling in Europe. The most notable visitor was Henry Barnard, the Connecticut and Rhode Island educational reformer, who in 1836–37 spent time with Emanuel von Fellenberg, a Swiss schoolmaster and one of Pestalozzi's most fervent followers.

But before a strictly graded educational program could win favor in the United States, it had to overcome the existing monitorial system, whose antecedents were English. In the late eighteenth century, two Britons, an Anglican missionary and a Quaker schoolmaster, had simultaneously developed a plan for teaching religious fundamentals more economically and efficiently than ever before. The plan involved using student assistants, or monitors, to aid in the instruction of classes that were too large for one teacher to manage.

Because the Church of England, like other things English, had little popularity in the newly independent United States, the plan developed by the Quaker schoolmaster, Joseph Lancaster, was the one introduced and accepted in this country. Adopted first in New York City in 1806, it spread quickly to most other densely settled regions. Known as the Lancasterian monitorial system, the scheme sorted children into small groups under the tutelage of student monitors who, as "youthful corporals of the teacher's regiment," instructed their charges in what they had learned directly from the teacher. In this fashion, one teacher, acting as a kind of master and inspector, could supervise a school of several hundred students. Though monitorial groupings now replaced the individual instruction of an earlier era, the divisions were not based on theories of age or child development. Rather, they separated pupils according to subject and ability, with the most clever children in each group acting as monitors. First used in the teaching of reading and the catechism, the Lancasterian system eventually was extended to other subjects and by the 1830s was firmly established, especially in the schools of eastern cities.[8]

Not all influences came from Europe; home-grown American theories also fed one of the streams that eventually converged to form the modern system of age-graded schools. One of the most important native writers was Samuel Harrison Smith, whose essay "Remarks on Education: Illustrating the Close Connection Between Virtue and Wisdom" won a prize from the American Academy of Arts and Sciences in 1795. Smith, the editor of the Philadelphia newspaper *National Intelligencer*, which later became the official organ of Thomas Jefferson's presidential administration, contended that it was the nation's duty to establish a system of education "independent of and superior to parental authority." He believed that when a child reached "a certain age," public education should take precedence over domestic (home) education. That age should be early enough "to anticipate the reign of prejudice and to render the first impression made on the mind subservient to virtue and truth." Accordingly, Smith offered an educational scheme based on an unrefined combination of age and subject divisions. His plan divided schools into two classes: in one, five- to ten-year-old children would be instructed in the rudiments of language, writing, and arithmetic; in the other, ten- to eighteen-year-olds would receive more thorough tutelage in English and arithmetic and also would study history, geography, and natural science.[9]

The nation's first widespread age-limited educational institution was the infant school, another reform borrowed from Great Britain. Infant schools originated in 1799 in New Lanark, Scotland, where manufacturer Robert Owen opened a school for very young working-class children to give them moral, physical, and intellectual training before they were old enough to become apprentices and factory helpers. The idea proved attractive to Americans because existing education systems in the United States purposely excluded children from grammar school until they were seven or eight, yet expected them to have been taught some elementary principles of reading and writing beforehand. Beginning in the 1820s, eastern cities established infant or primary schools to prepare young children, usually between ages three and seven, for more formal education. Housed in a quasi-domestic environment and staffed by female teachers, infant schools combined play with rudimentary mental training and discipline. Such schools were among the first to put into practice Pestalozzi's concept of having education follow the natural development of children, and in doing so they moved American education closer to adopting a developmental basis for instruction and a more formal sequencing of curriculum.[10]

Ironically, the early elaboration of child development theories and the formalization of public education doomed the infant school movement. One of Pestalozzi's principles was that, in matching education to natural growth, educators should be careful not to overtax the child. In the 1830s, this warning became the basis for a fear expressed by several American writers that young children's minds and bodies would be damaged by premature intellectual stress from infant school instruction. Rather, these writers urged, children should receive physical training to regulate growth and prepare their bodies for later intellectual exertion.

Explicit in these fears were some of the earliest expressions of age norms and prescriptions for proper scheduling of life course events. There were persistent warnings against educating children "too early," lest they develop "premature old age." One writer advised that giving children under the age of eight more than one hour of schooling a day would produce a "morbid condition" of the brain that could end with "epilepsy, insanity, or imbecility." An advice manual cautioned that intellectual training for children under age five was unsafe, and that play was the only suitable activity. Moreover, as public school systems began to be established in the 1850s, boards of education set entry age at six or seven. Thus, not only was public opinion militating against sending very young children to infant schools, but also bureaucratic reforms were lowering the age of entry to public schools, thereby siphoning off older infant school enrollees. Finally, public schools began employing more female teachers, a practice that cut into infant school personnel resources. Though infant school organizers protested that they were not overemphasizing intellectual instruction, as their detractors charged, the financing and staffing of infant schools became increasingly difficult, and the movement died by the 1850s.[11]

## THE ESTABLISHMENT OF GRADED COMMON SCHOOLS

At about the same time that infant schools were waning, the campaign to establish public, or common, schools was accelerating. It was in this movement that age grading first became extensively formalized in the United States. Common schools and the age divisions they established received direct impetus from several different forces. One influence was exerted simply by the combination of demography with practicality. By the 1840s, the nation's school-age population, especially in burgeoning cities, had grown too large for older forms of school organization. The Lancasterian system of monitors originally had been adopted to minister to increasing numbers of schoolchildren, but even it could not quell rising complaints about classes that contained indiscriminate collections of boys and girls of varying ages, sizes, and abilities. Henry Barnard articulated this viewpoint in his famous lecture, "Gradation of the Public Schools, with Special Reference to Cities and Villages," in which he maintained that a classroom containing such a mixture of students was inefficient and inhumane. In addition, there were now large enough numbers of pupils of all ages to justify the employment of more teachers. School officials, always wary of costs, could save money by hiring female instructors and paying them less than their male counterparts. But prevailing attitudes about female frailty militated against forcing a tender young lady into a classroom in which she might have to manage both squalling youngsters and rowdy teenagers. Some sort of system to separate students by age would ease a female teacher's responsibilities and allow for the assignment of older youths to male teachers.[12]

School architects, responding to the needs of increased school populations, began to incorporate in their buildings structural elements conducive to more formal class divisions. In the early nineteenth century, even in cities, school buildings usually contained just one room. When the Lancasterian system was utilized, each monitor tended to a row of students or was assigned to a particular section of the room. As numbers of pupils grew, however, some school buildings were built with recitation rooms adjacent to the main schoolroom. The newer the structure, the more recitation rooms it was likely to include. By the 1840s, many new schools were designed to facilitate the sorting of pupils into grades. The standard school building constructed in the last half of the nineteenth century contained three floors with four rooms to each floor.[13]

Philosophical antecedents and practical necessity provided the foundation, and building construction formed the framework, for the bureaucratic reform that instituted graded schools in the United States. By the mid-nineteenth century, a number of educators were convinced that the old tutorial systems of schooling were incapable of imparting democratic values efficiently and thoroughly. If the nation was to have an extensive system of public education, the schools must be reorganized according to some centralizing principles. Such principles, said many reformers, should include rationally constituted pedagogical groupings—that is, grades. The chief condition of success for a public school system, said Henry Barnard, was a "classification of scholars" that grouped together "a large number of *similar age and attainments* [emphasis added], at all times, and in every state of their advancement" within a classroom supervised by the same teacher.[14] Horace Mann, whose praise of the Prussian educational system in his *Seventh Annual Report of the Secretary of the Massachusetts Board of Education* (1844) stirred a controversy that eventually led to the establishment of fully graded schools, argued that the unifying and socializing goals of democratic schools could be accomplished only when pupils were taught in manageable groups. Though Mann would have such a system allow for individual differences in pupils' temperaments, abilities, and interests, he nevertheless called for a rational systematization that imposed a uniformity of classification, of curricula, of textbooks, and of discipline—in other words, bureaucratization.[15]

Efforts by reformers to systematize American education passed a watershed in 1848. That year, John D. Philbrick, a follower of Horace Mann, established the Quincy School in Boston. Philbrick's Quincy

School not only contained twelve classrooms and an assembly hall but also provided a teacher for each classroom and a separate desk and chair for each of the 660 pupils. Most importantly, the school was organized so as to divide the students on the basis of age and grade. In 1856 Philbrick published his scheme, which included a provision for promoting pupils every six months from one grade and teacher to the next.[16]

Over the next two decades, most cities and many rural communities established their own unified systems of graded elementary schools with defined courses of study. The systems created seven, eight, or nine grades, with eight being the most common. The normal sequence was for students to enter the first grade at age six and to leave the elementary school at age fourteen. By 1871, many cities had passed laws setting the legal age for starting school at five or six and the minimum age for starting high school—the next stage after elementary school—at twelve.

Thus, by the 1870s, formally structured age-graded institutions had become entrenched throughout the United States. Though compulsory school attendance laws had not yet taken root, in 1870 the proportion of white children ages five to nineteen who attended school exceeded 61 percent, up from 35 percent in 1830 and 50 percent in 1850.[17] Graded classes now locked a significant proportion of American children into age-determined groupings and engendered in adults the assumption that these groupings were intrinsic to the educational experience.

Through the standardization of grades, educators thought they had found a means of bringing order to the socially diverse and seemingly chaotic environment of American schools. To achieve their goals of efficient management, reformers explicitly copied the new factory system, in which a division of labor was used to create a product, from raw material, in successive stages of assembly, each stage building upon the previous one. Looking back in 1869, William T. Harris, superintendent of the St. Louis public schools, compared the old system of education to the "antiquated process by which [a] gun was made throughout—lock, stock and barrel—by one gunsmith." The new graded schools, he concluded, successfully adapted "the division-of-labor systems in the Springfield armory or the watch manufactories at Waltham or Elgin, where each manipulation has a different workman to perform it."[18]

The establishment of graded schools not only concentrated children of the same age together in a stage-based, factory-like setting but also eliminated incidences and tolerance of precocity. That is, the decline of infant schools and the establishment of an eight-grade institution for youths between ages six and fourteen imposed a structure on children's lives that made it more difficult for them to enter elementary school at age four or secondary school at age ten or college at age fourteen.

Figures from private academies testify to this development. In the mid-nineteenth century, these academies were the main providers of secondary education; the spread of public high schools did not occur until the end of the century. Before 1850, academy enrollments in Great Britain and the United States often included a mélange of boys, teenagers, and young men. But the onset of age grading in the elementary schools made secondary education much more an experience of the teen years. For example, in examining the student body at Philips Exeter Academy, Joseph Kett found that the percentage of students between the ages of thirteen and nineteen increased from 57.7 percent in 1810 to 69.7 percent in 1840 and to 87.3 percent in 1870.[19] In 1868, a British observer confirmed the trend in his country, stating that "it now has become a very common practice not to send boys to such a school as Harrow or Rugby till thirteen or fourteen, and to have them prepared at a preparatory school with boys their own age."[20]

The same compressing of age ranges and decreased tolerance of precocity that occurred in American and British secondary schools also occurred in colleges and universities, only with a slight time lag. Thus, in 1850, 36.1 percent of the students matriculating at Brown University were between ages eighteen and twenty-one, while 57.2 percent were in this age group in 1880.[21] In 1835, 27 percent of the matriculants to Oxford University were seventeen years of age or younger; by 1885, the figure had dropped to 6 percent.[22] Thus, institutions of higher education, like elementary schools, were creating much more standardized concentrations of youths by age than had ever before existed.

Not surprisingly, the age grading of schools was reflected in areas related to the teaching in those schools. Writers of school textbooks, which proliferated from the early nineteenth century onward, gradually adopted the developmental organization that schools were implementing, and they increasingly arranged and designated subject matter for specific grades and ages.

To some extent, textbooks had been age-graded long before the common school reforms of Mann, Barnard, and others. Because the skills used in reading, writing, and arithmetic are cumulative, any supplement to instruction had to have been organized according to the manner in which those skills are acquired. Thus, early spellers and readers were graded, with each successive volume more difficult than the previous one. The famous texts produced by Alexander H. McGuffey, for example, included an introductory primer followed by six graded readers, each more sophisticated in language and content and each requiring more knowledge than its predecessor.

Nevertheless, the grading of these texts did not fit a particular pattern of age development or school organization. As soon as a child had mastered one reader, he or she would move to the next one, but advancement could occur at any age. There was no norm.[23] Even widely used arithmetic texts, such as Frederic A. Adams's *Arithmetic in Two Parts* (1847) and Dana P. Colburn's *The Common School Arithmetic* (1860), presented the subject only as a method of thought and made no mention of a relationship between age and intellectual capacity for mastering the subject. Likewise, history texts published in the 1860s and 1870s made no reference to the ages or grades for which they were intended; they referred merely to their appropriateness for "young pupils" or "schoolchildren" in general. Some authors even asserted that their work was meant for "young and old."[24]

Around 1880, however, textbooks began to be produced for specific levels in the newly graded common schools. History texts, such as Samuel G. Goodrich's *Pictorial History of the World* (1881) and David H. Montgomery's *Leading Facts in History* (a series published in the 1890s), included various levels of lessons to match specific school grades.[25] In his *The Child and Nature: Geography Teaching With Sand Modeling* (1888), Alexander Frye provided a detailed, topical lesson outline for each of eight grades, to aid in the study of geography. Reminiscent of Pestalozzi, Frye, who had been a school principal in Quincy, Massachusetts, wrote, "It is the aim of this course of study to show what constitutes the science, or sequence of subjects, and assign them to different grades or stages of mental development."[26] Publishers of arithmetic texts also brought out numerous multivolume series of books designed for specific grades. The fit of the new developmental theory of education to arithmetic was expressed by George William Myers, who wrote in his preface to *Myers Arithmetic*: "The arrangement of number work for the grades must be in accordance with the natural unfolding of the child's mind. Too often this important fact is lost sight of in the logic of the subject itself."[27] Textbook writers and publishers thus accepted and perpetuated age-graded developmental schemes that the common schools had institutionalized.

## THE ARRESTED AGE GRADING OF SUNDAY SCHOOLS

As the second half of the nineteenth century progressed, age grading permeated the organization of secular education. But through much of the nineteenth century, religious instruction was a crucial part of people's lives, especially as it served to prepare youths for a lifetime of Christian piety. In this regard, Protestant Sunday schools were among the most important institutions. Unlike public schools, however, Sunday schools did not become age-graded permanently in the nineteenth century. A trend toward graded instruction started early in the century, then faded as the nature of Sunday school curricula shifted.

Carried to the United States from England in the 1780s and prevalent in most cities by the early nineteenth century, Protestant Sunday schools taught both secular and religious subjects, but the main course of study consisted of learning to read Scriptures, studying the catechism, and then participating in more advanced Bible study. The first Sunday schools had four divisions: "infant," in which children practiced the alphabet and words of one syllable; "elementary," for children who could read and spell longer words; "Scripture," which taught children to read from Scriptures; and "senior," which involved more extensive reading in the Old and New Testaments. But these four grades did not divide children by age; only when a pupil mastered the skills taught in one division did he or she advance to the next.[28]

When more formal catechism methods were adopted in the early nineteenth century, Sunday school curricula became more age-graded, predating graded common schools by at least forty years. The various catechisms were fashioned to fit the different ages and capabilities of Sunday school children. Thus, the catechisms compiled by Isaac Watts and first published by him in 1788 comprised three levels, each designed for a specific age group: the first for ages three to four, the second for ages seven to eight, and the third for ages twelve to fourteen. The Methodist catechisms also had three divisions: one for children of a "tender age," under seven; another for children over seven; and a third for "Young Persons." Yet many religious leaders came to believe that the subject matter of doctrinal catechisms—redemption, regeneration, salvation, the sacrifice of Jesus, the significance of the sacraments—defied age-graded simplification, and that Scriptures should be emphasized over doctrine. Thus, by the 1820s, the catechism—and accompanying age grades—fell out of favor, and the Bible moved to the center of religious education.[29]

Bible study, which became the major activity in Sunday schools after 1820, included the awarding of prizes and penalties based on a student's success or failure at memorizing and reciting certain passages. Because the Scriptures were less adaptable to different levels of learning than catechisms were, Bible reading was less age-graded. Teachers devised various lessons to make Bible study fall into beginning, intermediate, and advanced levels, and expectations and prizes were geared to each level. But grading followed the nature and mastery of the material rather than the age of the child. The age-graded organization of learning faded as the system of Bible study became more like the secular curricula of McGuffey's readers and similar texts.[30]

By the 1860s, Sunday school leaders of the various Protestant denominations had become dissatisfied with the Bible study method of teaching, and with the lack of uniformity in their curricula. Influenced in part by the common school reform movement, these leaders wanted the Sunday school to be a genuine teaching institution, not merely a place where children were forced to memorize Bible passages. Reformers such as Reverend John H. Vincent, secretary of the Chicago Sunday School Teachers' Union, and Reverend Edward Eggleston, editor of the *Sunday School Teacher*, did not explicitly link their reforms to age-graded theories of religious education; but their ideas foreshadowed the eventual development of lessons that would correspond with the age-related needs of Sunday school pupils. In his *Two Years With Jesus*, Vincent outlined a uniform lesson plan, based on study of the life of Jesus, that consisted of four grades: an "infant grade" for ages three to six, children who could not read; a "second grade" for ages six to ten, children with elementary reading abilities; a "third grade" for ages ten to sixteen; and a "senior grade" for older youths and adults.[31]

Plans like Vincent's, however, were exceptional and controversial. At its meeting in Indianapolis in 1872, the National Sunday School Convention debated whether to support a uniform lesson for all age groups. In the end, the convention appointed a committee to prepare a group of such lessons. Later that year, the committee published the *International Sunday School Lessons*, which were deemed suitable for all major denominations. The lessons emphasized Bible study and encompassed all age groups.[32] Though the lessons vaguely recognized that children had religious needs different from those of adults, the material-centered nature of instruction blocked the creation of a graded scheme that followed the age-related development of children. The more formal age grading of religious instruction would not occur until the beginning of the twentieth century, when Sunday school leaders began to accept the principles of modern educational and developmental psychology (see Chapter 5).

## AGE CONSCIOUSNESS AND THE ORIGINS OF PEDIATRICS

At the same time that philosophical, bureaucratic, and nascent psychological imperatives were propelling education toward age-graded organization, changes in scientific outlook were beginning to create another dimension of age consciousness. These changes, and their significance in making age an important concept in the United States, were manifested most clearly in the practice of medicine, particularly the medical treatment of children. The establishment and recognition of the medical specialty of pediatrics, like the formalization of graded schools, provided American society with a rationalized institution that fixed age-based considerations in the general culture.

Though in general people in pre-modern Western societies treated children as miniature adults worthy of no special consideration, medical practitioners did recognize that children had distinct peculiarities in their diseases and physiology. Hippocrates (c. 460–c. 370 B.C.), for example, penned a special treatise on the development and cutting of children's teeth. Galen (c. 130–c. 200) composed an advice manual on the medical care of children, and the Arabian physician Rhazes (850–923) wrote lengthy descriptions of children's diseases. Later writers focused special attention on newborns. Paolo Bagellardo, a Renaissance Italian physician, authored what was probably the first truly medical text on infant diseases, *Libellus de aegritudinbus infantium*, published in 1472. The German physician Euscharius Roesslin composed several influential works in the early sixteenth century on infant care and midwifery, and a treatise on infant diseases by the Swedish court physician Nils Rosen Rosenstein, published in 1774, marked an important step toward defining diseases that were distinctive to childhood.

Nevertheless, physicians did not yet recognize a special branch of medicine devoted to children, and there were no theories on the clinical treatment of age-related diseases. Sick children were treated in the same fashion as their elders—with traditional remedies such as emetics, purges, bleeding, and sweating, and with drug therapy consisting largely of calomel, tartar, quinine, and opium.[33] Many people applied home remedies that they found in almanacs, which were important sources of secular information for the American colonials. The only professional medical care that children received was chiefly from midwives, who tended to newborns and young infants, and from physicians whose province included older children and adults as well.

The only eighteenth-century age prescription that related to child care involved weaning. Most advice in this area derived from folk custom and the belief, based to some extent on biological regularity, that weaning should begin at the time of first dentition—that is, when the child was approximately one year old. But some experts refined prescriptions to accommodate individual differences. Thus, Culpepper's *English Physician*, published in Boston in 1708, advised, "The strong children must be sooner weaned than the weak, some in the twelfth,

41

some in the fifteenth month."[34] To others, however, the time of year at which to begin weaning was more important than any age prescription. Almost all medical writers warned against weaning a child during summer when the air was least healthy. For example, Lionel Chalmers wrote in 1776, "Even were [children] ever so strong and healthy, they should never be weaned till the month of October, when the weather begins to be cool and bracing."[35]

By the early nineteenth century, the new rationality of the Enlightenment had transformed both scientific outlook and popular attitudes toward life and health. Scientific theory increasingly was derived from controlled observation, experiment, and inference, rather than from reasoned speculation. Such a shift from opinion to experimentation opened the way for specialization within the practice of medicine. At the same time, the sanctity of life attained higher priority in the public consciousness, and growing faith in the ability of humans to control their environment stimulated efforts to reduce the high rates of mortality that prevailed especially among infants and children.

The medical renaissance that ensued from these changes in scientific outlook originated in France, where major developments in the fields of children's diseases and internal medicine occurred at the end of the eighteenth century and the beginning of the nineteenth. The principal French pioneer in child medicine was the physician Charles Michel Billard, who published the first modern text on the pathology of childhood diseases. His *Traites des Maladies des Enfans Nouveau-nes et a la Mamelle* (1828) not only categorized the diseases affecting children from birth to puberty but also was one of the first texts to list what Billard and other doctors believed to be the norms for the weight, size, and shape of growing children and their organs. Like Pestalozzi's theories relating education to child development, Billard's work provided an early framework for applying medical treatment to the developing child.

Billard and other French physicians had considerable influence on American medicine during this period. The national alignment with France and antipathy toward England prompted American medical journals to begin publishing a great number of French articles and many aspiring American doctors to travel to Paris to study. Unlike American medical writing at the time, which tended to be anecdotal descriptions of cures and drugs used in individual cases, French papers outlined detailed clinical studies that focused more directly on pathology and therapeutic measures.[36]

Even outside France, medical writers were beginning to affix more distinctiveness to childhood than they did before, but notions of developmental standards and their relationship to age remained vague. For example, British physicians Richard T. Evanson and Henry Maunsell, in the fourth edition of *Practical Treatise on the Management and Diseases of Children*, published in 1842, divided childhood into two age-based stages: birth to age one and age one to age eight. Their rationale for designating age one as the watershed year was because it usually marked the onset of dentition; age eight was the other boundary because after that age the "peculiarities characteristic of childhood" merge with those of adulthood.[37] Their survey of physiological development included no other age-specific references, and they recognized no differentiations among later ages, except for a brief mention of puberty. Even in their description of the second stage of childhood, Evanson and Maunsell wrote of growth in relative rather than age-related terms. Thus, "as an infant grows older, digestion ceases to be so active, . . . respiration becomes slower, and pulsations of heart less frequent."[38] American texts, such as John Forsythe Meigs's *A Practical Treatise on the Diseases of Children*—first published in 1848, followed by six succeeding editions, the last of which was published in 1882— also failed to discuss any age standardization in their descriptions of growth and pathology.

The most important practical step toward the recognition of children's medical needs as separate from those of adults was the establishment of children's hospitals. Though the British had opened a dispensary for treatment of the infant poor in 1796, the first hospital devoted exclusively to the care of children was the Hospital des Enfants Malades, built in Paris in 1802. This institution provided three hundred beds for sick children between ages two and fifteen. A half century elapsed before the Children's Hospital in Great Ormond Street was opened in London. In the United States, the first permanent pediatric institution was the Philadelphia Children's Hospital, inaugurated in 1855 to treat children suffering from acute diseases and serious injuries. A similar hospital was established in Boston in 1869.[39] These institutions provided an important foundation for the advancement and recognition of child care as a separate specialty of medicine.

By the 1870s, American physicians were paying greater attention to the medical care of children, because surveys were revealing that in almost every city one third or more of all children died before reaching their fifth year. Yet ironically, one of the most successful early movements pushing for the care of children as a separate class of the population grew not out of the medical profession but out of an organization founded to protect animals. In April of 1874, Henry Bergh, founder and president of the American Society for the Prevention of Cruelty to Animals (ASPCA), went before a New York court on behalf of "Mary Ellen," an eight-year-old girl who had been abused by her foster parents. A charity worker had discovered the maltreated child and had tried unsuccessfully to persuade several public and philanthropic institutions to assume care for her. As a last resort, the charity worker sought aid from the ASPCA. Bergh, while admitting that the girl's case did not fall within the organization's purview, decided it was his duty as a humanitarian to save the child. Thus, he and Elbridge T. Gerry, the ASPCA's legal adviser, obtained a warrant to have Mary Ellen removed from her cruel custodians and "placed in charge of some person or persons by whom she shall be more kindly treated."[40]

Mary Ellen's case, especially its catalogue of abuse that included beatings, confinement, withholding of food and clothing, and total lack of affection, attracted considerable publicity. Consequent to Bergh and Gerry's intervention, the child's foster mother was arrested, convicted, and sentenced for felonious assault. Mary Ellen was assigned to an institution known as Sheltered Arms, while the court sought her natural parents. More importantly, as a result of the case, Gerry and other philanthropists founded the Society for the Prevention of Cruelty to Children (SPCC) in December of 1874. From this point on, the number of organizations and agencies devoted to protecting children exclusively or children and animals jointly increased steadily until there were some 250 such societies by 1900.[41] The creation of the SPCC thus marked another major step toward recognizing childhood as a separate stage of life that required special efforts and organizations to protect it. The fields of both social welfare and medicine were now ready for a more formalized conception of childhood and its stages of development.

The culmination of this expansion in the amount and type of medical attention directed to children occurred when pediatrics became formally established as a recognized specialty. Though there were always certain doctors who had reputations for their effective treatment of children, the discipline of child medicine was unknown before the 1880s. In fact, the term *pediatrics* did not exist in the medical lexicon. Those specialists who tended to children usually were obstetricians. But the new philanthropic view that treated children as being different from adults, combined with research into pathologies of infant and childhood diseases, made a new medical specialty not only possible but acceptable. A few medical schools in the 1860s established special professorships in children's diseases, and one such professor, Abraham Jacobi, who had emigrated from Germany in the 1850s, established in New York City in 1862 the nation's first clinic for children's diseases. Around 1875, physicians who devoted themselves exclusively to the treatment of children began to call themselves *pediatrists*, and their specialty *pediatry* or *pedology*. Finally, in 1888, they organized themselves into the American Pediatric Society and chose Jacobi as their first president. (The terms *pediatrician* and *pediatrics* now replaced the former terms to prevent confusion with the term *podiatry*.) By the next year, the society included over thirty pediatric specialists, and the number of pediatric clinics was growing. By 1919, 64 of the nation's 119 medical schools had special professorships in pediatrics.[42]

Establishment of pediatrics as a recognized professional specialty promoted age consciousness and age grading in two ways. First, pediatrics provided a scientific rationale for considering children as more than diminutive adults. As medical historian Thomas Cone notes, physicians now were convinced "that psychological and biological differences between infants, children, and adults were sufficiently different to warrant establishing pediatrics as a specific discipline separate from internal medicine."[43] Or, as Abraham Jacobi wrote at the time: "Pediatrics does not deal with miniature men and women. . . . It has its own independent range and horizon. There are anomalies and diseases which are encountered in the infant and the child only."[44] Such thinking, though not revolutionary, confirmed with a certainty that had not previously existed that childhood was a special stage of life.

Second, growth of the pediatric specialty, when combined with new clinical and experimental research, enabled physicians to refine theories about child growth and development, and to affix age norms to growth stages and to the occurrence of specific diseases. Thus, Henry Bowditch, in an early article that foreshadowed modern pediatric research, wrote:

> It is probable that the accurate determination of the normal rate of growth in children would not only throw light upon the nature of diseases to which childhood is subject, but would also guide us in the explication of therapeutic measures. The statistics of growth taken in connection with those of disease might very possibly reveal unexpected relations between periods of slow and rapid growth and *the age at which certain diseases most frequently occur*. (Emphasis added.)[45]

As in education, age was becoming an organizing principle in medicine, and it would become more so as the century ended.

## AGE CONSCIOUSNESS IN EARLY YOUTH ORGANIZATIONS AND MAGAZINES

By the 1880s, then, reforms in education and medicine had not only generated new bureaucratic and scientific attitudes but also attached new significance to youth. Though theories of child development and adolescence remained unrefined, educators and physicians had alerted society to the special needs of young people. Not surprisingly, these attitudes began to influence activities in other segments of society that were only loosely associated with schools and hospitals.

For example, the Young Men's Christian Association (YMCA) reorganized itself in ways that reflected an impetus toward rationalization and age grading. Founded in London in 1844 by young, mostly white-collar men who sought a collective path to self-improvement and religious sustenance amid the temptations of city life, the YMCA spread to the United States and Canada in the 1850s. There, city associations at first accepted young men of all ages, usually imposing a maximum age limit of forty but granting membership to males as young as those in their mid-teens. In the late 1860s, however, YMCA leaders began to feel a greater need to rationalize association activities and to direct more attention to the needs of boys. Originally, all YMCAs expressed the goal of improving the spiritual, mental, and social condition of young men. But starting with the New York City chapter, the association began to add "physical" to the other three conditions. This addition provided the YMCA with its ultimate themes—body, mind, and spirit—and as a result, new YMCA buildings, such as that constructed in New York City, included a gymnasium. Not only was the organization becoming more secular, but also its structures were becoming more conducive to age divisions among its members.[46]

At first, only a few YMCA leaders had any desire to tend to boys' needs; the organization was based on the assumption that it should serve only young men who had left the family hearth, and that boys who remained under parental control needed less assistance. But as boys began to drift into YMCA buildings, attracted especially by the gymnasiums, various chapters gave them permission to use meeting rooms and athletic facilities, and some chapters began to organize programs for boys. The Salem, Massachusetts, YMCA established the first separate boys' department in 1869, and other branches followed suit. According to historian David Macleod, YMCA leaders' "awareness of boyhood as a separate and critical stage between the sheltered life of childhood and the relative independence of young manhood grew slowly out of concern that boys encountered moral dangers very young and out of a need to rationalize YMCA practice."[47] By the 1880s, most chapters that had created boys' departments used age sixteen or seventeen as the boundary between boyhood and young manhood, but the minimum age for membership in a boys' department varied between six and twelve. To standardize the structure of the organization, I. E. Brown, secretary of the Illinois YMCA, proposed in 1885 that boys' departments be restricted to ages ten to sixteen. This policy provided the national organization with its first fully defined age-graded criterion. Shortly thereafter, athletic leagues—the ultimate consequence of the emphasis on physical development and the construction of gymnasiums—were organized by age, further entrenching the YMCA's adoption of age-related standards.[48]

Just as organizations like the YMCA acknowledged the national impetus toward age grading, the rise of popular magazines for children reflected not only the stricter age divisions of childhood occurring in the schools but also a commercial effort to capitalize on the new divisions. As Frank Luther Mott, historian of American magazines, has observed, before the Civil War a few juvenile magazines existed, but they tended to be religious, "wooden and unnatural."[49] After 1865, however, just as graded common schools were beginning to spread, children's magazines began to proliferate and specialize. Though about half remained religious in content, the popularity of new secular magazines increased immensely. In fact, by 1885, *Youth's Companion*, with a circulation of over 385,000, quite likely had the highest readership of all American regular publications, with the possible exception of some mail-order newspapers.[50] Other new popular magazines that catered specifically to children's interests included *Frank Leslie's Boys' and Girls' Weekly*, *Frank Leslie's Chatterbox* (mainly for girls), *Boys of New York* (a cheap adventure weekly), and *Boys' Library of Sport, Story, and Adventure*.

Perhaps more importantly, a number of popular periodicals directed their content to specific sub-periods of childhood and youth. Thus, *The Nursery*, a magazine for "youngest readers"—between ages four and ten—first appeared in Boston in 1867. It was succeeded in 1880 by *Our Little Ones and the Nursery*, edited by the prolific and controversial writer William Taylor Adams (also known as Oliver Optic) and intended for readers between ages three and nine. Other publications for the tenderest age group included *Babyland*, "the baby's own magazine," founded in 1876, and *Little Folks*, established in 1897. Magazines for schoolchildren aged six to twelve included *Children's Hour*, founded in 1866; *Harper's Young People*, established in 1879; and *Our Little Men and Women*, founded in 1880. *Young People's Magazine*, founded in 1868; *Wide Awake*, first published in 1875; *The Boys' Champion*, established in 1881; and *Forward*, which began publication in 1882, ranked high among the burgeoning popular periodicals for older children. The editor of *Forward* explicitly recognized the new age specialization and announced in a passage published beneath the masthead that his publication was specifically intended for young people "say, sixteen, seventeen, or eighteen," who believed themselves too mature for "children's papers."[51]

As in medicine, specialization increasingly characterized the magazine medium: journals devoted specifically to art, music, sports, women's rights, and individual professions such as law and medicine proliferated. The new magazines for juveniles formed an important segment of this movement toward specialization and prompted cultural acceptance of segmented, eventually age-graded sub-stages of childhood.

As various strands of thought and culture began to interweave a social fabric of age consciousness, the pattern formed mostly around childhood. Such emphasis seems logical. American society, seeking to control the present and ensure the future, looked to children as redeemers of their hopes for knowledge, virtue, and purity. Children were malleable. Their minds were bottomless receptacles for knowledge; their bodies—threatened by often-mortal diseases—and their dependence made them ready subjects for medical experimentation; and their needs for recreation impelled writers and reformers to ensure that these needs were met in moral, productive ways. As the twentieth century drew nearer, movements to knit the social fabric according to an age-graded pattern continued to center on childhood, but other life stages began to enter the scheme. The result was the establishment of values and institutions that affected much of twentieth-century life.

Large families were characteristic of early American society. The roles of and age relationships among members of large families were less distinct than those in smaller families, which became more prevalent by the late nineteenth century. It is likely that several more children were born into this burgeoning family, resulting in the parents still having child raising responsibilities in their fifties and sixties and creating wide age differences between the youngest and oldest children.
*National Archives.*

Before the creation of graded schools and in sparsely populated rural areas even after the spread of graded schools, the one-room schoolhouse grouped together children of various ages.
*Library of Congress.*

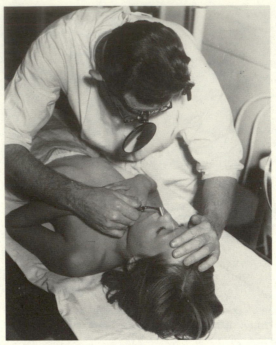

The establishment of the medical specialty of
pediatrics signaled recognition by physicians that
children had age-related diseases and experienced
physiological development that differed from the
diseases and development of older age groups.
*National Archives.*

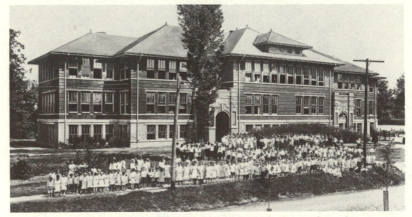

The clusters of children of similar heights signify the modern elementary
school's organization of children in strict age-graded groups.
*Library of Congress.*

By 1900, educators firmly believed that children in each grade in the
educational system should develop specific, age-related skills. Here, a
fifth grade class is measuring and recording heights and distances.
*Library of Congress.*

The junior high school, created in the early twentieth century, separated
the seventh, eighth, and ninth grades from the elementary and high
school grades, thereby isolating preadolescent youths from younger and
older children and further narrowing institutional peer groupings.
*Library of Congress.*

Age-graded activities extended beyond school classes into extracurricular organizations, such as this chapter of the Daughters of Woodcraft in Burlington, Vermont, in 1909. *Library of Congress.*

Formation of the Brownies, a sub-unit of the Girl Scouts for girls aged six to eight, reflected the movement toward finer age divisions in youth organizations and the creation of age-congruent peer groups. *National Archives.*

The intensification of peer associations was manifested in the activities
of adults as well as those of children. This photograph of the board of
management of the Daughters of the American Revolution in 1905
suggests that most of the members were of similar ages.
*Library of Congress.*

## AGE NORMS AND SCHEDULING: THE 1890S

Sometime in the 1870s, a new terminology entered American speech. The phrase *on time* and its concomitants, *behind time* and *ahead of time*, derived mainly from the standardized measurements essential to industrial capitalism. In pre-industrial America, clocks were rare and seldom accurate. People's activities, whether at the hearth or in fields and workshops, proceeded in haphazard fashion; rather than articulating phrases such as "on time" and other expressions of precision, they used more indefinite gauges such as "due time" and "when ready." Large-scale production of household clocks did not begin until the late 1830s, and cheap, mass-produced pocket watches were not available until the 1860s. Not until factories, with their regular working hours and production schedules, spread across the landscape did precise time become a serious matter.[1]

In addition, railroads and streetcars, with their explicit, regular schedules, forced people more than ever before to become conscious of, and submissive to, the clock. Time became even more fixed in everyday activity when, on November 18, 1882, American railroads, acting without any government or public sanction, imposed uniform time zones on the country. In 1884, representatives from twenty-five countries met in Washington and established Greenwich as the zero meridian, fixed the exact length of the day, and divided the planet into twenty-four time zones.[2]

Invention of the time clock around 1890 further compelled people to regulate their daily lives to meet production demands and maintain bureaucratic efficiency. Further, scientific management, Frederick W. Taylor's scheme for improving the efficiency of any particular task, began in the 1880s and 1890s to influence the workplace, so that increasingly time rather than quality became the major criterion for measuring productivity.[3] So drastic was the new American obsession with being on time that one observer in 1881 blamed clocks and watches for causing a particular kind of national nervousness, wherein "a delay of a few moments might destroy the hopes of a lifetime."[4] Concern with punctuality was not completely new at the end of the nineteenth century, but certainly it became more intense than ever before.[5]

In the 1890s, this new awareness of scheduling penetrated American culture in another way, one that influenced a person's entire life span, not just the hours of an ordinary day. Just as work, whether it involved production, record keeping, or management, became more standardized, so too did age-related life experiences. As the previous chapter has noted, educational and medical theories had begun to link certain developments and experiences of childhood to specific age ranges. As the nineteenth century closed, these theories were refined and applied to older age groups as well as to youths. Moreover, spokespersons in popular and professional journals and the institutions that their theories influenced began to delineate the ideal sequencing of a wide variety of experiences. Such delineations not only implied norms but also often specified them. As a result, the concept of being on, ahead of, or behind schedule referred to more than the arrival of a train or the completion of a task; it meant matching the timing of one's personal experiences and achievements to cultural standards.

By the late nineteenth century, social scientists had become fascinated with the way their surveys and census figures seemed to show powerful stabilities in certain social behavior—stabilities that seemed independent of the type and personality of government. There was uniformity from year to year not only in natural events like births and deaths but also in voluntary acts like marriage and crime. These discoveries prompted statisticians and those whom they influenced to define "statistical laws" and the predictable schedules inherent in such laws. Though it was impossible to explain the cause of every individual action, social scientists and popular writers came to believe that general, statistical truths about mass phenomena could increase our understanding of society. And when they examined behavior closely, they identified age as the underlying predictor of the schedules that the statistical laws dictated.[6]

## AGE PRESCRIPTIONS FOR MARRIAGE

In 1889, Frances Willard, temperance reformer and dauntless crusader for women's rights, published an etiquette manual titled *How to Win: A Book for Girls*. This book, full of sensible and quasi-scientific advice on how to behave and plan, contained one chapter, "At What Age Shall Girls Marry?" that constitutes an early statement of the new cultural emphasis on scheduling. This chapter discussed Willard's survey of "eight of the most distinguished physicians in America" and their theories about the proper timing of marriage. After reviewing this survey, Willard set the ideal marriage age within the range of eighteen to twenty-six.[7]

The range itself is less important than the emphasis on prescribing specific ages for marriage. Before Willard made her survey, few experts were willing to prescribe the "best" age at which women or men should marry. In 1867, for example, a writer in *Godey's Ladies Book and Magazine* offered that there was no correct age for marriage; rather, a woman should "fall in love as soon as you like, provided it be with a suitable person."[8] "Suitable" referred to status and character, not age. A decade later, a writer on the "Etiquette of Courtship and Marriage" declared that it was "impossible to fix any time at which marriage should be contracted," though he did advise that marriage was unwise for women under twenty.[9] The most common advice given about marriage in these early manuals was for a man or woman to resist impulsiveness and wait to marry the "right" person, but age prescriptions did not accompany such counsel.[10]

As Willard's chapter indicates, however, by the end of the century age norms for marriage had become more explicit and age prescriptions more insistent. Thus, although a writer for the *Ladies Home Journal* did not specify ages in an 1890 article on "Who Shall Be Younger?" the columnist's advice was quite firm: "It is always better for him [the groom] to be several years the senior of the bride."[11] The title of this piece reflects increased consciousness of life schedules, and the rationale for its prescription illustrates age-related values: according to the article, a wife must be younger than her husband so that she will not "be mistaken for his mother," and because as she ages an older woman is more "prone to jealousies" and becomes less attractive to her mate.[12]

Like Willard, other writers were steeping their advice in scientific research. Writing in *North American Review* in 1894, Cyrus Edson, health commissioner of New York City, expressed medical concern that women should not marry before their bodies had time to store up the strength they needed for childbearing. Using data from his own city, which showed that the average age of grooms was 28.8 and brides 24.5, Edson concluded that these were "proper ages" for marriage because they allowed for sufficient development of strength.[13] In addition, the title of Edson's article, "The Evils of Early Marriage," connoted both an awareness of the need to be "on time" and dire consequences for not adhering to the proper schedule. Specific age prescriptions would become even more common after 1900, but in the 1890s timing and scheduling were becoming more rigorously standardized than in previous years.

## PEDIATRICIANS AND THE SCHEDULES OF CHILDHOOD

Writers of prescriptive literature often based their advice on medical theory and with good reason: clinical observation enabled medical writers and practitioners to impart authoritative certainty to norms of scheduling and age-related experiences. Establishment of pediatrics as a recognized medical specialty in the 1880s had focused increased attention on the physical development and diseases of children as a distinct age group of the population (see Chapter 2). In the 1890s, several pediatricians refined findings of earlier investigators and more systematically divided childhood into age-graded sub-stages. Their work, in turn, informed nascent theories of mental and emotional development.

Louis Starr, who edited one of the most influential and widely quoted pediatric texts of the era, *An American Textbook on the Diseases of Children*, expressed the new preoccupation with standards and schedules when he announced in the book's introduction that "under normal circumstances" children grow in height and weight according to a "regular rate." By collecting and consulting data on growth, Starr continued, "it is quite possible to estimate what should be the normal size and weight of a child at any age. Consequently, if, on being measured and weighed, he should be found to fall short of the normal standard, it is proper to infer the existence of some fault in the nutritive process."[14] Though Starr was merely voicing what doctors had known for ages—that there is a logical sequence to a child's growth—he was among the first to articulate an age-graded schedule of growth, and to note that failure to meet the norms of that schedule represented a deficiency of some sort.

Starr detailed age-related norms of growth and development more extensively than any previous medical writers had. For very young children, he prescribed how feeding routines, bathing frequency, sleep requirements, and exercise regimens should change according to age. He listed the "normal" range of pulse rates for seven sub-periods of childhood between birth and age twelve. And each chapter on a specific disease set age norms for incidence and severity. Measles, for example, was identified as the most common infectious disease of childhood, and the "period of greatest susceptibility is between the second and sixth years." Regarding whooping cough, "age exercises a powerful influence. . . . By far the greater number of cases occur before the sixth year." In the incidence of chlorosis (a form of childhood anemia), "Age is an etiological factor of great importance, [with] most cases occurring between the thirteenth and twentieth years."[15] Whether these determinations were fallacious is irrelevant to the argument here; what is important is the association between scientific authority and age specificity.

L. Emmet Holt, who succeeded Abraham Jacobi as professor of the diseases of childhood at the Columbia University College of Physicians and Surgeons, further validated the concept of scheduling. His popular text on *The Diseases of Infancy and Childhood*, written in 1895 especially for parents, discussed at length the influence of nutrition on physical and mental development, and he outlined the changing nutritional needs of children according to their age. In subsequent books, he elaborated his theories about growth and diet, supplementing the text with numerous charts and tables that specified age-defined standards for the height and weight of children through their sixteenth year.[16]

Holt also emphasized the undesirable consequences of failure to meet scheduled norms. In a series of lectures and publications that spanned the 1890s to the 1920s, Holt argued that a child's failure to attain age standards for height and weight caused poor performance in school. He expanded this argument in *Food, Health, and Growth*, in which he concluded from survey data collected in 1893 that "retarded" boys had lower heights and weights than the average for their age and grade, and that "accelerated" boys had higher-than-average heights and weights.[17] In his prescriptions for caloric intake, Holt acknowledged that a child's needs vary according to metabolism and amount of activity; nevertheless, he organized his nutritional scheme around specific age norms and schedules. Significantly, in 1946 the Grolier Club of America included Holt's *The Care and Feeding of Children* among the one hundred books that most influenced American life and culture.

## New Consciousness of Old Age

Notions in the 1890s about the timing of diseases and the schedules of physical development drew increasing attention to stages of life and age-related transitions that separated those stages. Again, concepts of life stages were not new to late-nineteenth-century Western society. Ancient philosophers such as Aristotle and authors such as Shakespeare had depicted the "ages of man" in various degrees of detail. But by the 1890s, these stages were being defined with near-clinical precision, and more definite norms were being assigned to each stage. The newest dimension of such definitions consisted of normative characteristics of adult stages and transitions. For example, James Foster Scott, former obstetrician at the Columbia Hospital for Women and the Lying-In Asylum of Washington, D.C., expressed the new importance of timing as well as of stages when he wrote in 1898, "In order to learn how to live rightly we must understand ourselves at each stage of the march, lest a deadly blight settle upon us from which we may not be able to escape."[18]

Scott was particularly interested in sexual behavior at various ages, and he identified seven stages, from pre-birth to old age, each with different forms of sexual activity. He devoted special attention to the "climacteric," a concept from antiquity referring to the crisis years during which an individual completes one cycle and begins another. The ancient theory had been that humans experience climacterics at ages seven, fourteen, twenty-one, forty-nine, sixty-three, and eighty-four, with the "grand climacteric" occurring at sixty-three, the watershed between productive life and old age.[19] Scott was less exact about the age at which the climacteric occurred but more precise about what made old age different from one's previous life stages. He wrote: "The sexual life of both men and women continues until the climacteric, which is a momentous change or crisis . . . when the balance between tissue waste and restitution is disordered. After this event, the individual is in the afternoon of life and is again sexless from a physical standpoint."[20] This climacteric, said Scott, occurred in women between ages forty-two and fifty and in men between ages fifty and sixty-five. Clearly, Scott showed no knowledge of menopause or understanding about the sexuality of older people, but his ideas and writing reflected the expanding age and stage consciousness in American society.

Heightened interest in behavioral and sexual characteristics of later adult life was part of a broader social trend: new consciousness of and new attitudes toward old age. As historians W. Andrew Achenbaum and Carole Haber have posited, old people in the United States suffered a decline in status during the latter decades of the nineteenth century. Before that time, the aged generally had been accorded respect for their experience and accumulations of wisdom, as well as for their longevity. But as science and economic rationalization transformed the nation, attitudes toward the elderly shifted from ambivalence to disrespect and even to hostility.[21] This shift accompanied an increasingly explicit identification of old age as a separate stage of life, one marked by distinct age boundaries.

Every society has recognized that people who have lived to an advanced age differ in certain characteristics from those who are younger. Older people may be wiser, less nimble, more irascible, richer, poorer, surrounded by larger families, isolated by the death of a spouse, more infirm, more politically powerful, and the like. In many pre-modern societies, the elderly commanded respect simply by virtue of the fact that they had lived so long; they had survived the threats and temptations of life. Yet exactly when a person entered old age was never clear. Often a sixty-five-year-old person could plow a field or spin cloth as well as or better than a thirty-year-old. In societies with high birthrates and in which women continued to bear children well into their forties, parents' child raising responsibilities extended into their advanced years, precluding the onset of an "empty nest" period of family life that separated middle age from old age. There were no compulsory retirement or pension systems to launch workers into a new life stage in which they did not support themselves by their own work. Moreover, especially in early America, continued infusions of young immigrants and relatively short life expectancies kept low the proportions of old people in the total population. Thus, in 1850, when only 4 percent of the American people were age sixty or over (compared with nearly 15 percent today), old people did not constitute a very visible element of the population.[22] Near the end of the century, however, writers and experts increasingly focused on the infirmities and limitations of old age, thereby setting the increasing numbers of old people apart from the rest of society. This separation resulted from age-based assumptions.

The earliest and most important developments in this separation occurred in medicine; indeed, just as the evolution of pediatrics reflected new conceptions of the distinctiveness of childhood, a parallel movement did the same for old age and paved the way for the establishment of a new medical specialty for the treatment of old people. Before the nineteenth century, physicians administered to elderly individuals the same as they did to younger persons. They understood that certain diseases, such as gout and rheumatism, were more common among older people, but generally they acknowledged a relationship between age and adult diseases even less often than they recognized age relationships for childhood diseases.

When medical texts mentioned old age, they referred usually to the irremediable process of growing old. Since ancient times, physicians and laymen had believed that the human organism could store only a limited fund of energy, and they accepted the Biblical span of three score and ten years as the natural length of human life, seventy being the usual number of years it took for the body to exhaust itself. Some believed that by following certain rules for eating, dressing, and behaving, individuals might retard their loss of vitality, but because of the inevitability of infirmity and mental decline, few people could ever hope to surpass the limit of three score and ten.[23]

Ironically, however, by the mid-nineteenth century, as doctors began to examine physical, psychological, and pathological conditions of old people more closely, they concluded that the elderly should be viewed as a separate age group requiring special medical attention specifically *because* conditions of old age were so inevitable that proper diet and regimen could not prevent infirmity. French medical writers and clinicians were the first to focus on the unique pathological characteristics of old age. Research based on autopsies of elderly people who had been hospitalized because of indigence and illness enabled these physicians to theorize more systematically about the general degeneration characteristic of old age—a degeneration that included arteriosclerosis, fibrosis, and other forms of tissue deterioration. As historian Carole Haber has shown, these doctors concluded that the debilities of old age were irreversible; degenerated tissue, they deduced, could not be restored to a state more characteristic of a younger person.

Disease and degeneration were so much a part of old age that they were nearly the same. According to Jean Martin Charcot, the French doctor who helped lay the foundation for geriatric medicine in the mid-nineteenth century, "We shall have to note that the textual changes which old age induces in the organism sometimes attain such a point that the physiological and pathological seem to mingle by an imperceptible transition, and to be no longer distinguishable."[24] To medical researchers and practitioners, then, the elderly constituted a distinct life-cycle group, and they required treatment specific to their particular ailments and diseases.[25]

The findings of French clinicians prompted British and American physicians to identify with more accuracy the pathologies of old age, especially those that led to death. In doing so, they focused on the schedule of life and tried to define more precisely when old age began. This definition derived from the old concept of the climacteric. At first, physicians referred to a "climacteric disease," an abrupt change in the system that signaled the decline of vital energy and the onset of old age. Not only was an individual of advanced years more susceptible to life-threatening ailments, but that individual also took on the look of old age: stooped posture, sagging muscles, wrinkled skin. Equally important, the climacteric disease included a tendency toward insanity.

By the late nineteenth century, however, physicians conceived of the climacteric less as a disease than as a total biological and psychological condition that marked the division between maturity and senescence, "the turning point towards the downhill course," as one writer observed.[26] At this point in life, doctors noted, the two sexes merged in behavioral characteristics; men who had once been noble and brave and women who had once been nurturant and moral now became dependent, passive, and weak.[27] Moreover, as a result of work by American physicians on the climacteric condition, the terms *senile* and *senility* took on new and telling meanings.

As Haber has noted, before the nineteenth century, the term *senile* was a seldom-used neutral adjective referring to the quality of being old. It was not applied explicitly to the debilitation of mind or body. Thomas Jefferson, for example, wrote in 1794 that he eagerly awaited the time of life when he would exchange "the roars and tumults of the bulls and bears for the prattles of my grandchildren and senile rest."[28] But as doctors increasingly ascribed particular ailments to old age, the term acquired pathological and negative connotations. Even diseases that appeared among all age groups were given special names that represented new beliefs about the degeneration of old age. Thus, the medical lexicon enlarged to include "senile bronchitis," "senile gangrene," "senile pneumonia," and "senile chorea." Such a trend reflected and reinforced the notion that senility, the state of being old, was not only a distinct period of life but one in which debilitating illnesses were common, expected, and inevitably fatal.[29]

The use of the term senility to connote mental deterioration also evolved in the late nineteenth century. Senile dementia, the loss of reason in old age, had been a recognized affliction since Biblical times and was made a tragic theme in dramas such as Shakespeare's *King Lear*, but it was more often assumed to be an abnormal rather than a normal condition. In the nineteenth century, however, as physicians identified various forms of lesions and tissue decay among the elderly, they generally agreed that brain cells also suffered from the degenerative process. As the body decayed, so too did the mind. Thus, Dr. Charles Mercier wrote in 1890 that the psychological process of aging

> is a continuous, gradually progressive loss. Conduct, intelligence, feeling, and self-consciousness gradually diminish and at last cease to exist. . . . The decadence of old age is, in fact, a *dementia*, a deprivation of mind. It is a normal and psychological dementia, the natural and inevitable result of the gradual subsidence of the molecular movements of the nervous elements into stillness; the natural outcome of the exhaustion of the initial impetus which started the organism upon its course of life.[30]

Medical authorities now indicated not that loss of memory and intellect *could* happen in old age but that it *normally should* occur; such debility, they said, was natural and inevitable, because deterioration of tissue in the brain followed the same pattern as deterioration of tissue in other organs. Pushing these conclusions even further, some physicians warned that the brain decay and loss of reason that accompanied deterioration could also produce undesirable personality changes. Having lost moral judgment and self-control, people in old age could become antisocial, irrational, irritable, petulant, selfish, depressed, suicidal, or sexually perverse.[31] As with forgetfulness, these traits became equated with senility and came to be regarded as the normal behavioral characteristics of old age.

Such expectations prompted directors of some institutions to make marked changes in their policies toward the aged. Hospitals in the mid-nineteenth century had accepted and provided facilities for older people in declining health, even if the patients had no specifically diagnosed ailment. For example, Boston's Carney Hospital, a Roman Catholic institution that opened in 1869, reserved one floor exclusively for "old people who may not be sick but come here for a home."[32] Chicago's St. Luke's Hospital developed a similar policy in the 1860s, opening its wards to aged infirm men who had nowhere else to live.[33]

But in general, as doctors embraced the conclusion that old people's illnesses, whether physical or mental, were incurable manifestations of natural degeneration, they influenced hospital administrators away from accepting the elderly as patients. The modern hospital was viewed as a facility where new medical techniques could be used to cure acute illnesses and injuries.[34] Thus, administrators and their staffs preferred to admit those patients whose treatment promised improvement. (The same policy is in effect today.) They assumed that any individual who survived beyond age seventy inevitably suffered from chronic ailments and senility, conditions that offered no hope of being cured, and would degenerate into complete incapacity and dependence. Instead, medical personnel urged that the elderly in need of care be admitted to old-age homes, which could tend to them without the taint of the almshouse. Though the vast majority of older people needing care still lived with family members, by the end of the nineteenth century the number of superannuated inmates of old-age institutions was rapidly increasing (see Chapter 5). The city of Philadelphia had at least twenty-four such homes in 1900, and similar establishments had opened in a variety of places, including Charleston, South Carolina, and Minneapolis, Minnesota. Admission policies usually required that applicants be at least sixty or sixty-five, thereby creating a standardized boundary between adulthood and old age. As these institutions spread throughout all regions of the country, they became symptomatic of the new attitudes Americans were adopting toward the country's elderly population.[35]

The attitudes toward old women differed somewhat from the attitudes toward old men. As historian Lois Banner has noted, throughout much of the nineteenth century older women aroused more ambivalent feelings in the public mind than did older men. The image of the saintly grandmother, sweet and doting, existed side by side with that of the wrinkled, bent, and crabby hag. By the end of the century, according to Banner, society's new emphasis on youth prompted some popular writers to urge all women to look and act young. As a result, older women tried to enhance their physical appearance by looking and dressing younger. Yet even though the budding consumer industries of cosmetics and retail fashions strengthened the connection between beauty and youth, cultural prescriptions exhorting people, especially older people, to act their age were increasing. Thus, at the turn of the century, popular writer Celia Parker Woolley complained: "The haste and impetuosity so becoming to eighteen are immoral at fifty. . . . It is neither pleasant nor edifying to see an aging man or woman aping the behavior of the young."[36]

By the end of the nineteenth century, then, medical theorists and practitioners had defined old age in accordance with the rising public consciousness of age and life schedules. Expanding upon the concept of the climacteric and drawing from clinical studies of tissue and organ decay, they concluded that old age marked a unique stage of life when certain physiological processes and conditions not only occurred but were inevitable. As soon as individuals experienced these processes and became afflicted with these conditions, they entered the stage of senescence—a period when all others of the same age bore the same characteristics. Because of new scientific research on the link between advanced age and biological and mental decay, doctors had convincing reasons for treating old people as a separate group, and other experts and authorities had grounds for isolating, in the public mind if not physically, the aged from the rest of society. As individuals in need of constant medical attention because of their irreversible debilitation, and whose intellects suffered the same degeneration as their bodies, the old could no longer command respect as repositories of wisdom and experience. To medical experts and social observers, their separation was natural, necessary, and desirable.

## EDUCATION AND THE SCHEDULING OF CHILDREN'S LIVES

By 1890, the sequencing of elementary, secondary, and college education in America and the age grading on which it was based had been set. With the exception of a few New England systems that organized elementary schools into seven grades and some southern schools that provided for nine years of elementary education, the normal course (at least for middle-class whites) consisted of eight years of elementary schooling, plus (for a minority of youths) four years of secondary or high school instruction and four years of college. During the 1890s, however, a number of educators questioned this sequence and initiated discussions about how to reorganize it more efficiently. Though some minor reforms were adopted, the system resisted radical change. Nevertheless, the changes that did occur, and especially the debates that some of the recommended reforms provoked, reflected heightened consciousness of scheduling and age norms.

In 1888, Charles W. Eliot, president of Harvard University and one of the nation's leading education reformers, addressed a meeting of the National Education Association (NEA) on the subject "Can School Programmes Be Shortened and Enriched?" Eliot noted that in recent decades the average age at matriculation into Harvard had steadily risen until it currently stood at eighteen years ten months. Given that an individual normally spent four years at Harvard, and that the period for professional training after graduation had expanded to three or four years, "the average college graduate who fits himself for any one of the learned professions, including teaching, can hardly begin to support himself before he is 27 years old."[37] Eliot deemed this situation lamentable because it delayed a young man's entry into productive life longer than was the case among his European counterparts.

Eliot and the Harvard faculty had been grappling since the early 1880s with ways to condense school courses. They eventually made four recommendations: reduce college entrance requirements so that students could matriculate at younger ages; urge parents to send sons to college as soon as they seemed qualified (daughters remained an overlooked class); reduce the term of college education from four years to three; and persuade elementary and secondary school educators to shorten their courses.[38]

These suggestions inspired a plethora of discussions that expressed and reinforced the age consciousness that had become so pervasive in the educational system. Influenced by Eliot, the National Council of the NEA appointed in 1890 a Committee of Ten to sponsor a series of conferences between schoolteachers and college educators. These conferences were organized to discuss the best methods of instruction, the amount of time to be allotted to each school subject, and methods for assessing students' attainments. Eliot chaired the committee, which arranged meetings on nine separate curriculum subjects and issued a combined report later that year. Though the meetings originally were intended to assess secondary education, the conferees found that they could not make recommendations for secondary education without considering matters relating to elementary schools.

Age consciousness and references to explicit age norms pervaded the conference reports. For example, the meeting on Latin compared ages at which European and American students began the study of that language and advised "that such a modification of grammar-school courses can be made without delay as to render it possible that the high school course—and with it the subject of Latin—may be begun not later than the age of 14."[39] The conferees in the meeting on Greek language concurred that instruction in that subject could commence at the same age that pupils could begin learning Latin, and the meeting on modern languages concluded that students were ready to learn German and French in the fifth grade, when pupils were ten or eleven.[40]

Age requirements and norms became increasingly important considerations in other deliberations during the 1890s relating to the length of school terms. One often-discussed issue was whether the elementary school course should be reduced from eight to six grades and the high school course expanded from four to six years. The issue stimulated debates over the proper age at which a youth should begin high school. For example, the NEA Committee on College Entrance Requirements backed six-year courses for both elementary and high school. Committee members argued that because the seventh grade, when children were in their early teens, was the natural turning point in students' lives—rather than the ninth grade when they were in their mid-teens—they would be able to make an easier transition to high school between sixth and seventh grade.[41] In 1898, Nicholas Murray Butler, president of Columbia University and an influential spokesperson on education policy, voiced his support for the idea that an earlier transition to high school was desirable because it led to an earlier matriculation at college. Butler evoked emerging theories of youth development when he wrote: "The secondary period is essentially the period of adolescence, or what may be called active adolescence as distinguishable from later and less violent manifestations of physical and mental change. . . . The *normal* years [of adolescence] are, with us, from 12 to 16, or from 13 to 17. The *normal* boy or girl who is going to college *ought* to enter at 17 at the latest" (emphasis added).[42]

The statements and reports of Eliot, Butler, and the NEA committees criticized a graded sequence of education that they believed was too rigid. The existing system, they argued, extended schooling too long, beyond the age at which young people should have entered productive pursuits. Yet the various discussions and proposals seemed to impose age requirements that were as strict as or stricter than those of the system they hoped to reform. Some analysts recognized the consequences. For example, William Shearer, superintendent of schools in Elizabeth, New Jersey, complained in 1898 that the existing system of grades and age norms was too inflexible. To him, they kept "children of each grade in intellectual lock-step," regardless of their differences.[43] Shearer wanted to divide school terms into shorter intervals of a half year or less and to restore ungraded classes for the benefit of slow learners and brighter pupils. But his ideas did not fit with the tendency toward age standardization that even reformers like Eliot and Butler supported. Particularly as more four-year high schools were being established throughout the United States, the insularity of teenage students within an age-bounded environment was becoming uniform and accepted.[44] Proposals to end elementary school at the sixth grade and begin secondary schooling in the seventh grade ultimately led to creation of the junior high school in the early decades of the twentieth century (see Chapter 4), but this institution was the product of even more complex theories about age norms and adolescence.

## AGE NORMS AND POPULAR CULTURE

Enhanced consciousness of age and normative schedules can be identified in a variety of contexts other than formal institutions and thought in the 1890s. Schoolgirls' jump rope games and rhymes, for instance, began to specify age more explicitly than ever before. Usually played by girls in their preteen years, around ages nine to eleven, these contests included verses that the girls chanted in time to their hops over the swinging rope. One of the most popular games, which seems to date from the late 1890s or early 1900s, involved the recitation of sequential numbers, representing age, with the winner being the jumper who could count to the highest age without missing a hop over the rope:

> I was born in a frying pan,
> Can you guess how old I am?
> One, two, three, four . . .[45]

The second line is the important one here, for it signals explicit numerical expression of age.

At about the same time, a New York publisher printed *Maidenhead Stories*, a pornographic book that was deliberate and explicit in its mention of ages. This series of stories follows a somewhat prosaic model of one kind of prurience: a group of male students from a certain "Smith College" gather and one by one relate in lubricous detail the circumstances in which he lost his "maidenhead." Each tale is precise about its characters' ages, almost to the point of implying norms. Thus, "Tom Brown" lost his virginity at age fifteen to a "young servant girl"; a lad named "Burton," at age fourteen to a neighbor's wife; "Stuyvesant," at age thirteen to a twelve-year-old neighbor girl; "J. Richard," at age fifteen to a fifteen-year-old girl in a hayloft; "Winthrow," at age fifteen to a nineteen-year-old hired girl; and so on.[46]

On a related theme, autobiographer Flo Menninger was acutely conscious that the age at which she learned the "facts of life" in 1890 was later than the perceived norm. "I was nineteen years old," she wrote, looking back from the 1930s, "before I had a true idea of where a baby came from—an old maid told me during the time I was teaching my second term of school. Perhaps you can realize something of what it cost me to get this information in such a blunt way and to be laughed at and made fun of for my ignorance."[47] Menninger was embarrassed that her edification in this matter had been "behind time"—in other words, off schedule.

Debates over the so-called emancipation of women, published in popular periodicals from the late 1880s onward, also reflected new consciousness of scheduling norms when they focused on how expanded opportunities would affect a woman's traditional life course. The pages of magazines such as *Cosmopolitan* and *North American Review* reveal frequent challenges to and defenses of the customary sequence of schooling, marriage, and motherhood. In "The Emancipation of Women," David J. Hill, a university president, mused that increased college attendance and labor force participation might cause women to reject the traditional life course and create a society consisting "exclusively of [old] maids and bachelors." But in actuality, Hill concluded, the real consequence would be that women would simply postpone marriage and motherhood to "a later stage in their lives."[48] Hill's language implies awareness of both scheduling and norms.

Other writers, such as feminist Belva Lockwood, agreed that the timing of stages would change if women became emancipated, and she even urged such change. Lockwood not only noted that extended education would delay marriage for a woman but also advised that she should "look upon marriage not as a necessity, but as a sacred and inviolable contract into which she has no right to enter until able to be self supporting."[49] For our purposes here, the arguments in these and other articles are less important than the expression of concepts such as stage, delay, and postponement, all of which imply scheduling and norms.

THUS, as the nineteenth century drew to a close, the trend toward categorization, arrangement, and care of individuals according to their chronological age, which had developed first in the education and medical treatment of children, was now permeating other realms of American society and culture. But in addition to philosophical, bureaucratic, and biological justifications for age grading, new normative considerations were developing; that is, the early rationales and institutional reforms were fostering prescriptions not only as to what various individuals *could* be doing at particular ages but also as to what they *should* be doing. More than ever before, age was becoming a characteristic fraught with expectations.

# · 4 ·

## INTENSIFICATION OF AGE NORMS: 1900–1920

By the beginning of the twentieth century, age consciousness and age grading had become fixed in American institutions and culture. Publication in 1904 of a Bureau of the Census study, *Bulletin 13: A Discussion of Age Statistics*, symbolized and epitomized the new trend. This report, compiled from data collected in the 1900 federal census, marked the first time the census bureau had undertaken an extensive analysis of age and its significance. European statisticians had been studying age data for several decades before 1900, and in some ways *Bulletin 13* represented an attempt by the United States to keep abreast of other countries. But the analysis also reflected the heightened significance of age in national life and policy.

Allyn A. Young, assistant professor of finance at Dartmouth College and author of *Bulletin 13*, expressed this awareness when he wrote, "For the purpose of a scientific study of the population, the classification by age is only less important and fundamental than that based on sex."[1] Age data, said Young, were important not only because they provided crucial information about military strength, size of the electorate, economic potential of the work force, and characteristics of the coming generation, but also because they facilitated predictions about crime, pauperism, literacy, and mortality.

Such analytical opportunities existed because the 1900 census recorded ages more accurately than any previous census had. Significantly, before 1850 federal censuses did not include specific age information. Following census bureau guidelines, enumerators merely recorded people in age categories, usually set up in ten-year divisions. The numbers of people who were discrete ages were not compiled. Beginning in 1850 and continuing through 1880, census takers entered age at last birthday for every individual recorded. In 1890, the bureau changed the category to age at nearest birthday, but the revision proved too confusing. Age at last birthday was restored in 1900, but a new item, date of birth, was added as a check on age accuracy.

Data on age, together with wide-ranging information on other population characteristics, such as gender, birthplace, residence, race, occupation, marital status, and much more, made the census of 1900 the most detailed ever produced. Its myriad tables, percentages, and ratios manifested the burgeoning of American social science, with its passion for measurement and categorization. Systematic accumulation of information, it was believed, would facilitate creation of a well-ordered society, one in which there was no possibility that incomplete knowledge could hinder progress. A concomitant of this new emphasis on statistics was the consolidation and intensification of age norms in the first two decades of the new century.

## G. Stanley Hall, Child Development, and the Age Norms of Youth

The strengthening of age norms in institutions and thought in the early 1900s can be traced to one central figure: psychologist Granville Stanley Hall. Beginning with his studies of children in the 1880s and 1890s and culminating in 1904 with his landmark publication, *Adolescence: Its Psychology and Its Relations to Physiology, Anthropology, Sociology, Sex, Crime, Religion, and Education*, Hall's ideas influenced the course of both psychology and pedagogy, including the study of child development, curricular and organizational reform in the schools, physical education and recreation, and mental testing. Though Hall was not the only inspiration for developments in these areas, his theories influenced all of them.

Hall's career coincided with the rise of psychology, a new science devoted to the study of human behavior. Indeed, his contributions advanced the field in such a significant way that a friend once referred to him as "the Darwin of the mind." After earning a doctorate in psychology under William James at Harvard in 1878, Hall spent two years in Germany studying with leading figures in the fields of physics, physiology, and psychology. Though Hall was not originally interested in child development, he could not avoid being exposed to the activity in this field that was sweeping German psychological research at the time. Biologist Wilhelm Preyer had become especially influential among European scientists, and his publication of *The Mind of the Child* in 1881 intensified interest in the possibilities of understanding a child's mental development.[2]

Shortly after his return to the United States, Hall was appointed professor of psychology and pedagogy at The Johns Hopkins University in Baltimore, where he began research in experimental psychology and its applications to pedagogy. At Johns Hopkins, Hall trained a number of bright and ultimately influential young scholars, including educational reformer John Dewey, mental-testing pioneer Lewis Terman, and child psychologist Arnold Gesell. In 1888, Hall became president of newly established Clark University in Worcester, Massachusetts, and though he remained in that administrative post for over thirty years, he continued to research and publish, becoming the nation's leading figure in the child study movement.

Drawing from Charles Darwin's work in biology and from Herbert Spencer's social applications of Darwinism, Hall developed a psychological theory positing that the growing human organism recapitulated the stages of evolution experienced by the human race. That is, he believed an individual's physical and behavioral development passed through stages that corresponded closely to the periods through which humans evolved from pre-savagery to civilization. To Hall, the child was indeed parent to the adult. Because each stage of human development functioned as a crucial stimulus for the next, childhood was a particularly important period, warranting close attention and study. How successful and advanced a society was, in Hall's terms, depended on how well its children negotiated the perilous early stages. Thus, child study became the focus of Hall's research, and institutions of youth, especially schools, formed the nucleus of that research.[3]

Hall's theory of youth development contains an unusual blend of romanticism and scientific rationalism. According to Hall, the first eighteen years of life consists of three stages, each with a parallel in racial history and a requisite type of pedagogy to accompany it. Infancy and early childhood, he believed, constitute a period of primitive instincts and behavior, similar to the pre-savage stage of human evolution. During this stage, parents and teachers should leave the child to nature, encouraging activities with sand and blocks to foster development of the body's larger muscles. Then, at about age six or seven, the child experiences crises that lead into the preadolescent years of eight to twelve, when individualistic and unimaginative behavior harken back to the world of early pygmies and other so-called savages. At this point, the brain has grown almost to adult size, and the body resists fatigue. The child is now ready to enter school, though because the child's senses are so acute and vigorous, education at this stage should emphasize drill and obedience in order to inculcate self-discipline.

A new period of crisis then gives birth to adolescence, between ages thirteen and eighteen—a time of emotionalism, idealistism, and communal behavior, reminiscent of ancient and medieval civilizations. Adolescence is crucial, Hall asserted, because it prepares the youth for the acquisition of knowledge, mores, and skills that will determine the future of the individual and, by extension, that of the human race. "The dawn of puberty," he wrote, "is soon followed by a stormy period . . . when there is peculiar proneness to be either very good or very bad."[4]

Professional educators soon began to incorporate Hall's theories into their rationale for school reform. The previous chapter introduced the debates over changing the organization of grades to meet the newly perceived needs of teenagers. These debates extended into the early 1900s, as reformers continued to offer proposals based on age-prescriptive theories that meshed with Hall's ideas. In 1904, for example, the Commission of Twenty-One, a committee of the NEA, issued a report summarizing the main questions facing school reformers. Chaired by William Rainey Harper, president of the University of Chicago, the commission directed itself particularly to the issue of reducing the number of elementary grades to correspond to the period of childhood—ages six to twelve—and matching secondary grades to adolescence—ages thirteen to eighteen.[5] The report only raised questions concerning these issues and made no proposals other than that, in good bureaucratic style, a new commission of fifteen members be appointed to investigate them.

Though the NEA tabled this modest recommendation, the issues of reorganization and regrading continued to simmer. In 1909, a Chicago high school principal presented the NEA with a plan for a school system comprising four age-graded divisions: play-oriented classes for ages three to seven; "motor type" or elementary school for ages seven to twelve; "intermediate type" for ages twelve to fourteen; and "secondary type" for ages fourteen to eighteen. Supporting Hall's contention that children experienced crises just before adolescence, he justified the intermediate division by noting that "children at 12 to 14 should be isolated from younger and from more mature pupils in order to accord them proper environment for their peculiar condition."[6] Other reformers proposed different subdivisions, but all agreed that a major break should occur at age twelve to accommodate the needs of adolescence. For example, in 1913 James H. Baker, president of the NEA, offered his own plan for extending secondary education to encompass youths as young as twelve, asserting that "many processes of mental training are easier in the earlier years. Beginning high school methods at 12 will meet the needs of pupils who at that age are restless and are seeking larger and more varied interests."[7]

Notions of child development and age norms influenced religious as well as secular educational reformers. The Uniform Lessons instituted in Protestant Sunday schools in the 1870s had provoked objections that they were inappropriate for younger children as well as for adults. During the 1880s and 1890s, the American Sunday School Union entertained numerous proposals for lesson plans designed for distinct age groups but sanctioned none of them. Around 1900, however, scientific studies of child development published by Hall and others began to win recognition among religious educators such as Erastus Blakeslee, who introduced a series of age-graded lessons in the study of the Bible that successfully competed with the Uniform Lessons. Then, in 1906, a number of religious teachers and editors organized a Graded Lesson Conference in Newark, New Jersey, to revise the Uniform Lessons to fit specific age groups. As a result of the conference's influence, the International Lessons Committee of the International Sunday School Convention of 1908 recommended preparation of fully graded lessons. After accepting the recommendation, the convention authorized the publication of what came to be called the *International Graded Lessons*, the intention of which was "to meet the spiritual needs of the pupil in each stage of his development"; it thus offered age-specific lessons, usually centering on Bible stories. Sunday schools, like secular schools, now were being organized to move children along an age-graded ladder.[8]

Hall's ideas gave a stronger foothold to the concept of normative schedules in education—of fitting school grades and curricula to the age-based needs of growing children. Yet ironically, the concern over scheduling that had heightened in the 1890s gave way in the early 1900s to a concern over the failure of some children to meet standards set for specific grades. A more precise, scientific classification of the stages of mental and physical development resulted in greater emphasis on what was "normal" and, indirectly, on age criteria. Increasingly, educators focused on the incongruities between emerging age norms and actual conditions in the schools.

In particular, two problems associated with children who had fallen behind schedule vexed school officials. One problem was termed "retardation," the phenomenon of children whose abilities had not developed sufficiently to allow them to pass from one grade to the next, or who for other reasons were in less advanced grades than their ages warranted. The other problem was "elimination," the phenomenon of children dropping out of school before their educational training was deemed sufficient. In 1904, Dr. William H. Maxwell, superintendent of New York City schools, disclosed that 39 percent of his city's elementary school children were older than the normal age for their grade. Maxwell's report spurred superintendants of Philadelphia, Chicago, St. Louis, and Detroit to collect and express concern over similar data.[9] And in 1909, reformer Leonard Ayers published *Laggards in Our Schools*, an often-cited and provocative study that dramatized high rates of retardation and elimination in a number of city school systems.[10] Investigators like Ayers posited several reasons for such rates, but what is more important in the current context is the emphasis that these authors placed on "normal" ages for school grades. Indeed, psychologist Lightner Witmer asserted that age/grade statistics signified the extent of "backwardness" among American schoolchildren.[11]

Concern over age incongruities in American schools reached new intensity in 1911 with the publication of a U.S. Bureau of Education bulletin titled *Age and Grade Census of Schools and Colleges*. Like the 1904 Bureau of the Census *Bulletin 13* that compiled and analyzed age data for the entire population, this examination of school ages became another landmark in the development of American age consciousness. Using information collected in 1908 from 132 cities with populations of 25,000 or more and from 186 communities with populations of under 25,000, the report presented tables on the numbers and proportions of children in each community who were at, above, and below "normal" age for their grade.

George Dayton Strayer, professor of education administration at Columbia University and author of the 1911 bulletin's narrative section, was alarmed by the data because, he concluded, the tables showed that "grades are full of children who are two, three, or four years over age." Though Strayer did not believe that educators must ensure that all pupils be the "normal" age for their grade—urging instead that special schools be established for slow learners—he nevertheless expressed support for age criteria as the most bureaucratically efficient means of organizing schoolchildren. Thus, echoing early proponents of age-graded schools, he concluded: "When you may find in one grade children from 8 to 15 years of age, or from 6 to 12, the work of the teacher can not . . . be as effective as it should be. The situation demands grouping on the basis of maturity and educability rather than on the basis of ability to solve arithmetic problems or spell words not commonly used in the written expression of children."[12]

All the publicity about and discussions of retardation, elimination, and developmental needs of adolescents produced in the first decade of the twentieth century a major institutional reform in American education: creation of the junior high school. The fact that school dropout rates were soaring among youths aged twelve, thirteen, and fourteen seemed both to emphasize the distinctiveness of adolescence and to suggest that schools were not meeting the intellectual needs of students at these ages. With these factors in mind, the educational committee of the Minneapolis Commercial Club, a civic organization of prominent businessmen, designed and offered to the board of education in 1910 a plan for establishing "intermediate" schools that would comprise the seventh, eighth, and ninth grades exclusively. In rationalizing the need for intermediate schools board members must have had Hall in mind, for they recommended the plan to the superintendent with the advice that "at about 12 years of age, which usually marks the beginning of adolescence, children begin to differ markedly in their tastes and capacity; and to attempt longer to teach them . . . everything offered in these grades, or which may be profitably offered there, is in our opinion a grievous waste of the pupil's time, the teacher's energy, and the people's money."[13]

One of the driving forces in the national movement to establish junior high schools was Frank Forest Bunker, superintendent of schools in Berkeley, California. Bunker's critique of the eight-four division of school grades derived its logic directly from Hall. "The school system," he claimed, "in its organic form, and in the articulation of its parts, completely ignores the significant physiological and psychological changes which are ushered in with the advent of adolescence." Such ignorance, Bunker continued, accounted for the high dropout rates in the upper grammar school grades and in early high school.[14]

In 1910, Bunker instituted separate schools for the seventh, eighth, and ninth grades in Berkeley, and many other school systems followed suit. By 1930, there were some four thousand junior high schools across the nation, with enrollments totaling over a million and a quarter pupils.[15] The effects were important in the history of age grading, for the junior high school defined a new age group: youths between twelve and fourteen years old, whose biological and psychological development distinguished them from younger, elementary school children but who were not quite full-blown, high school adolescents. And by paring down high schools from four years to three and creating a new and separate three-year institution, educators helped to create and refine youth peer groups: a new group of junior high schoolers and, consequently, a more narrowly defined group of high schoolers.

As Joseph Kett, David Macleod, and other historians have observed, reforms in junior and senior high schools—often based on new psychological theories of child development, especially those of G. Stanley Hall—resulted in the prolongation of childhood dependence. As urbanization and industrialization transformed American society, imposing on youths new requirements for economic success and luring them with new temptations and diversions, middle-class reformers came to believe that extended isolation in schools would give children a chance to develop intellectual, physical, and moral capacities before they had to meet the challenges of adult life. Attending school became not only more standardized but more common. By 1919, 86 percent of all fourteen-year-old youths were attending some sort of school, and between 1890 and 1920, the number of all fourteen- to seventeen-year-olds in school rose markedly, from 203,000 to 2,200,000.[16]

The protected environment of schools, with their rigidly age-graded organization, herded together pupils into even tighter peer groups, which in turn enveloped youths in new patterns of socialization and sharpened their own sensitivities to age differences and age expectations. By the early 1900s, passage from elementary school to junior high school and from junior high school to senior high school marked important transitions for youths and nurtured precise expectations and norms for each age-bounded grade and type of school. A fourteen-year-old who was still in the sixth grade was keenly aware of being out of step with peers, as were boys who did not switch from knickers to long pants at thirteen.[17] Equally important, these peer groups and accompanying age expectations were bolstered by new scientific standards for physical and intellectual attainment.

## AGE AND PHYSICAL TRAINING

Child study, with its grounding in evolutionary and developmental theories, strongly influenced the burgeoning new field of physical education. Impulses to train children's bodies as well as their minds resulted in various efforts to formalize play and to make functional what formerly had been nonutilitarian activity. Equally significant, however, was the way the resulting increase in popularity of organized games and sports fostered age consciousness and age grading.

Early nineteenth-century private schools and academies included physical education in their curricula as a means of promoting good health. In 1823, for example, the founders of Round Hill School in Northampton, Massachusetts, announced that their academy encouraged "sports and gymnastic exercises" to develop "firmness of constitution and vigour of body."[18] By mid-century, a number of prominent reformers, including Thomas Wentworth Higginson, Catharine Beecher, and Henry Ward Beecher, were advocating a more active life for people of all ages. At about the same time, *Turner* societies—self-improvement clubs that were established by German immigrants and included physical fitness activities—were sprouting up around the country. Indeed, many schools hired *Turner* members as fitness instructors.

Reformers institutionalized systematic physical education within American public schools in the late 1860s. In 1866, California passed the first statewide law requiring physical training in public elementary and secondary schools, and other states soon copied the law.[19] The 1870s saw the introduction of Swedish gymnastics, with its regimen of calisthenics, which soon exerted a profound influence on education leaders.[20] But the age-organized development of formal games and sports did not occur until the turn of the century, when the play movement arose as one of the impulses of progressive reform. At this point, health educators joined with reformers who were seeking to manage children's spare-time activities, and the resulting movement reinforced age-graded divisions of youth and strengthened bonds within peer groups.

The leading American proponent of formal physical training in the early twentieth century was Luther Halsey Gulick, an educator whose work and writings promoted the view that physical activities should be geared to age-related needs. Gulick, who served as director of physical education at the YMCA International College in Springfield, Massachusetts, and later served in a similar position with the New York City public schools, was, not surprisingly, a friend and advocate of G. Stanley Hall. At Hall's urging, Gulick published in 1899 an article on "Psychological, Pedagogical, and Religious Aspects of Group Games," in which he outlined his theory of physical play as an expression of the body's hunger for exercise. In the article, he presented a chart listing common forms of play among various discrete age groups. Gulick's concept of an age-graded play order gave direction to the emerging field of physical education.[21]

The next year, Gulick became principal of Pratt Institute High School in Brooklyn, New York, and began elaborating his ideas on the interrelationships between physical and intellectual development. These theories prompted him to advocate what he called the "open door" policy, a scheme that promoted strict age grading in schools and emphasized the benefits of peer grouping over those of aggregating pupils by ability. The mastery of all subjects in a given grade, Gulick claimed, was not as important as enabling students to profit from social and intellectual contact with age peers. Physical maturity should take precedence over intellectual attainment. Thus, a nine-year-old who had not previously attended school should not be forced to start in kindergarten or first grade; rather, "the child should as rapidly as possible be put in with children of its [sic] own maturity."[22] Unless a student was hopelessly handicapped, he or she should be promoted with peers; and if the student reached the end of the education process without having completed all requirements, he or she then could take additional time to make up any deficiencies. The open door scheme derived from Gulick's earlier emphasis on physical education as vital to spiritual and intellectual development. To him, age-related needs constituted the basis for child training, and peers were as important as, or more important than, teachers and curriculum in the education process.

Gulick achieved his best-known accomplishments during his tenure as director of physical education in the New York City public schools, a post he assumed in 1903. There he created, as part of a citywide physical education program, the Public School Athletic League (PSAL) to systematize sports and physical activity for boys. (A girls' branch was established in 1905, though its predominant offering was dancing rather than athletics.) The league's purpose was to promote physical fitness through athletic competition, not just in team sports but also in individual contests such as chinning and rope climbing. Badges were awarded to those whose accomplishments in these events met certain standards. More importantly, Gulick wanted to avoid competition that was dominated by overgrown boys and older, semi-truants who played on school teams to give them competitive advantages. To encourage participation by all, he organized contests and events by age; when this proved unfair to slow maturers, he used a combination of age and weight.[23] As in the open door policy, Gulick stressed the value of peer grouping; though he recognized that children of the same age varied in size and ability, he believed capacities such as body control and endurance were mostly similar in children of the same age and therefore justified age-graded competition.[24] As a model for similar programs established nationally, the PSAL institutionalized age-graded athletics and, as a consequence, peer-group socialization.

After Gulick, the person most responsible for the extensive systematization of age-graded physical education was Jessie Hubbell Bancroft, Gulick's assistant director of physical training in the New York City public schools and the first woman member of the American Academy of Physical Education. Bancroft had become interested in athletics as a means of improving her own fragile health when she was a teenager in the 1880s. She studied German and Swedish gymnastics in Minneapolis and took courses on anatomy and gymnastics at the Harvard University Summer School of Physical Education. In 1893, she was appointed director of physical training in the Brooklyn public schools, a post she held until Gulick made her his assistant in 1904. In both positions, Bancroft devoted much of her time to organizing exercises and games for children in their ten- to fifteen-minute school recesses. One of her early publications was a pamphlet, printed in 1903, listing rules for sixty-one recess games and prescribing the age group for which each game was appropriate.[25]

Over the next several years, Bancroft engaged in further research and in 1920 presented a fuller compilation of games in *Games for the Playground, Home, School, and Gymnasium,* a book that was the most comprehensive catalog of games of its time. Significantly, each explanation of a game prescribed strict age limits. Bancroft clearly drew her rationale from Hall and other child development theorists. As she explained in her introduction: "The natural interests of a normal child lead him to care for different types of games at different periods of his development. In other words, his powers, in their natural evolution, seek instinctively the elements of play that will contribute to their own growth. When games are studied from this viewpoint of the child's interests, they are found to fall into groups having pronounced characteristics at different periods."[26] Though she acknowledged that variable conditions such as experience, fatigue, and environment could affect the suitability of specific games at specific times, and therefore made rigid age prescriptions artificial, Bancroft nevertheless defended a normative schedule of play. Thus, she urged, "if [proper play interests] should not appear in due time, they should be encouraged, just as attention is given to the hygiene of a child who is under weight for his age."[27]

On the one hand, Bancroft abjured rigid age prescription, because she believed that whatever is fun at any age should be acceptable. On the other hand, her developmentally oriented view of physical, mental, and emotional capacities prompted her to counsel that by a particular age children should be able to manage the requirements of certain games, and if they were not able to meet those requirements, they must be made to do so in order to keep up with their peers. Thus, she believed, certain games were not only more suitable for specific ages but also more functional. For example, young children responded best to short, repetitive games; as they grew older, they liked longer games with more suspense. By ages eleven and twelve, they no longer favored chase games; rather, she explained, in terms derived directly from Hall's recapitulation theory, they should play more strenuous team games that resembled primitive warfare.[28] In all, *Games for the Playground, Home, School, and Gymnasium* described some four hundred games and included rules, diagrams, and, most particularly, age boundaries for each.

The play movement, which was concerned with children's activities outside the organized environment of schools, also reinforced age grading in games. Impetus for the movement arose out of a concern over loss of healthy recreation for all ages because urbanization and industrialization had diminished opportunities and space for play.

Moreover, said play reformers, lack of adult supervision had allowed children's play to lapse into crime and vandalism, and commercialization of leisure activities was transforming recreation into idle spectator pursuits. Play reformers hoped to restore active, character-building recreation through the establishment of playgrounds, parks, social centers, music and drama clubs, and other organized activities. Their efforts, beginning with the introduction of sand gardens for very young children in Boston in 1885, reached full flower with the founding of the Playground Association of America in 1906 by Luther Gulick and Henry Curtis.[29]

Play reformers were concerned with recreation for all ages, but their various projects reflected a strong sense of peer grouping. In addition to sand gardens for preschool children, they supported special playgrounds for "little boys and girls," such as the New York City park at Ninety-ninth Street and Second Avenue, which was equipped with seesaws, swings, wheelbarrows, and wagons; "playgrounds for big boys," such as Boston's three summer playgrounds, for boys aged twelve to fifteen, which were equipped with gymnastic apparatus and supervised by trained physical educators; the "recreation centers" created for Chicago adolescents; and various classes and facilities for adults, including nighttime use of schools in Chicago, Los Angeles, Philadelphia, Boston, and New York. In fact, in response to the movement's expanded focus to include adult age groups as well as children, the Playground Association of America in 1911 changed its name to Playground and Recreation Association of America.[30]

Still, children remained at the center of play movement reforms and publications, and theories of child development not only inspired play reformers but also sharpened their age consciousness. A typical expression of this consciousness was the book *Education By Play and Games* (1907), written by George Ellsworth Johnson, superintendent of playgrounds, recreation parks, and vacation schools in Pittsburgh. In this publication, dedicated to G. Stanley Hall and including an introduction by Hall, Johnson tried to demonstrate how organized play contrasted with idleness and contributed to building character in a child. Just as school curricula were being adapted to the stages of a child's development, Johnson argued, so too must play. Using child development studies, he first outlined five age-graded stages of youth and summarized the physiological, neurological, intellectual, and emotional characteristics unique to each stage. The five divisions were: ages zero to three, four to six, seven to nine, ten to twelve, and thirteen to fifteen. Then, in addition to explaining what kinds of play are engaged in most frequently at each age, Johnson detailed what toys, songs, stories, music, and games are appropriate for each period. Even more than Bancroft, Johnson garbed his theories in scientific cloth, asserting:

> We must seek for the explanation of play in the study of evolution.
> . . . There is a law of child development which has to a degree been
> determined. Now since children unfold or develop in a general
> way according to a definite and universal law, we find occurring
> all along the line certain characteristic reactions to stimuli and
> environment, and these characteristic reactions . . . are the plays
> of children. Some make them reecho the historic activities of the
> race, harking back through the countless generations of human
> evolution; others make them look forward, preparing the child for
> future serious activities of life. . . . Let it suffice here to . . . think
> of play as the child's conforming to the law of his nature.[31]

Evolution and "laws of nature" dictated that play reformers and physical educators organize children's recreation in a way that would most properly correspond to and abet the growth process. The most appropriate type of organization, said Johnson, was one based on age.

By the early 1900s, then, several social movements were intertwining to reinforce the age uniformity of youth peer groups. Longer periods of formal schooling and increased proportions of children attending school prolonged dependency and postponed entry into adulthood. Most states increased the length of the school term to nine months—in some places it previously had been as brief as four months—and required school attendance up to age fourteen. At the same time, states also passed child labor laws, effectively barring children from the work force until, in most instances, they were at least fourteen. Compulsory school attendance laws and minimum-age labor laws reflected and sharpened age consciousness, because they established age fourteen as a new and meaningful milestone in an individual's life course, an institutionalized watershed between school career and work career. Keeping children and youths in their early teens out of the work force meant that they were no longer exposed to an environment that traditionally had been a source of socialization, where they had formal contacts with members of various age groups; instead, they were insulated within an environment that was peopled predominantly by their peers. Also, separation from the work force, in addition to their release from family chores such as milking and harvesting, left urban youths with more spare time than their counterparts in earlier and more rural communities had enjoyed. And concern over the sedentary, potentially wayward lives of these youngsters spurred parents and youth observers to try to manage children's physical and leisure activities.[32]

Educators, character builders, and social reformers tried to construct a new, total environment for youths, one that existed outside as well as inside the schools, and one that incorporated age-graded theories of development. As in the formalization of school curricula, an urge for bureaucratic efficiency in part propelled the age grading of organized physical activity. The writings of play reformers like Bancroft and Johnson prescribe precisely ordered schemes for play and games with strict rules and measurements. The objectives of these reformers were 1) to provide new opportunities for youths to build up their moral and bodily strength, and 2) to fill the void left by a perceived weakening of traditional socializing institutions: family, church, and small community.

But the urge for systematization would not have existed without evolutionary theory, its adaptation to pedagogy by G. Stanley Hall, and its implementation in the realm of physical training by Luther Gulick and his colleagues. These individuals not only recognized that physical capacities changed markedly with age but also believed that proper promotion of physical development, matching activities to age-based capacities, would benefit both individual and society. The results were profound. As numerous YMCAS, PSALs, city playground associations, summer park programs, and school recess programs became major sponsors of games and sports in the early twentieth century, they increasingly pressed youths into uniform age groups. Age-stratified groupings in both school and recreational activities combined to enclose youths in a potent environment that accustomed them to interacting almost exclusively with peers for a significant portion of their daily lives. These regular interactions nurtured in youths expectations for continued peer associations that they carried with them throughout their adult years (see Chapter 5).

## THE ORIGINS OF MENTAL TESTING

The early efforts to organize academic and physical training for children followed concepts of development based chiefly on biological age. But by the early twentieth century, another concept, that of mental age, was beginning to enter educational schemes and the culture at large. Derived from the seeds of developmental psychology and rooted in the rational empiricism of late-nineteenth-century Europe and America, theories of mental development reached full flower with the elaboration of intelligence testing in France and the United States after

1900. Americans, particularly, became obsessed with defining and measuring mental age, and their efforts to do so riveted age norms and developmental schedules in the public consciousness more tightly than ever before.

J. McKeon Cattell, professor of psychology at the University of Pennsylvania, introduced the term *mental test* into American empirical studies in the early 1890s. As a student in Europe, where he worked with such notable scientists as German psychologist Wilhelm Max Wundt and British anthropologist and statistician Sir Francis Galton, Cattell became convinced that study of human behavior and intelligence needed a firm foundation based on experimentation and accurate measurement. Upon his return to the United States, he worked out a series of tests to measure an individual's reaction time for identifying sound, for naming colors, for accurately bisecting a fifty-centimeter line, and for remembering a sequence of letters in one hearing. Cattell administered his tests to one hundred Columbia University freshmen in 1896, and the results were used by British psychologist Charles Edward Spearman in the early refinement of statistical correlation analysis. More importantly, Cattell's investigations, along with tests of children's vision, hearing, and memory undertaken by Clark University anthropologist Franz Boas in 1890, spurred other social scientists to launch their own studies.[33] Characteristically, the measurements obtained in these studies all were categorized by subjects' ages.

The science of mental testing, however, owed most to French psychologist Alfred Binet. Though he began his professional studies in law, Binet shifted early on to psychology and trained under the dictatorial Jean Martin Charcot at the Salpetrière hospital and asylum in Paris. In 1891, Binet left the Salpetrière to head a research laboratory connected with the Ecole Practique des Hautes Etudes, also in Paris. There he devised and conducted pioneering studies in experimental psychology. Heavily influenced by evolutionary theories of individual differences and convinced that industrial progress required universal education, Binet set out to identify individual differences in intellectual capacities as a means of aiding pedagogical instruction. In 1903, he published *Etude experimentale de l'intelligence*, a comparative study of his two daughters in which he concluded that how an individual performs with regard to a carefully determined assigned task provides the best method for predicting that individual's intellectual performance in general.

Building upon this conclusion, Binet began analyses of mentally abnormal children and by 1905 had developed a diagnostic method for measuring intelligence. Working with French psychiatrist Theodore

Simon, he devised a series of thirty intelligence tests and published them in his article "Methodes nouvelles pour la diagnostic du niveau intellectuel des anormaux," which appeared in *Année psychologique* in 1905. The Binet-Simon intelligence tests, revised in 1908 and again in 1911, had tremendous influence, especially after the revision in 1908, which introduced the concept of mental age—a scale of intelligence that matched item difficulty on each test to age expectations; that is, test problems were graded according to difficulty and to the age norms of different mental levels. More than their predecessors in England, Germany, and the United States, Binet and Simon had moved beyond tests of elemental reactions—reactions to colors, sound, and numbers—and posited that it was possible to ascertain higher mental functions more directly. Moreover, because the concept of mental age fit snugly into cultural consciousness and the impulse for rational categorization, the tests were clear and acceptable.[34]

For several years, psychologists in Europe and the United States used the Binet-Simon tests chiefly in diagnosing problems of mentally deficient and disturbed children. As part of his own research, Binet tried to measure deficiencies in intelligence by defining an "index of subnormality," arrived at by subtracting mental age, as determined by his intelligence tests, from chronological age. Then, in 1912, German psychologist William Stern published *The Psychological Methods of Testing Intelligence*, in which he suggested measuring intelligence by means of the ratio of mental age to chronological age, rather than by subtracting the first from the second. Stern, whose book was translated into English in 1914, seems to have been the first to express the concept of intelligence in mathematically relative terms. But the real impetus for acceptance of the ratio known as the intelligence quotient came from the work of American psychologist Lewis Madison Terman.[35]

After G. Stanley Hall, Lewis Terman probably most influenced the early development of psychological research in the United States. A doctoral candidate at Clark University, Terman's dissertation, directed by Hall, compared the intelligence of seven bright children with that of seven dull children on the basis of tests that he had designed himself. After receiving his degree in 1905, Terman joined the faculty at California State Normal School, where he learned of Binet's tests and began adapting them for American use. In 1910, Terman became professor of psychology at Stanford University and six years later published what became known as the Stanford Revision of the Binet-Simon Intelligence Scale.[36] The Stanford-Binet Intelligence tests had an immediate impact on the field of intelligence measurement, an impact that was soon to become even greater when the United States Army decided to administer the tests to men recruited for duty during World War I and appointed Terman to aid in the undertaking.

Terman's initial scheme established age norms from research on one thousand children between ages three and eighteen. He calibrated a scale of mental ages based on his conclusion that intelligence increased rapidly among young children, then slowed, and finally leveled at age sixteen, when the norm for adult intelligence was reached. To compare children, Terman used the Intelligence Quotient (IQ), the ratio of mental age to chronological age; that is, the IQ is calculated by dividing a subject's actual age into his or her mental age and multiplying the result by 100. A child whose mental and chronological ages are the same would have an IQ of 100 (average); one whose mental age is twelve but whose actual age is eight would have an IQ of 150 (what Terman dubbed "genius" level); and a child whose mental age is seven but whose chronological age is ten would have an IQ of 70 (retarded). Mental growth could be ascertained by applying the same tests to the same child over time. In addition, the tests made possible uniform comparisons among individuals of similar and different ages, genders, social classes, races, and so on.

As a dedicated scientist, Terman sought to establish standardized measurement and laws of predictability. He believed that uniform norms for mental age provided such measurement, and that the IQ was a constant index that could predict a child's mental development. Critics have since exposed flaws in these assumptions. The premises underlying the definition of mental age, an essentially subjective standard for the amount and difficulty of intellectual exercise a "normal" child is expected to accomplish at a given chronological age, are debatable. Moreover, the IQ does not accurately measure adult intelligence, and it does not sufficiently account for cultural differences among children of the same chronological age or for changes in the same child at different ages.[37] Nevertheless, by the sheer force of their work, Terman and other advocates of intelligence tests further sharpened consciousness of age norms. Indeed, the proliferation of intelligence testing in the 1910s and 1920s evidences a near-obsession with age norms in American social science. In addition to Terman's Stanford Revision of Binet-Simon, researchers developed and applied such variations as the Army Alpha and Beta test, the Otis Advanced, the National, the Illinois Examination, the Healy A, the Mare and Foal, the Knox Cubes, the Stanford Achievement, and the Otis Index, each with its own standards for intellectual achievement by age.[38]

Significantly, Terman opposed an educational system that divided children into grades on the basis of chronological age. He pointed out that children of the same chronological age showed wide differences in physical, intellectual, and emotional qualities; if such differences did not exist, he argued, there would have been no need to identify mental age. Because his tests showed differences in mental ability to be great, and especially because he believed such differences were immutable, Terman also contended that a school system that tried to squeeze all children through in the same number of years was unnatural. Though he admitted that serious problems could result from dropping or advancing children to a grade corresponding to their mental age rather than their chronological age, Terman advised that "the one criterion for fitness for promotion should be ability to meet the requirements for the next higher grade. . . . Instead of a single curriculum for all, . . . it would be better to arrange parallel courses of study for children of different grades of ability.[39]

Despite these objections to strict age grading, however, age norms rather than age flexibility prevailed. The emphasis on total child development, of which chronological age was the most expedient measurement and which guided John Dewey's educational reforms as well as Hall's, continued to intensify. Dewey's model curriculum at his famous Laboratory School at the University of Chicago, for example, was rigidly age-defined; each year—Dewey referred to "the sixes," "the sevens," "the eights," and so on—had its own developmental requisites to which the teacher was required to fit the curriculum in order to cultivate responsible and productive citizenship.[40] Intelligence testing provided merely another context in which age served as the determining criterion. The IQ became an important new concept in popular and social scientific circles, but by scientifically identifying relative differences among individuals it served chiefly to heighten still further awareness of age norms.

## AGE NORMS AND THE LAW

In 1905, the Supreme Court of New York State disposed of a case in a fashion ostensibly unrelated to the organization of schools but in fact derived from the same cultural milieu that was manifested in child development study and intelligence testing. The case involved an appeal of a custody decision made in 1903. In that earlier case, Ella Sinclair, who had been divorced from Daniel A. Sinclair, had been granted custody of their three-year-old son. Daniel Sinclair appealed the custody ruling, and in 1905 the court reversed the decision on the disposition of the boy. Speaking for the court, Judge Bischoff cited age as a determining factor in the decision, offering that at age three, a child "may be properly deemed to be of such tender age that . . . considerations of his welfare call for his having a mother's care, but the same cannot be said when the child has reached the age of five." Thus, according to the judge, at the younger age, the child duly belonged with the mother as long as that mother was relatively fit to carry out maternal responsibilities. But, the judge reasoned, by age five, a mother's care was no longer as crucial to the child's development, and a responsible father had a right to custody. Though Judge Bischoff did not cite scientific or social theory as the basis for his decision, he did place strong emphasis on age norms. "If," he asserted,

> the question of the child's tender years, as bearing upon the necessity of his having his mother's personal care, is not eliminated at the age of five years, it is difficult how it would be eliminated at the age of ten years, and I conclude, therefore, that "changed conditions" and lapse of time are sufficient for awarding the child to the father in this case.[41]

The Sinclair case was doubly important because it not only indicated judicial recognition of age norms but also used them to overturn a traditional common law right. Until 1905, an often-cited precedent in custody decisions was the 1842 case of *Barry v. Mercein*. Mary Mercein Barry, the defendant in that case, had left her husband, John Barry, and had taken their infant daughter to live in New York with Thomas Mercein, Mary's father. John Barry had agreed to let their daughter live with his estranged wife while he was traveling in search of work. John eventually settled in Nova Scotia and in 1839 filed a writ of *habeas corpus* in New York to obtain custody of his daughter. Various suits and appeals followed until the case reached the New York Supreme Court in 1842. The child was then four and one-half years old.

Like Ella Sinclair, Mary Barry had argued that she should retain custody of her daughter because of the daughter's "tender age and sickly nature." A child needed a mother's care, she asserted. But the court granted custody to John Barry, reasoning that law, under which a wife surrendered all "legal existence" to her husband upon marriage, took precedence over nurture. Under common law, moreover, a father was entitled to the benefits of a child's labor until that child was twenty-one years old; regardless of circumstances, the mother had no legal right to the child. The court admitted that when the father was a "wanderer," he may be required to surrender his right to the child. But when his circumstances changed, he could not be denied that right. Judge Cowan, speaking for the court, referred to the concept of "tender age," but not as a justification for a child's need to be with the mother; rather, he said, "Where a child is of such tender years as to be incapable of election, it should be delivered to the father, on his attending to receive it."[42]

Thus, in *Barry v. Mercein*, the court paid little attention to age and a child's age-related needs, resting its decision exclusively on the common law rights of husband and father. By 1905, sixty-three years later, both the interpretation of law and the cultural context in which legal decisions were made had changed. In *Sinclair v. Sinclair*, the court could render a decision influenced by age-based distinctions: a three-year-old was too young to be removed from a mother's care, and thus an estranged father should sacrifice his rights to the child. By age five, however, a child has reached a stage of maturity at which her or his welfare could be protected by the father just as adequately as it could be protected by the mother. Like other basic institutions in American society, the legal system had intensified age consciousness. In previous eras, the law had not been totally age-blind; the Constitution specified age qualifications, state laws regarding education and marriage set age limits, and various legal decisions like the Mercein case did take age into account. Nevertheless, by the twentieth century a new attitude characterized legal matters.

The Sinclair case and the increased awareness of age criteria reflected in judicial decisions stemmed from a new way of looking at, and treating, children that emerged in the second half of the nineteenth century. Pediatric medicine and various institutions devoted exclusively to children's welfare were consequences of the belief that children were not miniature adults; rather, they constituted a special, age-bounded biological and social group with its own needs and culture. Various laws and legal institutions manifested this belief, especially after the turn of the century, when age norms were being refined in other areas of society.

Juvenile courts were an embodiment of the changing attitudes that had resulted in separate treatment of children. First established in Cook County, Illinois, in 1899, special courts for juveniles generally were based upon the principle that children who broke the law were not to be regarded as criminals but rather as wards of the state. Like neglected or dependent children, youthful offenders were to receive the care, custody, and discipline that their parents should have furnished but were not able or willing to.

The major spokesperson for separate judicial treatment of children was Denver's Judge Benjamin B. Lindsey, whose work in the justice system paralleled that of Abraham Jacobi in medicine (see Chapter 2) and Luther Gulick in physical education. Lindsey asserted that courts could not treat youthful offenders as adults, because children could not be expected to carry the same responsibilities as adults. Just as Jacobi had argued that children had distinct medical conditions that merited special attention, Lindsey asserted the special moral status of children to justify his argument. Using a jurist's tight logic, he wrote:

> In caring for the financial affairs of minors, the State recognizes that it must accept the responsibility which it cannot in the case of adults. But in dealing with moral and personal affairs, the State expects from children the same respect for the law as it expects from grown men and women and deals out the same penalties. Such treatment is absurd. It might as well demand the same financial responsibility from children as the same moral and personal responsibility. Every case against a child must be judged from the standpoint of the child rather than from that of the man.[43]

But Lindsey also drew from the determinism of G. Stanley Hall and other child development pioneers in defending his ideas. "Certain well-defined rules," he announced, "regulate the actions of a child. These must be respected. This is one of the great advantages of the juvenile court system, that through it a means is devised of bringing about harmony between the Court of Boyville and the law of the adult."[44]

Lindsey proved to be one of the most influential of all progressive reformers, for by 1915 his recommendations for separate juvenile courts had been adopted by almost every state. Usually setting eighteen as the maximum age at which an offender could be brought before the juvenile court, state laws ratified the separation of childhood from adulthood and confirmed the age distinctiveness of adolescence as a legal, as well as a social, category. State laws not only established age-bounded courts exclusively for juvenile offenders but also fixed age limits below which children could not be jailed. As early as 1807, most states prohibited imprisonment of children under the age of fourteen.[45] Thus, older adolescents were deemed too young to fall under jurisdiction of ordinary criminal courts, but they also were considered old enough to be jailed with adults.

The distinctiveness of adolescence was also implicit in new efforts by states to tighten laws regulating age at marriage. Most states had passed age restrictions for marriage long before the twentieth century. Principles of English common law, adopted by statute in the United States, set the age at which a minor was deemed capable of marrying at fourteen for males and twelve for females. Marriage at younger ages required parental consent, though common law voided marriage below age seven even with parental consent. By 1886, laws in most American states had raised age limits considerably—usually to the mid-teens as the lower boundary of ages at which minors were deemed capable of marrying, and to twenty-one for males and eighteen for females as the upper limits for which parental consent was required.[46]

Between 1887 and 1906, however, heightened awareness of age norms spurred state legislatures and the federal government to direct more attention to marriage-age restrictions, with the aim of formalizing them and making them more uniform. Laws passed in seven states revised age limits upward, further isolating adolescents as a group by prohibiting marriage, even with parental consent, for males under eighteen and females under sixteen.[47] In addition, to enforce new age restrictions, those states that had not required formal solemnization or issuance of a marriage license passed laws making such procedures mandatory. By the end of 1906, a license was prerequisite to marriage in all states except New Jersey, New York, and South Carolina.[48] Publication in 1909 of a detailed census report on *Marriage and Divorce, 1867–1906* signaled heightened federal concern with age standards, a concern made especially evident by the report's presentation of extensive comparisons and contrasts between American marriage-age patterns and laws and those of various European nations.

At the same time that they were reviewing and tightening age restrictions on marriage, state legislators were placing age limits on sexual activity and on punishment for illegal sexual acts. These efforts flowed from the same reform and rationalization movements that established other age norms during the Progressive Era (1900–1920), but the immediate catalyst was the white slave—or prostitution—reform crusade of the early twentieth century, which was a response particularly to the fear that innocent teenage girls were being seduced, kidnapped, and forced into degenerate livelihoods. Women's and moral reform groups argued that common law protected "infants," that is, children under seven, from abuse and debauchment, but that laws did not sufficiently protect those over seven and under eighteen against exploitation by criminally minded men. These reformers focused on age of consent, the year below which no child, usually meaning a girl, could legally consent to have "carnal relations with the other sex." Before 1900, most states had set age of consent at fourteen or lower. But reform writers such as Anna Garlin Spencer cited investigations showing that large majorities of brothel inmates were between ages fifteen and eighteen, and that, in being lured from their homes by promises of money or other inducements, they had unknowingly contributed to their own eventual ruin. Spencer and others advocated raising age of consent in order to deter those who would debauch girls into vicious lives. As Spencer reasoned:

> If every man who debauched a child under fourteen or a young woman under eighteen were liable to punishment for rape, seduction, or procuring for immoral purposes, there would be more care taken to avoid such heavy penalties as these crimes entail. If, on the contrary, no child over seven years or ten years or twelve years is protected against the legal inference that she has consented to her own ruin, the number of men and women following the business of prostitution who are in any real danger of severe penalties is very small.[49]

After congressional passage of the White Slave Traffic (Mann) Act in 1910, states began revising their age of consent laws and enacting more explicit age restrictions on sexual activity. Though there was considerable variation, the age of sexual consent for women was usually raised to at least sixteen; carnal knowledge with a female below that age, regardless of consent, was punishable by imprisonment or, in some instances, death. Though reformers like Spencer also wished to protect boys against debauchment, age limits in regard to males tended to apply to the offender rather than to the victim. Thus, statutes made distinctions among offenders according to their ages, usually providing for lesser penalties for males under age eighteen. Several states also enacted a uniform provision that "no conviction may be held against a male who was under fourteen at the time of the act unless physical ability is established."[50] Obviously age was the most expedient criterion that reformers and legislators could use in making distinctions regarding sexual behavior. Nevertheless, the detailed age specifications that laws now incorporated were clearly part of the same wave of age consciousness that had been generated in the late nineteenth century.

Child labor provoked even more legislative activity than did sexual behavior, as humanitarian reformers worked to protect children from exploitation and dangerous environments. In doing so, they manifested both the general age consciousness of the culture at large and a heightened awareness of the age-related, developmental needs of youth. Legal limits on the ages at which children could be employed dated back to the 1840s, when industrialization began to accelerate in northeastern states. In 1848, Pennsylvania passed a law prohibiting employment of children under twelve in cotton, wool, and silk mills. Connecticut set its minimum age at nine in 1855, and Massachusetts fixed the limit at ten in 1866.[51]

Not until the 1880s and 1890s, however, did a broad movement to restrict child labor gather momentum. Not coincidentally, this movement arose at the same time that age norms, age consciousness, and new attitudes toward physical and mental development were emerging in education, medicine, and psychology. At its first annual convention in 1881, the American Federation of Labor adopted a resolution urging states to bar employment of all children under age fourteen. This resolution was aimed more toward reducing job competition than toward protecting children, but other organizations followed with prescriptions that were more consonant with reform goals. At its national convention in 1892, the Democratic party adopted as a platform plank the prohibition of factory labor for children under fifteen. And throughout the 1890s, women's groups such as the General Federation of Women's Clubs and the National Consumers' League called for an end to child labor.

Several states responded with legislation. Between 1885 and 1898, at least seventeen states set minimum age limits for the employment of children.[52] Yet the number of children in the work force continued to increase as families needing the income sent their children into the labor market and employers needing cheap, unskilled workers indiscriminately hired young hands. The 1900 federal census counted 1.8 million children between ages ten and fifteen in non-farm gainful occupations, an increase of 250 percent since 1880. This number did not include perhaps another 250,000 employed children under the age of ten and untold thousands, if not millions, engaged in part-time homework and street trades.

Disturbed by these figures, progressive reformers pressed harder for new legislation, and for more vigilant enforcement of existing laws. To achieve their ends more effectively, a number of reformers established the National Child Labor Committee (NCLC) in 1904 and met annually to discuss and promote their cause. Papers presented at these conferences, published in the committee's own *Proceedings* and in the *Annals of the American Academy of Political and Social Science*, reveal not only the movement's tactics and rhetoric but also its justification in the same principles that moved age-conscious reformers in other fields. Thus, Felix Adler, Columbia University professor of political and social ethics and long-serving chairman of the NCLC, wrote in 1905, "The reason why child labor must be abolished, apart from the sufferings of individuals, is one which biology and ethics combine to force upon us." The force of biology and ethics that Adler evoked resembled that which informed the theories of G. Stanley Hall and Lewis Terman. To Adler, growth depended upon a natural schedule that must be guarded and nurtured lest external pressures impair it. He grounded his argument on the needs of specific developmental stages and, in doing so, strongly implied age norms. Warning against the inappropriate timing of activities, he wrote:

> The human being requires a period of preparation extending over years before he is ready to take up the struggle for existence after the human fashion. First infancy, then childhood, then early youth; and during all that period he must remain dependent on the protection and nurture of adult kinfolk. If that period is curtailed the end of Nature in this highest type of living being—man—is thwarted. It is for this reason that premature toil is such a curse.[53]

Such norms and the developmental rationale that informed them were constantly elaborated by child labor reformers. In 1904, the Committee on Child Labor Legislation of the National Consumers' League published a survey of existing state age limits in various forms of employment and used them as the basis for the League's recommendation for a Standard Child Labor Law.[54] Moreover, the NCLC developed its own model child labor law, which included age-specific minimums that were related to physical and educational attainments.[55] As a result of lobbying by the NCLC and other reform groups, by 1911 twenty-three states had instituted regulations requiring employers to comply with child labor standards by validating the ages of children seeking employment.

To justify their support for stiffer regulations, NCLC leaders Albert Freiberg and Owen Lovejoy took Adler's views to more extreme limits. Nature, wrote Freiberg, echoing Gulick, demands that children under fourteen engage in running and jumping, rather than toiling, to develop proper blood circulation. And Lovejoy, taking his cue from Abraham Jacobi and the newly organized pediatricians, asserted, "Let the people be convinced that the child is not a little man or woman, but a being in the process of physical formation—with features of that development so delicate that no less caution is required at the age of ten or twelve than was required in infancy."[56]

However, as reformers worked to induce state legislatures to pass uniform child labor laws and to enforce them vigorously, many became convinced that real success could be achieved only through federal legislation. Thus, they increased pressure on Congress to act. The first federal child labor bill was the Beverage-Parsons Act, introduced in December 1906. The bill prohibited the interstate transport of products of any factory or mine that permitted employment of children under age sixteen. Beverage-Parsons failed passage, as did several subsequent bills. But in 1916, both parties finally agreed on legislation, and the Keating-Owens Act was signed by President Woodrow Wilson. The law forbade the interstate shipment of 1) products of a mine or quarry in which children under sixteen were permitted to work, and 2) products of a cannery or factory in which children under fourteen were permitted to work, and in which children between ages fourteen and sixteen had been employed more than eight hours per day or more than six days per week or between 7 P.M. and 6 A.M.[57]

In June 1918, nine months after Keating-Owens became effective, the United States Supreme Court invalidated the law as an illegitimate use of congressional power to regulate interstate commerce. In the majority opinion, delivered by Justice William R. Day, the Court recognized that the act was intended to standardize the ages at which children could be employed: "That there should be limitations upon the right to employ children in mines and factories in the interest of their own and the public welfare, all will admit." But, Day continued, a uniform law did not fall under Congress's constitutionally enumerated powers, and moreover, every state already had its own law controlling child labor.[58] Thus, the Court in theory accepted age as a basis for restricting activity, but it judged that restriction to lie within states' police powers, not within Congress's authority to regulate interstate commerce.

Stymied by the Court's decision, Congress in 1918 tried to invoke its taxing powers to control the ages at which children could be employed. As part of the Revenue Act of that year, an extra 10-percent tax was applied to profits from the sale of goods produced by establishments that knowingly employed children in violation of the age standards denoted in the defunct Keating-Owens Act. But in 1922, the Supreme Court voided this provision as well, again determining that it infringed upon state powers.[59] The Court made no objection to age standards but said that taxation was not a valid means to achieve them.

In spite of these defeats in the Supreme Court, various efforts to legally protect children as a special class of citizens achieved symbolic, and in some instances real, success in the early years of the twentieth century. In 1906, a bill creating a special government bureau to oversee children's needs was introduced into Congress. The measure languished in committee, chiefly because of strong opposition from business interests fearful of labor regulation. But lobbying for a special agency intensified, particularly during and after the historic White House Conference on Dependent Children in 1909, at which prominent social welfare workers such as Lillian Wald, Florence Kelley, Jane

Addams, and Homer Folks spoke strongly in favor of a federal agency. A bill to create a Federal Children's Bureau finally was passed by Congress and was signed into law by President Taft on April 9, 1912.[60] Creation of the agency marked the final phase in the process of isolating childhood as a legislatively special stage of life and implementing the age grading involved in such isolation. Just as educators, physicians, physical training advocates, and psychologists had certified the special nature of youth, so too had government and American law accepted children as a systematically defined, age-bounded class of citizens who merited a special protective relationship with the state.

By 1920, the process of rationalization and application of scientific expertise in education, psychology, and law had created environments for youths that reinforced age-related norms. Almost every formal institution was now organized around age-defined grades and expectations, and scientific theories of age-bounded development permeated official policy. In an era that prized efficiency and "scientific" data, age statistics were the most convenient criteria for measuring and evaluating social standards. Equally important, various institutions and organizations grouped youths together into strictly defined peer groups, not only creating powerful new forms of socialization but also accustoming youths to peer-based associations. The United States was fast becoming a peer-oriented society.

## EMERGENCE OF A PEER SOCIETY

"The gang's the thing!" exclaimed Paul Hanley Furfey in 1928. A sociologist at Catholic University in Washington, D.C., Furfey trod the path of child development study cleared a generation earlier by G. Stanley Hall. Furfey's main concern was to analyze preadolescent youths aged ten to fourteen—a period which he called "the gang age"—in order to provide social workers and recreation leaders with a better understanding of this turbulent time of life. Underlying his explanation for the tendency of boys at this age to form gangs was a significant principle: "It does not require very close observation," Furfey remarked, "to see that boys of [the same] age tend to stay together. Among other things, this must be due to the fact that tastes vary with age and that boys of the same age are likely to have the same tastes."[1] On the one hand, this simple statement reflected a self-evident truism; on the other, it epitomized the assumption that peer groups had become the dominant location for socialization in American society. Such an assumption was both a consequence of age-related developments in the previous decades and a driving force for contemporary and future social trends.

The dictionary definition of *peer* denotes only a person of the same rank or standing as another. But in the modern sociological and psychological lexicon, the term has come to connote one of the same age, and *peer group* refers to a number of persons of like age. Over the course of the twentieth century, *peer* has most often implied *age peer*.[2] And though peer groups originally were discussed as a phenomenon associated primarily with youth—G. Stanley Hall, for instance, described the "peer orientations" of adolescents, and Furfey identified the "tribal instinct" among preadolescents—the concept has been expanded across the entire life course to include a variety of same-age clusterings from childhood to old age.[3]

Peer groups are especially important and conspicuous in modern society, in which individual attainments are valued above those of the family, and in which, therefore, there is need to ease an individual's transition from the family to the larger society. Peer groups, in which age becomes the badge of collective identification, act as buffers between family and society, providing individuals with refuge from the demands of both worlds but also acting as a way station between the affectionate, nurturing environment of the former and the achievement-oriented norms of the latter.[4] In return for loyalty to the group, peer groups also supply emotional security and approbation, even to the extent of tolerating deviant values and behavior. Thus, peer groups not only function as socializing agencies but also can become, through their acceptance of deviancy and experimentation, fomenters of social change.[5]

As the twentieth century progressed, peer relationships, to which people became accustomed in childhood and adolescence, could and did extend into and through adulthood.[6] The institutionalized age grading and intensified age consciousness of society in the late nineteenth century relentlessly expanded the scope of peer groupings from schools to the occupational, leisure, organizational, and cultural lives of Americans and shifted their orientation from one of intergenerational contact to one of same-age association.

## A Family of Peers

As Chapter 1 of this study has noted, the pre-modern American family consisted of a pool of related—and sometimes nonfamily—members whose ages spanned a broad spectrum, and who arrived at and departed from the household with frequencies that kept it in constant flux. High fertility, which could extend childbearing over twenty years or more of parents' lives, continually enlarged household membership, while high mortality, especially among the very young, continually reduced household size. At the same time, households swelled and shrank from additions and subtractions of servants, laborers, apprentices, journeymen, and extended kin. In spite of high death rates, the fertility and survival rates in Western Europe and America usually were high enough to exert pressure on household space and, consequently, to force older children to move out and seek support and fortune elsewhere. In sixteenth- and seventeenth-century England, children often left home in their early teens, girls to become servants in other people's households, boys to work as apprentices or farm laborers. In seventeenth- and eighteenth-century American New England, males in their early twenties moved out of their parents' homes and away from their communities, because land divisions in previous generations left no property for them to inherit or settle.[7] Often the departure of these youths was not permanent; they returned to their parents' homes, left again, and returned again, suspended in a state of semidependence.[8]

As a consequence of these demographic patterns, siblings of any given family could have a wide range of ages. Families were quite large, and often twenty years or more could separate firstborn from lastborn children. There also could be great differences between the ages of spouses. Often men, waiting to inherit property or to acquire a trade in order to ensure independence, postponed marriage until their late twenties or early thirties, while women were ready for marriage in their early to mid-twenties. Thus, it was not uncommon for eight or more years to separate the ages of a wife and husband.[9] The age gulf could be even wider if, as sometimes happened, an older widower wed a much younger second wife.

By the late nineteenth century, however, two demographic trends were transforming age relations within the family, at least in the United States. These trends were the decline in birthrates and the narrowing in the age difference between spouses. Women who married in the seventeenth century bore an average of 7.4 children. But as the notion that people had the power to control their environment spread, and as economic development made such control possible, parents began to believe they could improve their and their children's lives by limiting family size. Thus, in contrast to women in the seventeenth century, those who married in the early nineteenth century averaged 4.9 children, and those marrying in the 1870s—and thus bearing children at or after the turn of the century—averaged only 2.8 children. Of those marrying in the eighteenth century, only 1 in 8 had 2 or fewer children, while 19.3 percent had at least 10. In contrast, of those marrying in the 1870s, over half had 2 or fewer children, while only 1 in 200 had 10 or more.[10] In 1910, 63 percent of the families of the urbanized business and professional classes had 2 or fewer children, compared with 45 percent as recently as 1890. Between 1890 and 1910, the proportion of working-class families having 3 or fewer children also rose remarkably, from 33 percent to 50 percent. Only farm families tended to remain large; in 1910, one third of farm families had 2 or fewer children, while another third had 5 or more.[11] Overall, birthrates dropped by half, from over 50 per 1,000 population in 1800 to 25 per 1,000 by 1920.[12]

The resultant decrease in family and household size was equally dramatic. Whereas in 1790, when the first census of the American population was taken, the average size of families was 5.8 persons, by 1920 the average had shrunk to 4.3, a decline of almost 25 percent.[13] In 1790, nearly 36 percent of all households (consisting of extended family members, servants, and boarders, as well as parents and children) contained 7 or more persons, while 37 percent contained 4 or fewer. By 1890, the proportions had shifted to 23 percent with 7 or more, 50 percent with 4 or fewer. And by 1930, the trend had accelerated: only 11 percent of all households had 7 or more persons and 68 percent had 4 or fewer.[14] To be sure, these gross figures obscure the wide variations in family and household size by region, race, ethnicity, and religion. Still, they indicate that a significant reduction in the number of persons in families and households was occurring at the same time that age norms and age congruity were pervading American culture and society.

With fewer children in the family, the age range of siblings became compressed; fewer years separated oldest from youngest, increasing the potential for siblings to interact as quasi-peers. Though such relationships had always developed, they assumed an intense quality in the era of reduced family size, when two or three children clustered in a narrow age range and, because there were no siblings who were much older, were more isolated from the older generation of their parents than would have been the case in a family with many children. Diaries of family life in this period contain virtually no mention of an older daughter acting "as a mother" to younger siblings; rather, siblings referred to each other, especially those of the same sex, as compatriots and friends. Even brothers and sisters could interact as peers.

Fewer children in a family not only set children apart as a quasi-peer group but also created a gap between generations. In large households, common in earlier eras, residents varied so much in age that lines between generations were blurred (see Chapter 1). At the same time, there were strong sanctions by which parents could control their children's behavior. In colonial Massachusetts, for example, a son wishing to marry and start his own farm often could not do so until he inherited land, or until his father sold or gave him a plot.

But the new family environment of the twentieth century, with its more isolated components, was more likely to promote solidarity among siblings-as-peers and the weakening of parental authority. Such potential for conflict and even revolt occurred not only in native families but especially in immigrant families, in which children had greater access than their parents to education, material goods, and commercial mass culture. For example, William I. Thomas and Florian Znaniecki's classic study of Polish peasants in America presents poignant examples of children reinforcing in each other individualistic goals that were in contrast to the familistic intentions of their old-world parents.[15]

Perhaps more important than peer-type patterns developing among children within any one family was another trend—that of men and women of marriageable age tending to choose partners closer to their own age than had been common among earlier generations. By the turn of the century, many young people, especially of the middle class, had grown up in small families and graded schools, and had enjoyed various types of social and recreational activities where they mixed commonly with others of their own age. Though many of their associations remained confined to others of the same sex, an increasing number of leisure, as well as educational, institutions combined males and females of similar ages. Such mixing occurred especially in dance halls, amusement parks, and movie theaters.[16] As a result, courtship became more peer-oriented, ending in marriage between people of nearly the same age.[17]

Figure 5.1 illustrates the emergence of peer marriages in the twentieth century by charting age differences between marriage partners in two quite different urban communities at two distinct periods in their histories. The data represent 689 marriages performed in Providence, Rhode Island, in 1864; 674 marriages in that city in 1921; 501 marriages performed in Omaha, Nebraska, in 1875 through 1877; and

FIGURE 5.1  INCREASE IN PEER MARRIAGES, 1864–1925

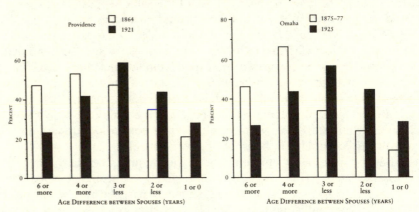

PERCENT OF MARRIAGES IN SELECTED AGE CATEGORIES

|  | Providence | | Omaha | |
|---|---|---|---|---|
|  | 1864 (N = 689) | 1921 (N = 674) | 1875–77 (N = 501) | 1925 (N = 804) |
| 6 or more | 47.1 | 23.1 | 46.0 | 26.5 |
| 4 or more | 52.9 | 41.4 | 66.4 | 43.4 |
| 3 or less | 47.1 | 58.6 | 33.6 | 56.6 |
| 2 or less | 34.7 | 43.3 | 23.6 | 44.4 |
| 1 or 0 | 20.8 | 27.6 | 13.6 | 28.1 |

804 marriages in that city in 1925.[18] Though the two cities do not together present a comprehensive picture of American urban life in the late nineteenth century and in the 1920s, their marriage-age statistics do show clear and consistent changes between a period before peer orientations had become pervasive and a period in which peer relationships had become paramount in American culture.

As Figure 5.1 indicates, there was a marked rise in the incidence of peer-type marriages in both cities between the 1860s and 1870s on the one hand and the 1920s on the other. The proportion of marriages in which spouses' ages were within two years of each other rose from 34.7 percent in Providence in 1864 and 23.6 percent in Omaha in the mid-1870s to 43.3 percent in the Rhode Island city in 1921 and to 44.4 percent in the Nebraska city in 1925. Equally remarkable increases occurred in the proportion of marriages in both Providence and Omaha in which spouses' ages were within three years of each other. Conversely, during the same span of time, the proportion of marriages in which six or more years separated the husband's and wife's ages dropped considerably.[19] Average marriage age was falling for both men and women during this period, but what is more important for our purposes here is that an increasing number of Americans were marrying age peers, whose accumulated experiences in school, in extracurricular activities, and perhaps even in family life matched their own.

Thus, demographic changes helped create the modern family of two distinct, sometimes conflicting, generations. The patriarchal control that previously had suppressed generational tensions weakened by the late nineteenth century, especially as a father's power over land and inheritance declined in the urban-industrial environment.[20] Instead, interactions among siblings and between spouses assumed the trappings of peer groups, as closeness in age fostered similarities in interests and goals. Conflict between generations broke out more openly on a number of fronts, as the household now lacked the buffer provided by members whose ages were spread over a broad spectrum. Popular writers sensed the change and tried to restore family harmony by dismantling barriers between children and parents. A writer in *Ladies Home Journal* in 1908, for example, expressed concern over the lack of empathy and understanding between modern fathers, who had become "money-making machines," and their daughters, who now received most of their solace and support from same-age friends. The writer suggested that the only way a father could bridge this distance was to become as a peer to his children, a wistful suggestion given the trend in social organization.[21] The family, once generationally inte-

97

grated in a functional and emotional sense, had become a way station for different peer groups.

## PEER-GROUP FORMATION IN SECONDARY SCHOOLS
## AND COLLEGES

Graded primary schools, which developed and spread across the United States in the second half of the nineteenth century, herded children into ever narrower age-homogeneous groupings. The increasing numbers of children ages six through fourteen attending school meant that ever larger percentages of youths were spending a considerable portion of their waking hours with age peers (see Chapters 2 and 4). Though within schools peer orientation and socialization intensified in important ways, schoolchildren nevertheless remained under tight adult supervision and thus were still subject to sustained intergenerational contact. The growth of junior high schools, high schools, and, especially, colleges after the turn of the century, however, provided environments in which adolescents and young adults could increasingly insulate themselves from adult influences and thereby create even more autonomous and exclusive peer contacts than they had experienced in elementary schools. As a result, peer groups became the generators of new values as well as of new organizations that came to characterize the social and cultural life of American youth in the 1920s, sharply distinguishing that life from the worlds of both children and adults.

Statistics show a remarkable increase in the numbers of youths who would have become exposed to influences of the secondary school environment. In 1889–90, enrollment in grades nine through twelve in American public and private secondary schools totaled only 360,000 youths, or 6.7 percent of the total population aged fourteen through seventeen. By 1919–20, enrollment in grades nine through twelve had ballooned to 2.5 million, or 32.3 percent of the population aged fourteen through seventeen. By 1929–30, enrollment had reached 4.8 million, or 51.4 percent of the high school–age population.[22] These youths and those a few years younger were placed in educational institutions structured in ways that separated pupils from even casual contact with those not of their own age. Establishment of junior high schools in the 1910s had pared high school terms from four years to three and detached the seventh, eighth, and ninth grades from primary schools, thereby refining and narrowing peer groupings in junior and senior high schools.

By 1900, secondary school students could choose from a large number of extracurricular, as well as curricular, organizations and activities that bolstered peer influences. School-sponsored clubs, drama productions, musical organizations, and sports fostered same-age associations before and after formal classes. Physical education and competitive sports held particular prominence among these activities, and they were intentionally structured by adult supervisors so as to enhance peer influence. Luther Halsey Gulick's "open door" policy, outlined in Chapter 4, explicitly exalted peer groupings over all other forms of organizing youth. To this dean of American physical education, peers were as or more important than teachers in the education process, and he stressed peer groupings in the activities of the Public School Athletic League that he founded in New York City in the early 1900s.[23] Gulick's ideas strongly influenced the establishment of organized sports in junior and senior high schools in the 1910s and 1920s, expanding the formal realms that promoted peer-group socialization. A study prepared by the White House Conference on Child Health and Protection confirmed the increase in peer interactions among adolescents—interactions that, by the early 1930s, predominated over other types of contact in their everyday lives. According to the report, based on a survey of three thousand families, the average urban adolescent spent four to six nights every week with peers and away from home and family.[24] These after-school associations combined with daytime activities, to fill a teenager's waking hours with peer contacts.

Peer influences were even more intense within colleges and the various associations that they generated. Especially for middle- and upper-class youths, and even more especially within those institutions in which students resided full time, college life provided the opportunity for continuous contact among age peers removed from the circumscriptions of family and adult surveillance. Though administrators tried to act *in loco parentis* and regulate student activities closely, college life promoted peer interaction in all three dimensions of its essence: studies, extracurricular activities, and social relationships. And though college students did venture away from the campus to visit their families, on whom many of them still depended for financial and emotional support, and to work at part-time jobs that brought them into contact with older adults, these counterbalancing influences were generally minimal.[25]

The first generator of peer solidarity in college had been the class-year system, which fostered common identities within individual freshman, sophomore, junior, and senior class-years. In the mid- and late-nineteenth century, not only were curricula organized by class-year, but also extracurricular competitions pitted class-years against each other. At Brown University, for example, one of the most important annual events in the 1880s was the mass football-rugby match between the entire membership of the freshman class and the combined sophomore, junior, and senior classes.[26] As intercollegiate sports evolved near the end of the century, they paved the way for students, both as participants and as spectators, to form new peer bonds distant from adult control. Football, said one professor, cultivated "a sense of friendship among the students—not fellowship in mischief, but friendship in pluck and manliness, in generous admiration of their mates."[27] College officials applauded the way sports seemed to encourage students to put aside differences and create peer values based on school spirit. President Arthur T. Hadley of Yale asserted in 1906 that football made social "class distinctions relatively unimportant" and allowed "the students [to] get together in the old-fashioned democratic way."[28] But, as noted in Chapter 2, the ages of college students ranged widely, and any one class-year could contain individuals in their midteens and individuals in their late twenties.

By the turn of the century, the age range of college students was narrowing and enrollments had become too large to sustain class-year as the premier locus of student identity. In 1880, college attendance stood at 116,000 students; by 1915, it had grown to 404,000. Numerous organizations and activities sprouting within student populations attracted particular kinds of participants while at the same time nurturing peer-group attachments. The curriculum, developing in new directions due to the creation of new elective courses, still followed somewhat of a standard progression, with freshman courses serving as prerequisites to sophomore courses, and so on. But in addition, more specialized peer groups were forming in response to the diversified curriculum, bound together by major area of study or approach to course work. Thus, by the 1920s, a large campus could consist of "art students," "science buffs," "grinds," "the social set," and other distinct groups, each with its own peer-based social and cultural values. Students then carried these identities outside the classroom.

The organizations that most decisively replaced class-year as the chief source of student identity and split campuses into peer-based subunits that exercised powerful influence over student culture in the early twentieth century were fraternities and sororities. Fraternities had existed at American colleges since the 1820s, but usually as secret societies. They expanded into social clubs after the Civil War and, aided by loyal alumni, began to build residences and hold meetings.[29] In 1883, American colleges and universities harbored over 500 fraternities and 16 sororities, with a total student membership of over 70,000. Already they were sponsoring sports competitions and holding dances and teas.[30] Even more dramatic expansion occurred after 1900, however, when college administrators encouraged the growth of fraternities and sororities because they could provide housing and dining services to swelling numbers of matriculants, and because alumni and alumnae contributed large sums of money to enhance the prestige of their clubs. By 1912, there were 1,560 chapters of national fraternities and sororities, and the number surged to 3,900 in 1930.[31] At many colleges in the 1920s, 35 to 40 percent of all students belonged to fraternities or sororities, and on some campuses the proportion reached as high as 65 percent.[32]

With their intimacy and ritual, fraternities and sororities offered young adults in college ready means of social identification and peer acceptance. The process of selection to the organizations could be brutally discriminatory, but it also protected corners of homogeneity within the growing complexity of college campuses. Peer sanctions strictly enforced this homogeneity. In return for the prestige and identity that the group could bestow, individuals had to conform to formal and informal rules of behavior. Those who deviated from those rules—in their dress, social tastes, or commitment to their political views—were ostracized from the group or excluded before they ever had a chance to join. As an observer at one college remarked in 1924:

> In the fraternities there is no marked individuality. The tendency is to mold a man to the fraternity type in the first two years; then they feel that his development is satisfactory in the last two years. Any man with an individual peculiarity has a bad time.[33]

Another observer testified:

> The sorority has certain advantages; the older girls help the younger ones and push them into activities, expecting each freshman to engage in three, and all above freshman year in two activities. Disadvantages are that the chaperonage is lax; the chapters are too large; girls meet too few types of girls and are narrow and self-satisfied; think their own group has all the good things.[34]

With their influence over campus social life, fraternities and sororities enforced peer norms that separated students from adult society. Yet at the same time, by inculcating the values of social demeanor, careerism, consumerism, and political awareness, the Greek organizations prepared young adults for the lives they would assume after their academic years ended.[35]

Fraternities and sororities were only the most identifiable arenas in which college peer society operated. As Paula Fass and others have suggested, peer-controlled behavior was manifested in a wide range of more informal groupings and gathering places, including parties, dances, movie theaters, cafeterias, and campus "hangouts." In these places, peer interaction followed less ritualized paths than it did inside Greek organizations, but such interaction nevertheless served to reinforce group norms.[36] Though without an academic curriculum college life would not have existed, the time that students spent on their burgeoning nonacademic activities increasingly competed with time spent on their studies. A survey of students at the University of Chicago in the 1920s found that on average a student spent thirty-five to forty hours per week on course work, and over one third devoted fewer than thirty-five hours to such activities. At the same time, the average student spent fifteen to twenty hours per week on extracurricular pursuits (presumably not including informal contacts and social events), and one fourth spent as much or more time on nonacademic activities as they did on academic matters.[37] Such figures serve to illustrate further the totality of the peer environment that surrounded increasing numbers of young adults in American institutions of higher learning.

## A SOCIETY OF PEERS

School and college life constituted only one of many contexts in which peer influences were cultivated. Throughout American society in the early twentieth century, new and existing associational groupings accelerated the tendency toward age-homogeneous organization. Gangs and clubs organized by and for youths, burgeoning forms of commercialized leisure, different treatment of and policies relating to old people—all acted to shift individuals away from family settings and muster them into peer associations that by 1930 were widely accepted as the most natural and efficient means of social organization. The result was a major transformation of American life-styles.

The streets of early American towns and villages had always harbored gangs of males who provided one another with fellowship but who also perpetrated various random acts of vandalism and harassment. Occasionally, the aggregations participated in, or even fomented, more sweeping violence with political overtones, as was the case in the Stamp Act riots and Boston Massacre in late-eighteenth-century Boston and the Draft Riots of New York City in 1863.[38] Generally, however, the gangs and mobs included men and boys of various ages. John Adams described the gathering that precipitated the Boston Massacre as a "motley rabble of saucy boys, Irish teagues, and out-

102

landish Jack Tars." Writing in 1873, author and editor Joel Tyler Headley portrayed New York's Dead-End Rabbits, a notorious gang of the 1850s, as made up of "mostly young men, some of them being mere boys."[39] Reformers Louis M. Pease and Charles Loring Brace also reported that New York gangs in the 1850s included boys as young as eight acting alongside youths in their middle and late teens.[40]

As cities grew in the late nineteenth century, gangs became more numerous and more age-homogeneous, making peer groups among working-class youths more evident. Social and economic changes, such as extension of formal schooling, industrialization and the withering of the apprenticeship system, and prolongation of the period during which youths lived with their parents, delayed the entrance of young people, especially teenagers, into the labor force and allowed them more time for informal association and disorderly activity on city streets.[41] Within these groupings, age became a distinguishing characteristic, resulting from and reinforcing peer relations fostered in graded schools and other nonfamilial institutions whose purpose was to organize and socialize youths. Sociologist Frederick Thrasher, in his classic study of 1927, categorized street gangs according to strict age-bounded groupings, noting that in "conventional gangs, a definite rule with regard to age is customary." He also identified the more finely age-graded subdivisions of "midgets," "juniors," and "seniors" within individual gangs.[42] Paul Hanley Furfey found that members of the Young Iroquois, one of the principal gangs he studied, "were all within twenty months of each other in age."[43] And J. Adams Puffer, another student of gang behavior in the early twentieth century, observed that members of the "Dowser Glums" were "for the most part seventeen or eighteen years of age," and that those of the "Island Gang" were "generally about fifteen."[44]

Though girls and young women had their own informal clubs and gangs, sometimes acting in tandem with male counterparts, their peer bonds and socialization were manifested in less mobilized ways. Young females depended on age mates for letter writing, library visits, tea parties, and other activities with intimate friends that often mimicked the adult women's world in the ways that boys' sports and fighting imitated the competitive activities of their fathers.

One feature that reflected peer identity among American girls was the autograph book. Immensely popular in England in the 1820s, these books were usually the property of upper-crust girls who strove to collect signatures and messages from known personalities, especially those in the arts. In the United States, however, the books—which came into wide use in the 1850s, grew into an absorbing fad in the

1870s and 1880s, and continued to enjoy strong popularity well into the twentieth century—were adopted by schoolgirls seeking remembrances from friends and classmates (and, occasionally, from teachers and relatives), not from artists, authors, and poets.

The verses written in these books signified the close communication and identity between peers. They might, for example, include sentimental vows, such as the entry in a Kansas girl's autograph book in 1901:

> When in my lonely grave I sleep
> And bending willows o'er me weep,
> 'Tis then, dear friend, and not before
> I think of thee, no more, no more.

Or, they could offer good-natured wishes for a successful future, as in this age-conscious rhyme inscribed in a New York City girl's book in 1909:

> I wish you love,
> I wish you plenty,
> I with you a husband
> Before you're twenty.

Or, they could express the corny, comic banter that close friends commonly exchange:

> When you get married
> And live in a truck,
> Order your children
> From Sears and Roebuck.[45]

When reformers began to combat miscreant behavior of unsupervised children and adolescents, they accepted the tight peer organization of youth culture and bolstered it by using age homogeneity as a principal means of structuring the formal play associations and character-building organizations that they established. Edgar Robinson, who in 1900 became administrator of YMCA activities for boys in the United States and Canada and in 1910 helped establish the Boy Scouts of America, argued that a youth group could hold its members for a maximum of only three years, beyond which time the boys would prefer to associate with those closer to their own age.[46] Thus, the junior divisions of the YMCA and YWCA, created for youths between ages twelve and sixteen; Cub Scouts, for ages eight through ten; Brownies, for ages six through eight; Senior Girl Scouts; and the Explorer and Sea Scout divisions of Boy Scouts—all represented efforts by early twentieth-century youth reformers to match youth organizational structures with assumed peer preferences and needs.[47] Social workers and other reformers, who tried to aid working-class children through clubs and Boys' Brigades in the 1890s and early 1900s, were less concerned with age distinctions; they were more intent on taking poor youths off the streets and teaching them morality than with fostering age-related personal development. Those reformers involved with middle-class youth in scouting and other organizations, however, stressed age calibration as the rationale for their various divisions.

Youth reformers had to compete not only with street gangs for the souls and loyalties of young people but also with the enormous expansion of commercialized leisure in the early twentieth century. The "cheap amusements" that proliferated in every city came to embody modern American culture, particularly the values of individualism and consumerism, and the resulting world of pleasure was one that emphasized youth and the escape from adult supervision. Some of the new leisure institutions sustained the gender segregation characteristic of society previously, while at the same time fostering age segregation. For example, poolrooms and young men's social clubs became the domains of young working-class males in their twenties, who avoided the saloons and lodges frequented by older males of the same socioeconomic status.[48]

More important were the dance halls, amusement parks, and movie theaters that mingled young men and young women in a new environment of peers. Such commercialized recreation centers provided an arena for friendship, courtship, and even illicit behavior that, like college dormitories and fraternity and sorority houses, nurtured peer orientation and values. Dancing especially was, from 1910 onward, a favorite peer activity of older youths, and, according to historian Kathy Peiss, "going to the city's dance halls marked a particular stage in the life cycle."[49] New York City alone had over five hundred public dance halls and more than one hundred dancing academies. Patrons, who almost always were under the age of twenty-five, developed particular peer dance styles that symbolized their age identities.[50] Movie theaters also provided settings for youth-peer socialization, sparking generational conflict between adolescents and adults because of the tensions created between new-world commercialized leisure and old-world traditions of family and home. For example, a New York social worker, writing in 1914, described the case of a Hungarian immigrant mother who expressed a desire to go to the movies with her teenage children and met strong resistance from her husband and children because, according to her family, she would be doing something unseemly for someone her age.[51]

The lure of commercialized leisure and the changed context of waged labor had a particular affect on life-styles of young working-class women. Newly available jobs in department stores, offices, rationalized factories, and service establishments such as restaurants and beauty salons offered shorter hours and better pay than domestic service, sweatshops, and household production—the types of labor in which most women were engaged in the nineteenth century. By the early twentieth century, nearly 60 percent of New York City women aged sixteen to twenty held paid jobs, and in many cities women's labor force participation began to signal an important individual career transition from childhood to adulthood as well as a supplement to family income.[52] Young working women now had the time, income, and desire to seek good times with friends.

Several historians recently have noted that these women, especially second-generation immigrants, aroused family tensions when they balked at turning over all of their earnings to their parents, preferring to reserve at least some wages for expenditures on the clothes and entertainment necessary to maintain peer relations.[53] Also, the need for time and money to pursue the social life of the dance hall and movie house may have contributed to the relative decline of domestic service as an occupation among young white women (though not among black women). Explaining why she disdained domestic work, a young factory laborer told a YWCA worker in 1915, "A factory girl is out more . . . and has more time to be in the society of others, and so is able to have high social standing if she is of good character."[54] Thus, the tug of peer-based leisure could affect occupational choices as well as family allegiance.

A variety of institutions reflected and reinforced peer organization among adults as well as among children and youths. Adults did not always associate exclusively with people their own age, but by the turn of the century urbanization had brought increasing numbers of Americans into a world in which many more choices and opportunities for peer association existed. A wide range of social organizations, formal and informal, arose, many of which were specialized in ways that included age criteria. Society had become more organized at all levels, and age groupings often, though not always, resulted from the organization process.

Though the memberships of some fraternal and benevolent associations spanned a broad age spectrum, leadership in both men's and women's organizations in the early twentieth century seemed to be concentrated in narrower age ranges, reflecting the development of cliquish clusters of age peers dedicated to organizational administration. In women's benevolent organizations, such as the Providence, Rhode Island, YWCA and Women's City Missionary Society, the ages of officers in the 1870s showed a wide distribution, with nearly as many officers under age thirty-five as over fifty. By the early 1900s, however, no officers of either organization were under thirty-five, and from two thirds to four fifths were between ages fifty and sixty.[55] Also, the memberships of some organizations did seem to contain large clusters of age peers. Writing in 1900, Margaret Sangster labeled women's clubs "schools for the middle-aged woman," where a woman of fifty could find "friends who like her are on the middle way of life."[56] And men's associations split into age-graded, peer segments. For example, the Junior Chamber of Commerce, founded in 1920, limited membership to men no older than thirty-six, thereby extending into adulthood peer associational patterns begun in graded elementary schools and carried forward through adolescence, college years, and young adulthood.

Heightened consciousness of distinct adult stages reflected age grading and peer groupings beyond childhood and adolescence. In the decade following World War I, serious and popular writers filled journals with analyses of age-based characteristics that clarified the distinctions between young adulthood, middle age, and old age. In 1919, for example, physical fitness expert and sports author Walter Camp asserted that the period between ages thirty-one and thirty-five marked a watershed in male adult lives. At that point, according to Camp, a man "knows more and he can get bigger results with a smaller effort. But physically he is at the top of his ladder. And most men begin to slip back, so far as physical condition is concerned, from that time."[57] Camp was echoing an old maxim that set the peak of life at thirty or thirty-five, but he wrapped it in the scientific veneer of the twentieth century by prescribing a series of nine exercises appropriate for each age-bounded stage of adulthood. Sociologist E. A. Ross used social scientific terms when he concluded that people under forty differed markedly from those over fifty in their values and education, and that the sub-stage between forty and fifty represented a period of awkward transition.[58]

Indeed, the "discovery" of middle age as a distinct life stage climaxed the postwar discussions of age in American culture. Before the twentieth century, middle age was seldom considered as a separate time of life. The few writers who noticed middle age saw it only as a fleeting, vacant transitional period between adulthood and old age. In his poem *Don Juan*, for example, Byron mused:

107

Of all the barbarous middle ages, that
    Which is most barbarous is the middle age
Of man; it is—I really scarce know what;
    But when we hover between fool and sage.[59]

But by the 1900s, several developments had served to draw greater attention to the period of life that seemed to commence in the forties. For one thing, the growth of formal retirement, old-age homes, and other institutional aspects of old age (see below) had increasingly advanced the onset of old age until it was now sixty-five or seventy—rather than a younger age as had been the norm in the nineteenth century—thereby creating a wider gap between peak of life and ultimate decline. Second, improvements in medical care, sanitation, diet, and general living conditions had extended adult life expectancies so that there were more old people in contrast with those who were now not quite old—that is, those, say, over sixty-five contrasted with those between forty and sixty-five. In 1920, 7.4 percent of the population, or nearly 8 million people, were at least sixty years old, and 13.2 percent, or 14 million, were between forty-five and fifty-nine. By contrast, in 1870, only 5.0 percent of the population, or 2 million people, were at least sixty, while about 10.0 percent, or 4 million, were between forty-five and fifty-nine.[60] Social analysts expressed increasing awareness of this new group, who differed not only from those older than them but also from those younger than them. Reformer and judge Ben Lindsey of Denver, for example, identified a definite peer group of middle-agers, people in their forties and fifties who had grown up in the 1890s and who, by the 1920s, were still so much in the grip of traditional moral values that they gasped when a character in a play invited another to her bedroom. In contrast, he observed, the younger generation in the audience accepted the scene and made fun of their elders' reactions.[61]

Walter Pitkin's bestselling book, *Life Begins at Forty*, published in 1932, ratified the recognition of middle age in American culture. Proclaiming that his title reflected "the supreme reward of the Machine Age," Pitkin, a psychologist and journalist, urged that one's middle and later years could be productive and enjoyable. According to his scheme of adulthood, the years between ages seventeen and twenty-four were a sort of apprenticeship, when "we learn the social life." Between twenty-four and forty, the demanding tasks of getting a job, buying a house, and raising children consumed a person's energies. In previous eras, Pitkin observed, "men wore out at forty." But now, because of new technology, better standards of living, and increased access to leisure time, "life after forty has been much more exciting and profitable than before forty."[62] To prove his point, Pitkin listed famous people who had "blossomed" after age forty, and he asserted further that "in some fields, the woman past forty is best qualified to think and to lead."[63]

Pitkin's book was intended to uplift people languishing in the depths of the Depression, but it also had a great impact on other areas of popular culture. The book was the largest-selling nonfiction title in 1933 and the second largest in 1934, and the adoption of its title at large by the popular media turned it into a truism. Newspaper and magazine writers, radio shows, movie scripts, and common conversation repeated the phrase so frequently that it became a symbol for the onset of middle age. Thus, popular songstress Sophie Tucker could write in her autobiography that one of her favorite songs to perform was Jack Yellen's "Life Begins at Forty," because the song expressed "what everybody who shivers at the word 'middle aged' feels."[64] Such an immediate and widespread embrace of Pitkin's simple declaration could occur only in an age- and peer-conscious society.

## THE ISOLATION OF OLD AGE

In 1922, when he was seventy-eight years old, G. Stanley Hall published *Senescence: The Last Half of Life*, the first important American study of the psychological aspects of aging. Though Hall identified the early forties as the age when senescence normally begins—he labeled post-climacteric old age *senectitude*[65] rather than *senescence*—most of his discussion focused on qualities and problems associated with the most advanced years of life. Topics ranged from mortality statistics to mental health to constipation, and the book even contained excerpts from literature. It helped open a new field of study and social service, gerontology, and it also signaled a final step in the process of separating old age as a distinct life stage that merited special treatment in policy making and institutions. This process of isolation created a special age, or peer, group of elderly people.

Hall did not "discover" senescence as he had discovered adolescence. Throughout the nineteenth century, welfare workers, medical practitioners, and social reformers had increasingly defined old age as a period marked of special characteristics, especially poverty, unemployment, physical decline, and mental derangement. Charity workers and sociologists, confronting the harsh effects of urbanization and industrialization, viewed advanced age as a time of dependence. Accord-

109

ing to one writer in 1912, life after sixty in industrial society had bleak prospects:

> Property gone, friends passed away or removed, relatives become few, ambition collapsed, only a few short years left to live, with death a final and welcome end to it all—such conclusions inevitably sweep the wage-earner from the class of hopeful and independent citizens into that of the hopeless poor.[66]

Physicians had their own medical model of senescence which considered old people as continual patients whose organic pathology rendered their ailments incurable; the physiological destiny of death made old age itself a disease. Advances in medical treatment and preventive measures had reduced the number of deaths due to previously feared acute diseases such as typhoid, pneumonia, and digestive disorders, but the number of deaths due to chronic illnesses of old age rose dramatically, attracting popular and medical attention to the problems, as well as the numbers, of older people in the population. Between 1900 and 1913, for example, the death rate from cancer rose from 62.9 per 100,000 people to 78.9 per 100,000, an increase of 25 percent.[67] Such a trend boded ominously for those reaching old age. "For a person in the seventies," wrote one doctor in 1904, "it is not worth while to make any great sacrifice in the way of money and associations to go in search of health."[68] Thus, according to professionals, old age had none of the prospects of other life stages and more than its share of afflictions.[69]

One response by professionals to this situation was institutional segregation of old people. As historians Carole Haber and W. Andrew Achenbaum have demonstrated, almshouse populations in the late nineteenth century increasingly consisted of the dependent elderly, especially in industrialized states. Between 1864 and 1904, for example, the proportion of older people in Massachusetts almshouses swelled from 26 percent to 48 percent. Yet even at the later date, only 8 percent of the Massachusetts population was over sixty years old.[70] Nationally, in 1910, some 45 percent of native-born almshouse inmates and 70 percent of foreign-born inmates were at least sixty.[71] As administrators came to believe that institutionalization was the cheapest means of supporting needy older people—unlike younger paupers, the old could not be expected to become self-sufficient eventually—they established more and more old-age homes as alternative havens to almshouses and hospitals. Mostly accommodating incapacitated, widowed, and needy elderly, these benevolent asylums proliferated by the turn of the century. New York State in 1894 had fifty-eight such institutions, harboring nearly five thousand aged individuals.[72] By 1900, the city of Philadelphia had twenty-four old-age homes, each devoted to a particular type of resident, such as widows, couples, blacks, or the previously wealthy.[73]

By attempting to meet the perceived special needs of older people more humanely than almshouses did, old-age homes became a popular means for institutionalizing the elderly while at the same time reinforcing the uniqueness and isolation of senescence. This belief in humane isolation was clearly revealed in a settlement worker's letter to *Charities and the Commons* in 1907. "Kindhearted people," he wrote,

> provide refuges for stray dogs and cats, and work up elaborate entertainments for the benefit of the homes for such animals. Would it not become seemly to provide decent shelter for the helpless and aged of our own species?
> More homes for the aged![74]

Only a tiny percentage of all older people lived in institutions. But many of the uninstitutionalized older people were separated by equally significant barriers from the adult world they formerly inhabited. Mandatory retirement from the work force and pensions both derived from and supported concepts of uselessness and poverty in old age but also created a rigid age criterion for defining precisely when a person became old. Before the late nineteenth century, individuals retired when they were too debilitated to work or because they were wealthy enough not to have to work. Age was not directly linked to a person's work force status. Following the Civil War, however, public and private employers began to discharge and, at the same time, reward long-serving employees whom they considered too old to work productively. In the rationalized, bureaucratized economy that emerged by the turn of the century, forced retirement became a handy means of reducing unemployment and diminishing pressures from a surplus of younger, allegedly more efficient workers. Pensions and annuities, which formerly had served as charity and disability payments, became a means of pacifying older workers until they reached retirement age, and then of inducing them to retire quietly. But because pension payments were so meager and so few companies actually implemented them, by the 1910s progressive reformers were urging government to assume responsibilities for old-age assistance.[75]

Public and private concerns were slow and inconsistent in developing retirement policies. At the federal level, a congressional act of 1861 required naval officers below the rank of vice-admiral to resign their commissions at age sixty-two, and an 1869 act allowed, but did not

111

force, federal judges with at least ten years of service to retire at age seventy with a pension equal to their current salary. But before World War I, there were few other retirement provisions for federal employees.[76] Transportation companies pioneered the establishment of pension and retirement programs. Following the example set by the American Express Company in 1875 and the Baltimore and Ohio Railroad in 1884, 49 major companies had established pension plans by 1910; 370 had done so by 1926.[77] Increasingly, executives justified these plans in terms of productive efficiency. Experts deemed that an employee's long years of service—by which they meant the aging process—inevitably resulted in slower work pace and reduced output. The key word that they used to describe this condition was *superannuation*, a polite term for human obsolescence but which derived from the late-nineteenth-century view that irreversible physical and mental decline characterized the advanced years of life. Pensions thus became a means of eliminating underproductive "dead weight," those workers who had become superannuated.[78]

Such drives for efficiency sparked movements in the early 1900s to establish pensions for state and municipal employees. In 1910, for example, a *Report of the Massachusetts Commission on Old Age Pensions, Annuities, and Insurance* identified 491 state employees over age sixty-five and strongly implied that more efficient service could be attained by pensioning off elderly workers and replacing them with young people.[79] Public workers such as teachers, policemen, and firemen often supported pension plans, because their low salaries had not enabled them to save for their advanced years. Pensions, they said, would enable them to avoid poverty. But these and other employees, public and private, expected to retire and to receive pensions only when they chose or when some disability prevented them from working. Instead, however, they found themselves betrayed by what Haber has labeled the bureaucratic impulse "to measure and categorize man's physical and mental capacities."[80] This rationalization, just as in education and mental testing, set specific age, not individual capacity, as the paramount criterion for determining who should retire and who was pensionable. Some agencies used age sixty-five, some seventy, some sixty; but what was more important than the ages used was the formulation of specific age as a determinant of inefficient senescence and the reduced social status that superannuation implied.

In the 1910s and 1920s, a few states created old-age pensions for some of their elderly population, chiefly as a humanitarian move to ease old-age dependency but also in an effort to save money by offering direct payments instead of maintaining indigent older people in poorhouses. Lurking beneath the legislation, however, was the assumption that poverty and uselessness had become defining characteristics of old age. Thus, the Montana Industrial Accident Board, which studied old-age dependency and recommended a pension plan in 1923, observed:

> The haunting fear that grows at the heart of every normal man and woman is the fear that he or she, through misfortune, will be deprived of a competency during old age and be left penniless and friendless, as an object of charity or as a subject for the poorhouse. The continual press of the race for industrial supremacy, the commercial battle that is more and more becoming a survival of the fittest, must provide relief to those who are worn in struggle to the point where they can no longer care for themselves.[81]

Arizona became the first state to establish a noncontributory pension system when in 1914 the legislature passed a law, stimulated by voter initiative, that abolished all almshouses and authorized monthly stipends for indigent mothers and needy persons aged sixty and over. The state supreme court declared the law unconstitutional on the basis of its vagueness regarding almshouses and mothers with dependent children. But in 1923, Montana, Nevada, and Pennsylvania passed old-age assistance acts, and they were followed over the next few years by Wisconsin, Kentucky, Colorado, Maryland, and Massachusetts. By 1931, there were eighteen state programs, with age eligibilities set at either sixty-five or seventy. The movement for government-funded old-age assistance received further impetus in 1927 with the formation of the American Association for Old Age Security, which lobbied for pensions in both the private and public sectors.[82]

Though pension and retirement plans often imposed strict means tests for eligibility and were seriously underfunded, their establishment helped to solidify notions of an age-limited work cycle. Transformation of the definition of *retirement* reflected this development. No longer did the term simply mean withdrawal from public notice. Instead, as Achenbaum has shown, the term now connoted that a person was no longer qualified, on account of old age, for active service or employment.[83] According to Haber, pensions systems "not only arose out of changing ideas about the elderly's need and ability to work but legitimated the demand that the aged should no longer be employed."[84] Such systems also distinguished the elderly as an economic group distinctly separate from the rest of society. What was on the one hand a humanitarian movement and on the other a calculated efficiency measure helped further to solidify peer-group organization of that society.[85]

Simultaneous with the separation of elderly people by old-age assistance programs, medical theories about old age began to coalesce into a new field of specialized treatment that, like pensions and retirement plans, institutionalized old age as a distinct life stage. As a consequence, older people were further set apart as a separate, age-determined social group. As Chapter 3 indicated, nineteenth-century physicians, influenced by the work of researchers in France and Germany, had begun to believe that the infirmities and diseases of old age were inevitably incurable. From this assumption, it was but a short step to the definition of old age as normally a period of degeneration and disability, a time when the elderly individual, beset by senile conditions of mind and body, needed to be left to a doctor's constant care.[86] Just as social and economic theorists linked dependence and low productivity to old age, doctors emphasized pathological deterioration. Both views pointed toward socially isolating elderly people from the rest of society.

By the early twentieth century, some American physicians were assembling theories into a new medical specialty, a field devoted exclusively to the care and treatment of old people: geriatrics. The leader in this new field was New York physician I. L. Nascher. Born in Austria and educated in New York City, Nascher blended scientific rigor with compassion for the biological ordeal of the elderly. He seems to have coined the term for the new medical specialty when he wrote, in 1909, "Geriatrics, from geras, old age, and iatrikos, relating to the physician, is a term I would suggest as an addition to our vocabulary, to cover the same field in old age that is covered by the term pediatrics in childhood."[87] Like Abraham Jacobi, the pioneer of pediatrics a generation earlier, Nascher believed old age was a "physiological entity" with discrete, prevalent conditions that, though disadvantageous to the individual, were normal to that period of life. Just as lack of physical coordination was a normal quality of infancy and labor pains were normal for a childbearing woman, so too were degenerated organs and mental senility normal for an elderly person.

These conditions of old age, Nascher argued, required particular treatments. The medication that might be used on a diseased younger adult would be inappropriate for the same malady in senility.[88] Thus, Nascher wrote, just as "the pediatrist [sic] does not look on the child as an adult with incompletely developed organs and tissues, but as a child . . . [so too] the geriatrist does not look on the aged person as an adult having pathologically degenerated organs and tissues, but as an aged person."[89] This belief prompted Nascher to organize in New

York City in 1912 a "Society of Geriatry," forerunner to the American Geriatric Society.

By 1930, the medical establishment, private industry, and government bureaucracy had converged in their definitions and treatment of old age. This consensus served to lend to old age a more exclusive distinctiveness, physical, social, and policy-wise, than had previously existed. The climax to this form of age grading occurred with passage of the Social Security Act in 1935. Establishment of national old-age pension and insurance schemes in numerous European countries by the 1920s, as well as private and state plans in the United States, had inspired introduction of similar measures in the United States Congress from 1911 onward. The bills provided weekly stipends (usually one to four dollars) to aged persons (usually at least sixty or sixty-five) whose weekly incomes fell below a certain level (usually six to ten dollars). Provisions also required citizenship of sixteen to twenty years and proof of sound moral character.[90] None of the bills succeeded, though in 1920 Congress did pass the Civil Service Retirement Act, which mandated retirement of federal civil service employees by age seventy and offered annuities to retirees depending upon their years of service. Mechanics and postal employees could become eligible for benefits at age sixty-five, railway clerks at sixty-two. This measure, along with the Railroad Retirement Act of 1934, set the stage for Social Security.[91]

The political process leading to passage of the Social Security Act has been traced elsewhere and need not be repeated here.[92] Chiefly, the measure was intended to establish unemployment insurance and to aid needy persons who were unemployable. The act's old-age provisions derived from work done by the Committee on Economic Security (CES), appointed by President Franklin Roosevelt in 1934. These measures were lodged in Title I and Title II. Title I created grants-in-aid for needy aged individuals, and Title II established an insurance system to pay old-age benefits to retired workers beginning at age sixty-five.

The decision to set the age threshold at sixty-five seems to have been partly arbitrary and partly rational. The majority of existing state old-age pension plans used sixty-five as the standard age for eligibility, and the most established European programs, especially those of Germany and Great Britain, also used age sixty-five. The CES accepted that age almost without question, and all its recommendations followed from that basis. Alternatives received only brief attention; a lower age, the committee believed, would make the insurance program too costly, and a higher age would provoke opposition from members of Congress who wished to alleviate unemployment of younger workers by removing older workers from the labor force.[93] President Roosevelt accepted the CES's proposals in December 1934 without commentary on the proposed retirement age.

When the bill containing the various old-age provisions reached Congress, the age threshold generated almost no discussion, perhaps because the omnibus bill contained so many new and controversial issues that the age issue was overlooked. According to Wilbur Cohen, who helped formulate the bill and later wrote its history, no Senate or House committee requested a justification of age sixty-five, and the House voted down those few amendments from the floor that attempted to reduce the age for old-age assistance to sixty.[94] Though in all probability neither gerontologists nor politicians expected that Social Security would rigidify the definition and isolation of old age, the facile acceptance of age sixty-five created momentous consequences.

LOOKING back from 1934, writer and editor Henry Seidel Canby reminisced, "In the American nineties generally, home was the most impressive experience in life."[95] By the 1930s, however, social reorganization had confounded that simple vision. Sociologist William F. Ogburn, writing in the *Report of the President's Research Committee on Social Trends*, commissioned by President Herbert Hoover, concluded that there currently was "a greater individualization of the members of the family."[96] Though asserting that the family still retained vital "personality functions" in its serving as the locus for affection and nurture, Ogburn observed that the family had yielded to outside agencies its traditional economic, protective, educational, and entertainment functions. As a result, especially in urban areas, children associated more with playmates, a gap opened and then widened between generations, and husbands and wives had more friendships outside the family circle. These patterns developed in conjunction with other trends, such as the increase in clubs, commercialized entertainment, and automobile travel.[97] In another section of the report, Warren S. Thompson and P. K. Whelpton noted the accelerating increase in the number of older people in the population and speculated on the effects this burgeoning age group would have on the nation.[98] What all of these observers were noting was the culmination of a major social transformation. In the family, the schools, the workplace, and the society at large, peer groups and age homogeneity had become dominant organizing principles.

By the end of the nineteenth century, increasing
proportions of marriages were taking place
between people who were of, or near, the same
age, and a trip to Niagara Falls was becoming a
popular honeymoon for these age-peer couples.
*Library of Congress.*

In the early twentieth century, peer-based youth gangs
prompted reformers and psychologists to become more
concerned than they ever were before with the
distinctive characteristics and needs of adolescents.
*Library of Congress.*

This photograph of the residents of an old-age home in Ohio depicts the institutional segregation of elderly people from other age groups that began in the early twentieth century. *Library of Congress*.

Whether within the family or among peers, the birthday party has become Americans' most ritualized recognition of age. *Library of Congress*.

The first birthday cards, such as this one published by Louis Prang and Company in 1875, expressed the theme "happy returns of the day," emphasizing the hope for a continuation of present happiness. *Courtesy of Hallmark Cards.*

By the early twentieth century, birthday cards and their messages focused on the present—the significance of attaining a specific age. *Courtesy of Hallmark Cards.*

"Silver Threads Among the Gold," published in 1873, was probably the most popular song in the 1870s and 1880s sentimentalizing old age. *John Hay Library, Brown University.*

Songs such as "When I Was Twenty-One and You Were Sweet Sixteen," published in 1911, signaled an explicitness in the expression of age and age norms that was new in the early twentieth century. *John Hay Library, Brown University.*

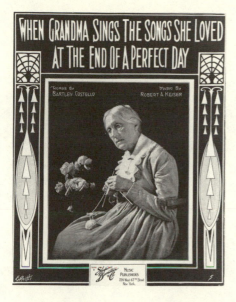

Sheet music covers such as this one, published in 1916, helped spread the image of old age as a time of doddering sweetness tinged with confusion. Note how numerous characteristics— thinning hair, wire-rimmed eyeglasses, shapeless dress, knitting—are used to distinguish an elderly person from someone in a younger age group. *John Hay Library, Brown University. Reproduced with permission from Shapiro, Bernstein and Company, New York.*

Beginning in the 1960s, formal organizations of older people, such as the National Council of Senior Citizens, formed to lobby for their own age-related needs. *Library of Congress.*

ACT YOUR AGE: THE CULTURE OF AGE, 1900–1935

In 1893, a simple ditty titled "Good Morning to All" appeared on page three of *Songs for the Kindergarten*, a book of children's tunes published in Chicago. Two young sisters, Mildred J. Hill and Patty Smith Hill, from Louisville, Kentucky, were listed as the song's composers and copyrighters, though later a third sister, Jessica M. Hill, claimed to have been a collaborator. The three Hill sisters subsequently distinguished themselves professionally: Mildred as an organist, pianist, and authority on Negro spirituals; Patty as education professor at Columbia University and an authority on the kindergarten movement; and Jessica as an English instructor at Columbia Teachers College. But their personal fame paled beside that of their youthful creation, because while the sisters were building their careers, their innocent little composition was being transformed into America's most frequently sung musical piece.

The Hills' song appeared again in 1924, when Robert H. Coleman, a publisher from Dallas, Texas, included "Good Morning to All" among the songs he compiled and edited for *Harvest Hymns*. The book recorded no authors for the song and no copyright notice. More importantly, however, the second stanza of "Good Morning to All" now included the words "Happy Birthday to You." Coleman incorporated this stanza into at least three other song collections that he published between 1930 and 1933. In 1934, "Happy Birthday to You" was sung in the Irving Berlin and Moss Hart musical production *As Thousands Cheer*, and it quickly became a hit.[1] At this point, Jessica Hill sued Sam H. Harris, publisher of *As Thousands Cheer*, for plagiarizing from the song "Good Morning to All," asking two hundred and fifty dollars in damages for each performance of the Berlin and Hart show.[2] The suit was apparently settled out of court, and later that year the Clayton Summy Company of Chicago republished the melody without lyrics, crediting Mildred and Patty Hill as composers. In 1935, Clayton Summy published two other arrangements, this time with words, and used the title "Happy Birthday to You" instead of "Good Morning to All." Again the Hill sisters were listed as the composers.[3]

Between the first publication of "Good Morning to All" and its emergence on Broadway in the form of a birthday song—a song so popular that it generated a lawsuit and publishing scramble to establish its authorship—American society had changed markedly. By the time "Happy Birthday to You" had become fixed as a verse in the Hills' original song, age consciousness had flowed through American institutions and was permeating the general culture. A strong current of age norms now guided people's behavior and expectations, admonishing each individual to "act your age." And the anniversary of one's birth, hardly recognized in past eras, now not only afforded cause for elaborate celebration but also represented a distinct life-course milestone by which the individual could—indeed, should—measure status and accomplishments in comparison with those of age peers. This chapter examines the culture—the reservoir of goals, values, and behavioral patterns—which manifested itself in popular attitudes about age.

## THE ASCENDANCE OF AGE CONSCIOUSNESS

In 1919, *American Magazine* sponsored an essay contest on "The Age I Would Most Like to Be." The very occurrence of the contest itself is significant because it reflects the powerful age consciousness prevalent in American society at that time. Equally significant were the prize-winning compositions, which the magazine published at the end of the year. First prize was awarded to "R. B." for her essay "How Life Seems at 73." The author of this essay not only cheerfully accepted the distinctions of old age but also recognized the age-normative qualities of other life stages. She stated with confidence that she would like to remain at age seventy-three "indefinitely." Though she knew seventy-three was old and she looked old, she considered old age restful, not burdensome. To her, youth had pleasures but also many pitfalls, and "middle age is the storm period," especially for mothers. "Old age," she explained, "is sweet and restful, the calm after the storm."[4]

"M.M.R." won second prize for "From a Young Man of 21." This author envied a friend of fifty who had so much more experience and seemed to be able to enjoy so much more of life. He was also envious because his friend seemed so much more comfortable than he was in the company of women, and because his friend could rejoice in another person's success and did not fear death. At the end of the essay, the author revealed that his "friend" was his father.[5] Though a sentimental paean to a parent, this essay nevertheless evidences acute awareness of generational differences and age-related characteristics.

Third prize went to "V.M.M." for "Why I Would Like to Keep on Being 14." This piece expressed innocent adolescent dreams and fears, with a modicum of age norms. The author conceded that age fourteen was a time of dreams and ambitions; even if those visions might dissolve in the future, she still could dote on them. She disliked boys of her own age and feared having to socialize with them (peer grouping); what she liked best was to daydream about her teachers and about her favorite movie star, Madame Nazimova. She ended by stating that she wanted to stay at age fourteen because she did not "*want* to grow old and toothless, and have [her] grandchildren have to stay home" to care for her.[6] Conceivably, V.M.M.'s fear derived from a real situation in her own family and therefore was idiosyncratic. Even so, her stereotyped conceptions of youth and old age highlight distinctions and generational rifts that, though they existed before the twentieth century, had become increasingly acute and dominant in the culture of her own era.

Popular media expressed consciousness of age in a variety of ways. Publications such as *Living Age* and *Ladies Home Journal* offered regular advice columns on the raising of children, including definitions of childhood's sub-stages and prescriptions for how to satisfy children's age-related psychological and intellectual needs. Such issues as at what age treatment of a child as an infant should end, at what age a child should be sent to school, and at what age he or she should "go forth into the wide world" were the subjects of constant attention from self-proclaimed experts.

Many writers of autobiographies and memoirs, especially women, also described the age-related values and events of their youth with a precision that generally was absent from comparable works in previous eras. These authors used specific age references in two major ways. First, age for them was a guidepost, a means of chronologically situating events and accomplishments in one's personal career. Statements such as "I first met———when I was eight years old" and "I was twenty-two and my brother was eighteen when our mother died" commonly appeared in these reminiscences.[7] This kind of reference certainly was not new in the twentieth century, but its use seems to have expanded considerably. Second, authors of personal reminiscences used age to categorize individual development and to express norms by which to compare themselves with their peers. Thus, the writer of one memoir recalled that one of her most vivid childhood memories was at age thirteen being "very tall for my age."[8] Another remembered a special dance class for pupils aged sixteen to eighteen, who were "girls of what might be called the conscious age; conscious of their clothes, conscious of the desirability of male dancing partners, and conscious that schoolboys of a like age are in reality very much younger than themselves."[9] Though these authors were describing sit-

119

uations that had occurred many years before the time at which they were writing their recollections, the contemporary norms and language of the culture that surrounded them resulted in their almost unconscious expression of age references.

Mass-market publications directed particular attention to young adulthood, in part because of the emergence of a youth culture in the first third of the twentieth century. Popular writers mused on, and fretted over, numerous topics pertaining to early adulthood, from life at home and at work to sexuality and marriage. Some authors seemed obsessed with distinguishing between youth and adulthood. One self-styled expert, for example, asserted that "a *man* of *twenty-five* and a *boy* of *seventeen* cannot meet on equal terms." Calculating that "the average boy is, to be exact, sixteen and two months old" (such exactitude was rare before the twentieth century), the author cautioned that boys who adopted adult values would prematurely pass their prime, and that men who believed they could linger at age sixteen would be demeaning themselves. Rather, he advised, at age eighteen or nineteen, a boy becomes a young man and should "take his place in the world." Age, according to this writer, served as a crucial determinant of appropriate behavior.[10]

Female diarists and autobiographers were particularly reflective when it came to the age-related social and psychological changes they experienced in the transition between girlhood and womanhood. Writing from her perspective in the 1920s, Mabel Osgood Wright, a popular essayist and daughter of a New York Unitarian minister, recalled in her autobiography that her life changed markedly—as it was supposed to change—when she left her teens. "At nineteen," she mused, "one is contented merely to live, to bite into the ripening fruit of life hungrily, with sharp teeth and let the sweet juice trickle down the throat; . . . but at twenty, one thinks a bit more about taste and quality of the fruit and as to what is coming next."[11] The next year of her life was even more important. Wright devoted an entire chapter to "One and Twenty," declaring that "any other year in my life might have been lived through imagination or make believe, but for me one and twenty stands alone. For me it was a year of reconstruction, for during it everything that had been or ever was to be, ended and was reborn."[12] In part, this watershed effect derived from the fact that Wright's favorite aunt had died that year, but again what is significant is her attempting to link personal assessment with specific age.

One of the most vivid representations of early twentieth-century awareness of age and the transition to womanhood is the poignant and introspective diary of Wanda Gág. Later a famous fashion illustrator for *Harper's Bazaar*, Gág penned her diary between 1908 and 1917, during her teen years and early twenties, when she attended boarding school and art school in Minnesota. In her diary, she not only chronicled personal experiences but also often used them to launch into ruminations about her personal development. These reflections almost always included age and peer comparisons, which served as guideposts.

Physical maturity and sexual awakening provoked Gág into intense self-examination. In the spring of 1914, when she was twenty-one, Gág made several entries into her diary that expressed apprehension over the physical and emotional strains of being child and woman at the same time. While visiting school friend Paula Hershl, Wanda was drawn to making comparisons between herself and her peer. After inspecting herself in Paula's mirror, Wanda confided to her diary:

> I look so much like a child. No wonder Armand [her first true beau] is afraid the Woman in me hasn't spoken. But this I know: I look more childish than I am. My soul and heart and mind feel sedate but my body doesn't. My body is only twenty-one years young—my heart and soul and mind are older than that.[13]

A few days later, Wanda became more petulant. She wrote:

> Paula thought there was more of the Woman in her than in me. I don't think so. It is true that there is more of the Child in me than in her, but I will not grant that there is more of the Woman in her than in me.[14]

Gág was also profoundly conscious of where she stood among age peers with regard to romance and sexual contact. Her vexation about "the Woman in me" prompted her to conclude:

> I think I have a pretty sensible record as far as love affairs is [sic] concerned. Nearly every girl of about my age [twenty-one] that I have met lately has been engaged once or twice or even thrice. Nina for instance, has been engaged three times, and Mary is engaged for the third time at present. I think, without much trouble I might have been engaged twice. In fact it was more trouble to prevent it from happening than otherwise, I think.[15]

A discussion with Paula over "how much liberty one should allow a boy to take" caused Wanda to review the three instances when a young man had put his arm around her shoulder or held her hand, and then to observe, "I have found since that it is not very often that a girl has reached the age of twenty before she has had a boy's arm about her, so my record is comparatively good."[16] Three years later, however, her self-assurance dissolved when a fellow art student gave Wanda her first romantic kiss. "And now I have done it," she confided to her diary. "I knew it would come but didn't think it would happen so soon." At age twenty-four, Wanda fretted over whether to relate her kissing experience to a friend, then kept silent out of embarrassment.[17] Gág's credibility is not at issue here; rather, her sensitivities about the connection between age and personal experiences represent an acute awareness of age that her ancestors would not have possessed.

Scheduling norms for marriage, established in prescriptive manuals from the 1890s onward, occupied many popular writers in the first third of the twentieth century (see Chapter 3). Journalists and diarists frequently expressed cultural age norms for marriage when discussing the pitfalls of "early" or "late" marriage. Almost every reference to marriage included age specificity. A writer for the *Ladies Home Journal* in 1909 warned that no one should marry before age twenty-two, because "puppy love," common among youths between fifteen and twenty, was only a false imitation of true love.[18] A "career woman" complained that her family treated her with condescension when she became engaged, "too late," at age thirty. "I suppose," she grumbled, "if I had been twenty instead of thirty when I became engaged, I should have walked through a golden door."[19] A seventeen-year-old diarist made special note of the conditions she observed when visiting her twenty-two-year-old sister who had run away from home and married when she was sixteen. The diarist wrote that seeing her sister "made me kinda sick. There she is with a house full of squalling brats. She looks 30 if she is a day, and she's only five years older than I am." Her sister told her, "I was too young to get married but things went wrong and so Mom and Pop raised the dickens and Arthur and I ran away and got married. . . . But look at me now! I'm an old woman at 22. I ought to be just thinking about getting married. I've been cheated out of my good times."[20]

In spite of such regrets about early marriage, many writers still warned against waiting too long to marry. Irrational caution, advised the authors of the 1927 publication *Wholesome Marriage*, could be as dangerous as youthful impetuosity.

So much has been said about the danger of marrying in haste that we are likely to overlook the equally important fact that young people can be over-prudent. The reckless years are followed quickly by the overcautious ones. These too careful years are likely to come in the late twenties. It is easy as one comes toward the thirties to construct arbitrary conditions that must be fulfilled before marriage can be thought about, with the result that often there is no marriage at all for these young people who are unwilling to trust themselves to the adventure of home-making."[21]

In the 1920s, the proper age for marriage concerned experts in a variety of fields. Even health enthusiast and maverick publisher Bernarr MacFadden became involved with the issue when he sponsored publication of *How Can I Get Married?* an anonymously authored recollection of a young woman's search for a husband. In his preface, MacFadden stated that the book was meant to "teach a girl what she should do to prepare properly for marriage." The manual's author, a woman named "Molly," devoted a full chapter to "It's Time You Were Married." In this segment, Molly related that when she was sixteen, her mother strongly protested every time she wanted to discuss marriage, admonishing her that "I must not think of marriage at my age." But four years later, when she was twenty, Molly was made to feel out of step because she had not yet married. Then, she complained, "mother tells me quite plainly that it is time I was married. 'What's the matter with me?' I ask myself."[22] Such explicit expression of age norms and guilt suggests the kinds of cultural pressure that was being applied to young adults.

Popular writers had been attaching specific age norms to marriage since the 1880s, but in the early twentieth century they expressed for the first time age consciousness in relation to middle adulthood. For example, in 1908 a writer for *Living Age* lamented what was happening to people "on the right side of thirty" who might soon find themselves "too old at forty" to be respected in the business world. The premium on youth, wrote the author, meant that "the places for the not young men are becoming fewer."[23] Other writers reflecting on their middle years used age-specific references seldom voiced a generation earlier. Upon reaching his fiftieth birthday in 1919, popular author Ellis Parker Butler noted, "At 20 my life was a feverish adventure, at 30 it was a problem, at 40 it was a labor, at 50 it is a playful journey well begun."[24] Taking stock at midlife was not completely new; age specificity was.

Significantly, advertisers quickly integrated the age consciousness of adults into their sales pitches. A striking example is the magazine ad for Pyorrhocide Powder, an antiseptic dentrifice manufactured by the

Dentinol and Pyorrhocide Company, Inc., of New York City. "HOW OLD ARE YOU?" the ad challenges in bold print, continuing:

> If you are over  60—have you lost all of your teeth?
> 50—have you lost some of your teeth?
> 40—are some of your teeth loose?
> 30—have you sore, bleeding, receding gums?

> Now take a mental glance at the condition of your mouth, teeth, and gums. THEN think of your age.

The company, of course, was trying to sell its product by cashing in on adults' new age-related expectations of physical well-being.[25]

Such expectations virtually spilled out of popular books and articles on old age, a topic addressed frequently in the 1910s and 1920s. Some writers showed how pervasive the age norms of senescence were by seeking ways to undermine them. In a profile of Joseph C. Butler, an active seventy-eight-year-old businessman in Youngstown, Ohio, journalist William Bruce Hart observed in 1919, "Many people believe a man has reached the point of greatest efficiency at around forty-five years of age. A man of fifty years old to them is on the brink of the grave. And when he is sixty, they are convinced he is only cheating the undertaker." Hart was indulging in overstatement for effect, but his use of specific age grading is revealing nonetheless. He concluded his article on Butler by stating, "When one sees other men of similar age hobbling around on canes, one marvels at Mr. Butler's ability to keep his health under a strain unusual for a man of his age."[26]

Another author related a ruder awakening to the physical plights of old age when he injured himself trying to kick a cat. His physician told him, "A man who is sound . . . should increase in strength until he is forty; from forty to fifty he should hold his own; after fifty he begins to go to pieces." The writer was forced to admit that he had entered that last stage. "Old age," he bemoaned, "is a thing of dread. One associates it with slippers and . . . white whiskers and crutches." He resolved to do everything possible to evade the stereotypes of old age by working hard, maintaining his optimism, and paying more attention to grooming. Yet, like the medical theorists and practitioners, he was forced to admit in maudlin resignation that "no matter how much fun we get out of life, there comes a time when the pilgrim grows tired and footsore, beaten by the storm of years, and he should be glad to see the inn at the end of the road, though the windows be dark. If it is cool and silent, so much the better for sleeping."[27]

Themes of isolation and dependency haunted popular accounts of old age. Numerous books, articles, and stories evidenced a heightened awareness that older people had become increasingly segregated in American society. Discussions were tinged with both calm resignation and bittersweet complaint. In *The Felicities of Sixty*, Isaac Lionberger saw himself entering a more placid stage of life, in which he and others of like age could disengage themselves from the world's cares. He wrote, "We watch without anxiety the restless and incoherent progress of society from blunder to blunder and experiment to betterment. We never despair, and are never foolishly hopeful. . . . If we hope less, we fear less. Death does not appall us for we have lived long enough to know that death cannot be evil."[28] And in a moving and poignant personal statement, feminist Mary Vorse, writing in the person of her aged mother, regretted the ways that age had separated elderly individuals from active family life. "As one advanced further into the Land of Old Age," she lamented, "one sees more and more how isolated each generation is from the other. We begin . . . playing Providence to our children. We end . . . a spectator to the drama of our children's lives. You will not be able to turn the tragedy into comedy."[29]

Isolation was linked to need in various ways. The president of Prudential Insurance Company warned that people had to plan for the inevitable helplessness of old age, and he listed stark statistics to underscore his point:

Out of 100 average healthy men 25 years of age, 64 will reach age 65. Of these:

1 will be rich
4 will be well-to-do
5 will be earning their living
54 will be dependent on friends or charity.[30]

And in the short story, "Scattergood Borrows a Grandmother," Scattergood Baines, the popular small-town busybody created by Clarence Budington Kelland, discovers that a "Grandmother Penny" was unhappy because "her family looked upon her white hair and wrinkles, and arrived at the erroneous conclusion that her interest in life was gone, in short that she was content to cumber the earth and to wait for the long sleep." Scattergood decides that what Grandmother Penny really needs is independence, so he finds a sixty-six-year-old widower, Spackles, and introduces him to Penny. The two elderly people eventually decide to marry, but their children forbid the union because Spackles and Penny would have to use their burial money to support themselves. When the older people try to invest their savings and instead lose it to a swindler, Scattergood intervenes, swindles the swindler, and returns the original money plus an extra ten thousand dollars to Penny and Spackles, allowing them to wed. Though not intended as social commentary, this sentimental and amusing tale emphasizes the difficulties of loneliness and of maintaining economic independence in old age.[31]

Popular American writers had described stages of life long before the twentieth century but seldom with the age specificity and awareness of distinct separateness that had become so common by the 1910s and 1920s. Consciousness and expression of age norms resulted from and reinforced the peer society that had coalesced out of demographic and institutional developments at the end of the nineteenth century. The cultural emphasis on precise age and on social organization by age induced Americans not only to assess themselves through comparison with their peers but also to attach greater significance to age-defined milestones in their lives. This process endowed birthdays with a meaning and importance they never before had carried, and the celebration of a birthday became one of the, if not *the*, most significant annual events in an individual's personal career.

### "Happy Birthday to Me!"

At the dawning of the twentieth century, author and editor Margaret Sangster urged American mothers and wives to pay attention to a very important responsibility. "We should make much of the home anniversaries," she wrote. "Let every birthday be a festival, a time when the gladness of the house finds expression in flowers, in gifts, in a little fête. Never should a birthday be passed over without note, or as if it were a common day, never should it cease to be a garlanded milestone in the road of life."[32] Sangster's entreaties reflected a trend in which birthdays were becoming more elaborately celebrated events than they had ever been before. In a culture that regarded age as a defining characteristic of social status and responsibility, and that accepted age as a label with the capacity to explain an individual to self and to others, the day that announced the attainment of a certain age became more than just a personal holiday. It became a crucial aspect of one's own definition of self.

In ancient, medieval, and early modern Western societies, birthday celebrations were not as customary as might be assumed. In fact, their occurrence on such a large scale is a rather recent phenomenon.[33] Because a birthday depends on a date, no one could regularly observe a celebration of one's own birth until a consistently accurate calendar had evolved. Such a calendar seems to have been perfected in ancient Mesopotamia and Egypt.[34] But in addition, until the modern era, large proportions of people could not read and would have been unable to identify their birthdays on a calendar even if they had owned one. Moreover, the official recording of birth dates was sporadic. In ancient times, birth records were deemed important, especially by the aristocracy, because they were needed to cast a horoscope. Early Egyptians, Greeks, and Romans did celebrate birthdays of royalty and other important personages, but it is unlikely that commoners had any notion of their own birthdays. When the societies of antiquity abandoned their census-taking practices, birth records ceased to be kept. The only exceptions occurred among families to whom marriage contracts and dowries were important. Not until around the twelfth century did parish priests revive the recording of exact birth date on an extensive basis.[35]

Before the Reformation, even when people knew their date of birth, they seldom celebrated it—except for nobility—because the Church deemed such festivities to be pagan, unholy practices of the pre-Christian past. More important in terms of personal and family observance was name day. At baptism, a child received the name of a patron saint who was to become the child's guardian. Henceforth, the individual annually would celebrate the day sacred to the saint whose name he or she bore.[36] Among Roman Catholics, name day retained importance into the twentieth century and continued to mark the occasion for celebration and gift giving. In 1911, for example, a Polish peasant wrote his father in the United States and expressed gratitude for his father's name-day gift. "I inform you that I received your letter with wishes and three roubles for my name-day on my name-day itself. I thank you very much, father, for the wishes and the three roubles."[37] But name day did not really commemorate an individual's age or birth; rather, it focused on an external personage, the protecting saint, rather than on the individual who might have been attaining a new status in life.

The only birthday that was widely recognized in pre-modern times was Christmas, the birth date of the Christian son of God. But even this birthday was secondary, at least in the Middle Ages, to Twelfth Night, the celebration of the baptism of the baby Jesus. It was this occasion which may have provided the precedent for modern birthday celebrations, for Twelfth Night festivities often included joyous activities, exchanges of gifts, eating of cakes and sweets, and candlelighting. In Germany, the Twelfth Night Epiphany, which also commemorated the visit of the Magi and the manifestation of Christ to the gentiles, evolved from a cheerful family festival into children's celebrations called *kinderfesten*. Then, in the nineteenth century, Queen Victoria of England, presumably calling upon her German antecedents, adapted the *kinderfesten* into birthday celebrations for her own children, setting an example for broader observance of children's birthdays.[38]

After the Reformation, celebration of the birthdays of royalty revived and furnished another model for modern practices. Especially notable were festivities on the thirteenth birthday of England's King Charles II, May 29, 1660, a day that also marked restoration of the monarchy and an end to Oliver Cromwell's Puritan reign.[39] In the infant United States a century later, some patriots worried that growing sentiment in favor of celebrating George Washington's birthday intimated too closely the European customs of honoring royalty. Thus, as Washington's birthday approached in 1819, Thomas Jefferson wrote to James Madison: "A great ball is to be given here [Philadelphia] on the 22nd, and in other great towns of the Union. This is, at least, very indelicate, and probably excites uneasy sensations in some. I see in it, however, this useful deduction, that the birthdays which have been kept, have been, not those of the President, but of the General."[40] Jefferson had cause for fearing that a public birthday celebration would be a first step toward considering Washington royalty. Troops at Valley Forge had begun celebrating Washington's birthday in 1778, and during his presidency Washington annually received accolades on the anniversary of his birth. When he died in 1799, Congress designated his birthday, February 22, as a day of mourning, and President John Adams continued to honor the occasion. Jefferson discontinued the practice when he became president in 1801. Observance became irregular until 1832, when the centenary of Washington's birth sparked renewed celebration. Thereafter, February 22, along with July 4, marked an occasion for patriotic fervor, but it also awakened new interest in birthday observances.[41]

After the Civil War, birthday observance became the vehicle for honoring another of the nation's revered heroes, Abraham Lincoln. A group of Lincoln's admirers initiated the first formal commemoration of his birthday in the Capitol on February 12, 1866. Thereafter, unofficial observances occurred around the country. Then, in 1891, Hannibal Hamlin, Lincoln's first vice president, spoke before the Lincoln Club of New York and suggested that the birth date be made a national holiday. In 1892, Illinois became the first state to make Lincoln's birthday a legal holiday, and within a few years more states took similar action.[42] At the same time, published calendars began to show birthdays of other notable personages, and although widespread official celebration of these persons' birthdays did not become regular occurrences, recognition of the dates reinforced the growing importance of the concept of birthdays in the national culture.

In the case of more ordinary people, birthdays were seldom celebrated before the end of the nineteenth century, both because such observance was not deemed important and because records were not always accurate or consistent enough to allow people to identify their birth dates. The first broad public survey that tried to include precise information on birth dates was the 1845 census of Boston, compiled by Lemuel Shattuck. The schedule for this census included the questions "Age of each male person on the last birth day" and "Age of each female person on the last birth day."[43] These questions did presume that people knew their exact age and birth date, but when Shattuck compiled the age data, he aggregated them in five-year categories, not single-year designations, suggesting that he was trying to minimize the age heaping (lumping of ages in years ending in zero or five) that would have resulted from people guessing their age because they did not know when the anniversary of their birth actually was.

Diaries and memoirs from the mid-nineteenth century reveal either no recognition of birthdays or no special observance of them. For example, Anna Reed, a California temperance advocate, wrote in her diary on Sunday, December 19, 1869, the occasion of her twentieth birthday: "This is my birthday. Went to church with Will Vineyard."[44] No mention is made of gifts or parties to celebrate that birthday. In fact, though it describes numerous parties, balls, and other celebrations, Reed's diary, which she began in 1863, does not refer to any other birthday, hers or anyone else's, until her birthday in 1919, when, at a time when birthday celebrations had become common, she recalled a surprise birthday dinner given for her the previous year.[45]

The journal of Agnes Lee, fifth child of Mary Custis and Robert E. Lee, refers to a birthday only once in its entries between 1852 and 1858, when Agnes was a teenager, and this reference illustrates the triviality of birthdays in the popular mind. On June 18, 1854, Agnes wrote, "This is Annie's [her sister's] birthday, but I suppose she has forgotten all about it."[46] She never mentions her own birthday. Flo Menninger, a Kansas teacher reflecting on her youth in the 1860s from the perspective of the 1930s, was conscious of her birthday; but though she elaborately described celebrations of Christmas, Thanksgiving, and even May Day, she made no mention of birthday festivities. Thus, she wrote, "On my fifth birthday, I had finished all but three patches for a quilt." That is all; as with Anna Reed, there were no gifts, no party. The birthday was simply a means of gauging time.[47] Lottie Spikes, recalling her childhood in Georgia in the 1860s and 1870s, failed to mention any birthdays at all in her memoirs, in spite of her many descriptions of family and social events.[48]

As the nineteenth century advanced, however, birthdays began to occupy a more prominent place in popular thought and culture. Birthday celebrations, with parties and cakes (adopted from the German practice of baking *Geburtstagtorten* on birthdays), in part resulted from the new conception that children were special beings distinct from older youths and adults.[49] By the 1870s, birthday parties for children of the elite had become particularly elaborate. Mabel Osgood Wright recalled one celebration that included "a sitdown luncheon at one; afternoon jugglers, and oh bliss, performing dogs!"[50] Birthday books, in which the owner would record birthdays of friends and relatives, were widely bought and circulated.[51] Parties and cakes became common among urban working-class and poor rural families.[52] It appears also that a variety of popular rituals attached to birthday celebrations became common in the late nineteenth century. Although dates are uncertain, certain beliefs and practices—for example, birthday spankings for good luck ("and one to grow on," etc.); wishing on the candles of the birthday cake and blowing them all out to make the wish come true; and predicting the future by putting a coin, a button, a ring, and a thimble in the birthday cake and then ordaining a fate of wealth, poverty, marriage, and bachelorhood to the respective recipients of these objects—seem to have been customary by the early twentieth century.[53]

Diaries from this period, unlike those of earlier eras, abound in birthday references, so much so that birthdays appear to be a primary event for the diarists. For example, from 1908 onward, Wanda Gág made diary entries not only for her own birthdays but also for those of her siblings. Thus:

December 7, Wednesday
    December 4th was Dehli's [sister] birthday. She didn't get anything from us because we didn't have enough time and money to give her anything. Perhaps Asta and Tusey [more sisters] made her some pictures or cards tho.

May 25, Tuesday (in school)
    Yesterday was baby's [Asta, youngest sister] birthday. She was two years old and got 2 presents.

September 5, Sunday
    Fine day to-day. Drew 12 pictures in my birthday book. The birthday book is going to be one in which people write their names and birthdays.

December 5, Saturday

Dehli's birthday was yesterday, and she got, besides 5 cts. worth of candy, (which she had to share with us all) a paper doll set, some cloth and a drawing book.

March 10, Wednesday

The girls in St. Paul are going to give a spread for my birthday tomorrow.[54]

Similarly, the letters of Lella Faye Secor, a Michigan journalist and peace activist during World War I, frequently contained lengthy descriptions of the birthdays of family members.[55]

More significant than simple references to or descriptions of birthdays were the ways individuals used the occasion of a birthday to take stock of themselves, assessing their past and present careers, and to peek at an uncertain future. Personal timetables, comparisons with peers, and, above all, age norms pervaded these reflections. Again, this practice was not completely new, especially among wealthy and literate persons. A revealing self-assessment written early in the modern era comes from Charlotte Brontë, who in the spring of 1847 reflected upon her impending birthday with melancholy: "I shall be 31. . . . My youth is gone like a dream; and very little use have I made of it. What have I done these last 30 years? Precious little."[56] By the century's end, however, it was common for birthdays to prompt age-reflective outpourings. On her twenty-fifth birthday, November 10, 1893, Alice Weston Smith wrote in a letter:

Birthdays? yes in a general way for the most if not the best of men and Martin Luther, Shelley, and I chose this rather grim date for putting in an appearance on this troublous globe.—*Figurez vous* I am absolutely twenty-five years old and I naturally turn to my Aunt Boosie [actually, a peer friend rather than an aunt] for sympathy, knowing that she too has touched that high water mark and survived it. You will be twenty-six on January 17th is it? (My mind is going, you see) but twenty-six is mere child's play compared to a quarter of a century.[57]

Another young woman had similar apprehensions about an age milestone. "I'll be 18 in August," she wrote, "and I used to look forward to that birthday. But there aren't any marriage proposals in sight—and what else does being 18 bring me? I used to think that when I was 18 I could do anything I wanted to. That's a laugh now."[58]

Again, Wanda Gág exemplifies the sensitivity felt by many to the implications of the birthday as a milestone. On March 11, 1911, her eighteenth birthday, Gág confessed to her diary:

131

Eighteen, sensible eighteen—Oh glory, if I'm sensible I misjudge myself entirely. Of course I can't get sensible all at one jump after having been Silly Seventeen for 365 days, but somehow I have a premonition that I shall be endowed with that characteristic for some time to come. However, "We can only hope to get better as we grow older" and I sincerely hope that I will.[59]

On the same date two years later, she wrote, "Well today I am 20 years old. Out of my teens. It is time I began doing something worth while."[60] And when she turned twenty-three, Gág voiced a common assessment about age-normative growth: "I was twenty-three years old a week ago. How can I be 23 and sometimes feel 17, sometimes 25, and sometimes 7?"[61] Alice Dunbar-Nelson, black poet, journalist, feminist, and widow of poet Paul Lawrence Dunbar, expressed similar themes on her birthdays. In 1921, she wrote in her diary, "I lay in bed this morning thinking, 'forty-six years old and nowhere yet.' It is a pretty sure guess that if you haven't gotten anywhere by the time you're forty-six, you're not going to get very far."[62] In 1927, she wrote, "My birthday! 52 years old. Ye gods! Can you believe it? I feel about 32, look 42." The next year: "My birthday! Fifty-three today. Feel much younger than when I was 33." The next year: "My birthday! . . . I am fifty-four, feel twenty-five, look forty." And the next year: "My 55th! Ye gods! Can it be that I am sliding down the other side of the hill!"[63]

The heightened awareness and regular celebration of birthdays by the early twentieth century underscore the fact that age had come to represent social status as well as the completion of a span of years. In a society characterized by ladders of age-graded experiences, attainment of a specific age denoted an important landmark in one's personal career. It marked the entry into a stratum with socially defined characteristics, attitudes, and behaviors. The aging process thus became a more patterned form of social mobility than it had been in previous eras, endowing the individual not only with changing sets of roles but also with greater or lesser rewards than were to be had at each previous age.[64] In this way, the birthday became a rite of passage itself, affording cause for celebration and provoking introspection about one's individual history and schedule.

## The History of Birthday Cards

Early in 1910, Mrs. Wilbur A. Simpson sent a seemingly innocuous postcard to a friend. Printed on one side of the card were some flowers, bows, and a simple statement, "Happy Birthday." On the other side, Mrs. Simpson confessed in longhand, "We are supposed to write some-thing original but I can't do that—so I simply write my wish that all your birthdays may be happy ones."[65] In spite of its innocence, this card reflects important developments in the national culture of age. First, it illustrates the cultural significance of birthdays in the early twentieth century and the popular impulse to celebrate them. Second, it exemplifies the rise of the birthday celebration as a commercial en-terprise. And third, it marks a transition from private, individual expression to packaged, standardized birthday messages—that is, the creation of a birthday industry. Age consciousness had reached its most explicit degree of development.

The custom of sending birthday cards, indeed the exchange of any sort of greeting cards, is a relatively recent phenomenon. According to one historian, the first modern greeting cards were Christmas cards, which seem to have originated in England in the 1840s.[66] Shortly thereafter, American printers and lithographers began producing Christmas cards, with one firm, Louis Prang and Co. of Boston, be-coming particularly successful in this business.[67] By the 1870s and 1880s, however, producers began marketing cards that used the same designs as Christmas cards—birds, flowers, children, pastoral scenes—but changed the titles and sentiments to express birthday, rather than Christmas, greetings. Most early messages were in the form of simple verse, such as:

> May each recurring day that marks thy birth
> Find thee possessed of all that gladdens earth.

Or, a bit more elaborate (and maudlin):

> What makes the sum of a year?
> Now a hope, now a fear,
> Now a smile, now a tear.
> What makes the sum of life's day?
> Time to work, time to pray,
> Then good night and away.[68]

The most common form that these cards took was that of a small postcard. Postcards of many types came into wide use after the United States Postal Service legalized them in 1898, but most birthday post-cards contained on one side a blank space for address and personal message and on the other side artwork depicting flowers, pastoral scenes, or birds, along with a brief printed message or simple phrase such as "Birthday Greetings."

By the 1910s, American publishers had begun to produce cards exclusively for birthdays, not just revamped Christmas cards, and had begun to replace postcards with folded, folio-type engraved cards. One entrepreneur helped transform the manufacture and sale of all cards, including birthday cards, into a new growth industry. Joyce Clyde Hall opened his business in Kansas City in 1910, selling postcards by mail order to drugstores in nearby communities. The cards generally carried birthday messages or sentiments of cheer or congratulation. In 1913, Hall began marketing valentine "greetings" in the form of lightweight folders, "pulls," and "honeycombs," often bordered by paper lace. That year Hall also opened his first retail store, which sold gifts and stationery as well as cards. Within a few years, he was also selling Christmas, Easter, and birthday cards in the same format as the valentines. In 1915, when his largest supplier of Christmas cards went out of business, Hall bought some die printers and began manufacturing his own products. The entrance of the United States into World War I gave huge impetus to the birthday card industry. Families and friends wanted to send birthday greetings to servicemen overseas, and they bought thousands of cards produced by Hall and other manufacturers. By 1920, Hall also was taking advantage of the growing market for cards for Easter, Mother's Day, Father's Day, Halloween, and Thanksgiving.[69] Hallmark Cards, Inc., had helped turn sacred and secular holidays into a commercial bonanza.

The rise of birthday cards as a common artifact in American culture reflects the institutionalized age consciousness that emerged in the late nineteenth century. In addition, the changing content of these cards reveals how Americans refined their attitudes toward birthdays and made the celebration of them increasingly important. By far the most common messages printed on the earliest birthday cards used the occasion to wish the celebrant a long life of health and happiness. The enduring sentiment "Many happy returns of the day" expressed this wish, and the statement and its variations, such as the abbreviation "Many happy returns," appeared commonly on birthday cards of the 1870s and 1880s.[70] The expression used the present to anticipate a rosy future, rather than focusing on the anniversary of birth as a celebration of accomplishment and a major milestone. Thus, though the statement "Many happy returns" did bestow on the occasion a certain significance and bolstered age consciousness, the phrase's future-oriented implication did not attract as much attention to the specific birthday as would be the case in later cards.

Around the mid-1880s, the messages on birthday cards slowly began to shift from the future to the present status of the recipient and all the implications of the celebrant's current age. Instead of "Many happy returns," messages began to contain statements such as "Congratulations on reaching this day." By the early 1900s, the focus had sharpened; instead of containing sentimental aphorisms, many cards substituted gentle, prodding humor that highlighted attainment of a specific age and the incidence of the birthday itself. Thus, a card printed in 1908 reads, "It is your birthday and I wish you happiness. *You are passing another milestone*" (emphasis added).[71] A popular Hallmark card from the 1920s carried the idea further:

> The king of England has 'em,
> The First Lady of the Land has 'em,
> You have 'em—I have 'em—
> everybody has 'em—
> There's nothing to worry about
> until you *quit having 'em*!
> HAPPY BIRTHDAY![72]

Another card evinced heightened age consciousness by jokingly promising to keep age a secret:

> Cheer up
> I know your age
> But I'll keep it mum
> If you'll do the same
> When my birthdays come.[73]

Though messages such as "May you always feel as young as you look" mirrored society's youth consciousness, others revealed the harsher awareness that birthdays represented the troublesome process of aging. Thus, a card from the early 1900s smugly chided:

> Another Birthday? That's a Shame
> Feelin' sort of tired and shakey?
> Bones a little stiff and achey?
> Frame a little cracked and creaky?
> Eyesight kind of dim and weakey? . . .
> That's too bad. It's AGE I'll betcha!
> FATHER TIME IS BOUND TO GETCHA.[74]

In the late 1920s, companies began to print cards celebrating the attainment of a specific age. Most of these cards were designed for children's birthdays. The most common age-specific cards were those commemorating a child's first birthday, but among Hallmark's best-selling cards in 1929 was one that read, "12 years old! Happy Birthday." The next year, the company produced a series of cards that included each individual age between two and twelve. Other cards emphasized the special nature of older ages. A Hallmark card titled "Twenty One! Congratulations!" proclaimed:

> You can *do* what you please
> in the *way* that you please!
> You can be your own boss!
> You can take your own ease!
> So here's hoping you'll please
> to have joy by the ton
> And still be on the go
> at one *hundred* and one![75]

Though cards and messages did not yet mention exact ages for older adults, some cards in the 1920s were intended for celebrants in a particular stage of life, thereby reflecting the age-graded fragmentation of the life course. A Hallmark card of 1926, for example, was titled "A Birthday in Life's Autumn" and read:

> In the beautiful Autumn of life
> With memories golden all through
> I'm hoping each day brings you gladness
> As I wish Happy Birthday to you.[76]

At the same time, Hallmark and other companies began to print cards meant for specific adult family members, such as "Mom," "Dad," "Grandmother," and "Grandfather." Also, Hallmark printed cocktail napkins with special birthday messages, expanding the artifacts of birthday celebration.

The birthday card industry grew dramatically after World War II, when companies produced increasing numbers of cards for age-specific celebrations. Late in the 1940s, Hallmark brought out a card series for elderly birthday celebrants, which included special messages directed at people in their sixties, seventies, eighties, and even nineties.[77] In 1950, Hallmark produced a "Life Begins at Forty" birthday card and another that included the message:

> This birthday's pretty special,
> For when all is said and done
> *there's not a more important time*
> *Than when you're twenty-one.* (Emphasis added)[78]

During the 1950s, companies introduced "studio" cards, whose humorous themes and messages included the mocking of age—another, and perhaps even more extreme, form of age consciousness. A 1956 card, for example, pictured a saddled horse saying, "Only your 29th birthday? Get off my back." Another from 1959, used a photograph of age-conscious comedian Jack Benny, who advised, "How to stay young forever—Lie about your age."[79]

By the middle of the twentieth century, then, the booming trade in birthday cards had fulfilled the prophecy of Ernest Dudley Chase, who in 1926 had predicted that sales of birthday cards would soon match those of Christmas cards, because "everyone has a birthday once a year and more and more people are keeping the date in mind."[80] Birthday celebrations, diary entries, popular media, and more—all in their various ways reflected the fact that age and age norms had come to occupy a prominent place in the public consciousness. This was the environment that made it possible for the Hill sisters' "Happy Birthday to You" to become such a widely popular and recognized expression of twentieth-century American culture.

## · 7 ·

AGE CONSCIOUSNESS IN AMERICAN POPULAR MUSIC

At first hearing, "Just One Girl" resembles countless other love ballads popular in the 1890s, though it was longer-lived. The song first was published in 1898 but remained a favorite as late as 1953 when it was sung by Gordon MacRae in the motion-picture musical *By the Light of the Silvery Moon*. A smitten lad sings the lyrics, which begin with his description of how he and his "sweet girlie" meet "each morning quite early" and walk to work together. The implication that the young woman is employed is interesting in and of itself, because it points to an important economic trend in the late nineteenth century; but that is an issue extraneous to the topic at hand here. It is the second verse, in its expression of the observations and attitudes germane to the foregoing chapters, that gives the song its distinctiveness:

> To be married we're old enough plenty,
>     she and I, she and I.
> She's eighteen and I will be twenty,
>     by and by, by and by.
> Although we're short as to money,
>     what care we, what care we?
> There are only two flies in the honey,
>     just one little girl and me.[1]

This simple verse contains explicit age references and the statement of an age norm, both of which mirrored the heightened age consciousness of the society that made the song popular.

"Just One Girl" was one tiny component of the expanding mass popular culture that has enveloped American life since the late nineteenth century. In its modern sense, the term *popular culture* refers to the various art forms, artifacts, and media products that are explicitly designed for and disseminated to a mass audience. Popular culture is distinct from high culture, which is associated with high social status, and the artists of which are more concerned with personal expression than with mass consumption; and popular culture differs as well from folk culture, the artists of which are considered members of and intermediaries by their audiences.[2] More than high culture or folk culture, popular culture is produced with an aim to sell, to arouse feelings and tastes in mass consumers in ways that will result in commercial success. Thus, the elements of modern popular culture are closely identified with entertainment. Yet even though those "artists" who intentionally appeal to mass audiences have been accused of manipulating vulgar tastes, they could not achieve their goal of commercial success unless they also were responding to mass values.

Many elements of popular culture embodied changing values and expressions of age in the nineteenth and early twentieth centuries. Among these were newspapers, magazines, pulp fiction, photographs, fashion, cartoons and other popular art, toys, vaudeville, popular theater, and motion pictures. Popular music, an often-neglected source of historical information, frequently gives expression to prevailing attitudes and tastes. As commercial commodities, successful songs have had to appeal to a broad audience and have had to reflect contemporary values. Though songwriters tended to portray those values in simple, even naive, terms, they generally did so in a manner that directly voiced what people believed to be fundamental truths. Obvious, basic, and sincere, popular song lyrics matched the mood of the times and shifted in the direction of changing attitudes and norms. Such qualities illuminate why popular music was, and is, popular.[3]

### PRE—1880 SONGS:
### SENTIMENTS OF STAGE BUT NOT AGE

Arguably, one could contend that popular music did not exist in modern form before the late nineteenth century, because the mass culture and audiences from which commercial songs derived their appeal were too amorphous. Rather, songs written and sung in the mid-nineteenth century and earlier could be classified chiefly as folk music, antecedents of, but not technically qualifying as, modern popular music. Yet, two arguments counter such a conclusion. First, as early as the 1830s, when federal copyright law first began protecting musical compositions, commercial publishing companies were printing sheet music expressly written for mass consumption. Composers in cities across the continent were churning out simple tunes and verses for family and group enjoyment. Sheet music often was bought as much for its artwork as for its melodies and lyrics. Lithographer Nathaniel Currier, of Currier and Ives fame, began his career as a designer of sheet music covers, and his success prompted scores of others to follow him in that profession. By 1870, the designing of sheet music cover pages was a major component of the output of hundreds of artist-lithographers, and millions of copies were purchased annually.[4]

Second, themes and styles of much of this early sheet music could be labeled "urban music," written to reflect and appeal to a public that became the foundation of American mass society. Songs appreciative of new urban services in the 1830s, such as "The Fireman's Heart Is Brave and Free"; songs commenting on increased immigration in the 1840s and 1850s, such as "The Lament of the Irish Emigrant"; songs lampooning urban fads in the 1860s, such as "The Grecian Bend" (which satirized the posture that bustles forced women to assume); and songs extolling new urban sports teams in the 1860s, such as "Home Run Galop" [sic], dedicated to the Atlantic Club of Chicago—all addressed urban themes in a highly commercial style.[5] Moreover, mid-century marked the takeoff period in the mass manufacture of pianos, an important stimulus to the spread of popular music, especially to urban households. In 1829, only 2,500 pianos were produced in the United States; in 1851, the number manufactured annually had grown to 9,000; by 1860, it had passed 21,000; and by 1910 it had swelled to 370,000.[6]

Before the 1880s, a number of popular songs expressed social norms in their lyrics, but, like the early etiquette manuals and other types of prescriptive literature described in Chapter 1, they almost never lectured or advised in age-conscious or age-specific terms. Rather, lyrics tended to communicate norms in the form of contrasts between life stages—usually the nonspecific periods of youth and old age. Thus, one of the earliest copyrighted songs, "An Old Man Would Be Young," published in Philadelphia in 1833, warned that in marriage old and young should not mix:

> An old man would be wooing,
> A damsel gay and young;
> But she when he was suing,
> For ever laugh'd and sung:
>
> An Old Man, an Old Man
> Will ne'er do for me,
> For May and December,
> Can never, can never agree.[7]

The lyrics assume distinctions between youth and old age that would be commonly accepted, but the unexpressed boundaries of those categories—was a damsel "young" at, say, twenty-six? was a man "old" at forty-four?—signal lack of a cultural need for age-based precision.

Old age seemed to receive more attention in popular song lyrics of the mid-nineteenth century than did any other stage of life. The sentiments of these songs prove revealing about attitudes toward old age and the place of the elderly in American society during this period.

Indeed, one of the most commonly expressed emotions was a maudlin apprehension about one's general condition and prospects in old age. This theme is starkly presented in the lugubrious ballad "When I Am Old," published in 1851:

> When I am old, this breezy earth
> Will lose for me its voice of mirth;
> The streams will have an undertone
> Of sadness, not by right their own,
> And spring's sweet pow'r in vain unfold
> Its rosy charms when I am old.
>
> When I am old, my friends will be
> Old and infirm and bowed, like me;
> Or else, their bodies 'neath the sod,
> Their spirits dwelling safe with God;
> The old church bell will then have tolled
> Above their rest, when I am old.[8]

Though not as gloomy, other songs voiced similar apprehensions about loss of love and contentment in old age. For example, the 1867 song "When You and I Grow Old" asks, "Will you be as truly mine, Annie/When you and I Grow Old?" And the 1872 imitation "When You and I Are Old" asks, "Will it seem the same in years to come/ When You and I Are Old . . . Will our days be happy then as now/ When You and I Are Old?"[9]

References to old age, like those to youth, revealed a sense of distinct life stages, but stages defined by qualities, not by age. If a young damsel was "gay," an aged person was "infirm and bowed." The features of the latter stage reflected developing images of old age based upon new medical research and theory (see Chapter 3). Such images contributed to the declining status of older people in American society.[10] Significantly, however, songwriters did not attach age norms to the characteristics or conceptions of old age presented in their lyrics. The song title declared "When I Am Old," not "When I Am Sixty-Five" or "When I Am Fifty." Rhyming scheme aside, the lyrics of "When You and I Are Old" did not read "Will our days be as happy as when we were twenty-five/When you and I are sixty?" As in other aspects of mid-nineteenth-century culture, song lyrics blurred transitions between the stages of youth and old age, leaving age boundaries unarticulated.

Songs representing the gloomy perspective of young people looking ahead to the prospect of old age were balanced by songs written from the perspective of old people taking stock of their current condition and reminiscing about younger days. Compositions like "When You and I Were Young, Maggie" (1866) and "When Your Silver Locks Were Gold" (1874) were not drenched with foreboding pessimism as songs about growing old were, but they did contain strong expressions of melancholy and consolation over lost youth. Thus, after describing a wistful visit to the scene of their early courtship, the singer of "When You and I Were Young, Maggie" concludes:

> And now we are aged and gray, Maggie,
> The trials of life nearly done.
> Let's sing of the days that are gone, Maggie,
> When you and I were young.[11]

Mixed with the sentimental reminiscences of these songs was a kind of reassurance that old age was not an empty time of life. Lyrics to "The Old Folks" (1867) declared:

> We are old folks, now, my darling
> Our beards are growing grey,
> But taking the year, all around, my dear,
> You will always find a May.[12]

And "Old Folks Love Song" (1869) concluded:

> Though the light on our path grows dim, love,
> And our faltering steps are slow,
> Though we know we are drawing near, love,
> The gates where mourners go;
>
> Still love makes life beautiful,
> Our waning day shall cheer,
> 'Til we join our hands in Heaven, love,
> My love of many a year.[13]

The most representative of these sentimental and melancholy ballads of old age—indeed, one of the most successful songs of the late nineteenth and early twentieth centuries—was "Silver Threads Among the Gold." Written by Eben Rexford and H. P. Danks, and first published in 1873, this song sold over a million copies of sheet music before 1900 and became a standard of barbershop quartets after the turn of the century. Certainly, the song's lingering, mournful tune contributed to its popularity, but so did its comforting lyrics, which acknowledged the distinctiveness and isolation of old age and the need for reassurance in the face of distant youth on one side and impending death on the other. The song begins:

> Darling, I am growing old,
> Silver threads among the gold,
> Shine upon my brow today;
> Life is fading fast away.
> But my darling, you will be, will be,
> Always young and fair to me,
> Yes! my darling, you will be,
> Always young and fair to me.[14]

The same themes—resigning oneself to life's final stage and consoling one another through reminiscence and encouragement—pervade many other contemporary songs, some obviously inspired by "Silver Threads Among the Gold."[15] These compositions evidence two contrasting but not necessarily contradictory sentiments about old age. On the one hand, these songs can be interpreted as positive assertions that though the "path grows dim," love remains, and one can always view a sweetheart as "young and fair." On the other hand, such statements represent a whistling past the graveyard, a self-deception that rationalizes and makes palatable for the singer the "waning day" and the fact that life is "fading fast away." Still, these songs never specify age. Though there was an awareness of the characteristics attributed to old age—faltering step, silver hair—the elderly in these songs were not characterized by explicit ages.

Researching scores of songs published before 1880 yielded only one that mentioned explicit ages. "The Old Maid," published in 1860, is the lament of a woman who lost all her chances to marry. The narrator of the song relates that when she was eighteen, she was pretty and spirited, and she attracted many suitors. But over the years, she ended up rejecting each potential beau, until the last one departed when she was forty-four. Now she was fifty-three and regretted that she had been too particular. She concludes with the advice:

> Then all ye young ladies, by me, warning take,
> Who, scornful or cold, chance to be;
> Lest ye, from your fond silly dreams should awake,
> Old maidens of fifty-three.[16]

In part, this song constitutes an exception to the rule of no age specificity in mid-nineteenth-century popular music. But it also lacks a precise sense of norms. To be sure, it warns that women should not wait until age forty-four or fifty-three to marry, and it implies that unmarried women at those ages acquire the social stigma of lamentable old maidenhood. But, like contemporary marriage manuals and advice books, it does not prescribe an ideal range of ages at which women should marry or the accepted age by which women should be married. There is no developed sense of schedule or of meeting age-defined standards. Like the society that made it and songs such as "When I Am Old" and "Silver Threads Among the Gold" popular, it did not reflect any developed awareness of age and age grading.

## AGE INVADES TIN PAN ALLEY

By the end of the nineteenth century, momentous changes in American society were transforming the content and context of popular music. Mass production and mass marketing of consumer goods and services, which in turn created new demands; increased leisure time, which resulted from mechanization and higher productivity; rapidly expanding communications media, which united distant regions of the country more effectively than ever before and provided people greater access to new products; and generally rising standards of living, which gave people more spendable cash—all created myriad new institutions and opportunities. Technological and bureaucratic developments, along with the impulses for profitability and productive efficiency, enhanced the importance of time and scheduling. The urge for efficiency generated institutional reforms, such as standardization of graded schools in which scientific theories of physical and intellectual development increasingly determined organization and policy, and values related to rational and uniform scheduling were translated into norms associated with the stages of life. Proliferating medical and advice literature began to set forth age-explicit behavioral characteristics of childhood, young adulthood, and old age. Indeed, childhood increasingly took on both special attributes and protected status, and old age received more distinct definition than in earlier eras.

The content of American popular music incorporated and mirrored all of these developments. As mass entertainment emerged as an important component of mass culture, and as professional show business became an ever-expanding segment of mass entertainment, popular music increasingly became more distinct from other forms, such as folk and religious music. Variety shows, which had replaced older minstrel performances and which by the 1890s were rechristened "vaudeville," included in their fare popular music that appealed to expanding urban audiences composed of women and children as well as men. At the same time, the genre of American musical comedy shed its dependence

144

on European models and became a unique indigenous art form with its own distinctive songs. Show business entrepreneurs, such as Tony Pastor, F. F. Proctor, B. F. Keith, and E. F. Albee in vaudeville and George M. Cohan and Florenz Ziegfeld in musical comedy, provided new opportunities for popular music composers to reach the public.[17]

Also in the 1890s, music publishers, spurred on by these opportunities, began to market and promote their songs more aggressively by increasing their output, distributing sheet music in department stores and five-and-ten-cent stores, and inducing producers of traveling musical-variety shows to adopt new tunes. After the turn of the century, many of these publishers clustered on 28th Street in Manhattan, a location soon nicknamed Tin Pan Alley, probably because of the numerous cheap pianos heard from the offices that lined this street. Acting as music factories, these places catered to public tastes, producing songs that could readily be sung on the stage and, more importantly, could be played and sung at home. Writers and publishers kept close watch on shifts in public interest, quickly incorporating current fads—be they bicycles, automobiles, the "new woman," or clothing fashions—into their music. And their efforts reaped sizable financial rewards. Between 1900 and 1910 alone, there were nearly one hundred songs that each sold over a million copies of sheet music.[18]

Products of this booming popular music industry not only reflected contemporary fads and fancies but also expressed shifting attitudes toward age. The song "Where Did You Get That Hat?" which was published in 1888 and became one of the most popular vaudeville ditties of its time, was also one of the first to refer to explicit age and normative scheduling. Its verses tell of humorous incidents in which the singer incongruously wore his battered old hat. One verse, about his betrothal, begins:

> At twenty-one I thought I would
> to my sweetheart be married,
> For people in the neighborhood had said
> too long we'd tarried.[19]

Though not definitively prescriptive or intended to arouse guilt in one who did not adhere to certain social norms, these lines do represent an important early link between a normative term—"tarried"—a specific age—"twenty-one"—and a life course event—"married."[20] Moreover, the verse serves as an important antecedent to "Just One Girl," written ten years later, in which the song's speaker asserts normatively that he and his sweetheart are "old enough" to marry at the explicit ages of twenty and eighteen, respectively.

145

In marked contrast to song verses of the 1860s, 1870s, and early 1880s, lyrics in the 1890s and early 1900s frequently mentioned explicit ages and did so in ways that were at least implicitly, if not explicitly, normative. The earlier songs depicted life stages in terms of physical characteristics, such as golden hair, silver hair, mirthful voice, bowed posture, rosy cheeks, and wrinkled brow; or in terms of seasonal metaphors, such as summer, winter, May, and December. Songs of the latter period, though still often containing such images, were far more age-conscious and age-specific. For example, probably the most popular ballad written by the successful and prolific turn-of-the-century songwriter James Thornton was "When You Were Sweet Sixteen," the lyrics of which imply that age sixteen is the time when a person first falls (or is supposed to fall) in love.[21] The profusion of age-specific love ballads written during this era included "Feather Queen," published in 1905, which also describes falling in love at age sweet sixteen; "When I Was Twenty-One and You Were Sweet Sixteen," a 1911 publication capitalizing on Thornton's earlier hit; "When You Were Six and I Was Eight," which depicts childhood as a carefree, idyllic time of life; and "When I Was Twenty-One," in which the singer specifies the age at which he began (and, by implication, the age at which one should begin) his courting of women.[22]

A number of songs surpassed "Where Did You Get That Hat" and "Just One Girl" in their level of consciousness and rigorous judgments of normative schedules. Typical of these songs was "Old Before His Time," from the musical comedy of 1894, *The Passing Show*. The title and lyrics of this air suggested social values in terms extremely rare among songs that predated it; they offered a clear warning against habits and behavior inappropriate to certain stages of life and listed the characteristics that would make one appear to be in the wrong stage: "There's loss of wealth, there's loss of health, and also loss of hair;/There's loss of sleep and appetite, and also hope or heart . . ."[23] Another judgmental song, this one age-specific, was "Old Maid Blues," originally written for the *Cohan Review of 1916*. The opening lines of this show tune expressed profound awareness of age-based scheduling norms for marriage:

> Getting old,—twenty-five today
> I've been told
> Don't like sitting, cats, or knitting. No!
> Want a man to keep me on the go.
>
> Oh, if you want me, Oh, if you'll have me
> Just come and take me, just come and make me
> Obey you and do as you please . . .[24]

Together, the title and lyrics of "Old Maid Blues" convey the guilt and desperation that an unmarried twenty-five-year-old woman was made to feel by an age-conscious society.

In some respects, references to and portrayals of older people in turn-of-the-century popular songs resembled those of the earlier era. The theme made so popular by "Silver Threads Among the Gold"—that of wistfully looking back to headier days and trying to feel reassured about present old age—continued to inform songs about lost youth. A verse from "When You Were Six and I Was Eight," for example, concedes that "now that we are older [and] the world [is] more bitter and more strange,"

> And though we love each other dearly
> Our home's as happy as can be,
> We cannot help to long and wish again
> Those merry, happy days to see.[25]

Yet in contrast to earlier ballads, songs of the early 1900s expressed greater reassurance, less apprehension, and a gentler, if not more optimistic, acceptance of old age. The chorus to "The Days When We Were Young," a 1912 love song, proclaimed:

> Golden hair now turned to silver
> All through life we sweetly clung,
> And I love you just as dearly
> As the days when we were young.[26]

Similarly, "When You're Five Times Sweet Sixteen" (1916) looked forward to old age—calculated in explicit mathematical terms—with less apprehension than did a song such as "When You and I Are Old" (1872), confidently asserting:

> When your hair turns to gray I will sing of the day,
> When you were my own village queen
> You'll be nearer to me and dearer you'll be,
> When you're five times sweet sixteen.[27]

Songwriters' views of old age in this period seem subtly to mirror the complex changes that were redefining the position of the elderly in American society. A number of factors were coming together and resulting in the social and cultural isolation of older people. Medical researchers were certifying old age as a biologically distinct life stage, and the specialty of geriatrics was created to tend to the special medical needs of old people. Technology and productivity requirements were placing a premium on youth and agility, making older workers a liability and prompting employers to pressure them to retire from the work force. Reduced family size and accelerating geographical mobility were physically separating generations more than in previous eras. And a burgeoning youth culture was segregating generations psychologically. All of these developments combined to create consciousness of old age as a "social problem."[28]

Though not age-specific about old age to the extent that songs like "When You Were Sweet Sixteen" were about youth, many song verses after 1900 did heighten awareness of old age as a distinct time of life. Moreover, they exemplified new attitudes toward the elderly that contributed to their social segregation by characterizing them in sympathetic yet condescending fashion. Historian David Hackett Fischer has theorized that by the twentieth century, as older people lost the authority and respect they traditionally had commanded, young people were more likely to make them objects of affection and sympathy. The weakening of the rigid generational hierarchy that, because of their ownership of land and their skills old people once had dominated, disposed young people to adopt new images of the elderly as complaisant—if not docile—and doting grandparents.[29]

Sheet music portrayed these images in their artwork as well as in their titles and lyrics. For example, the cover page of "When Grandma Sings the Songs She Loved at the End of a Perfect Day"—a syrupy ballad of 1916—shows a stereotypical grandmother knitting in a rocking chair next to a vase of flowers. She is wrinkled and gray, with thinning hair pulled back in a bun, and with wire-framed spectacles. She wears a heavy, apparently wool dress with a white lace collar, and her expression is one of sweetness, though there also is a hint of confusion in her countenance.[30] It is apparent, then, that songs helped smooth the rough edges of old age while further characterizing it as a separate, norm-defined life stage.

Even more than they did old age, turn-of-the-century popular songs from Tin Pan Alley highlighted childhood as a special time, and in doing so mirrored contemporary social attitudes. Medical developments leading to and resulting from the establishment of pediatrics as a separate specialty, in addition to emerging psychological theories of child development and the relationship of those theories to education, were increasingly contributing to the delineation of childhood as a period with needs and characteristics vastly different from those of older age groups. Institutional developments such as passage of compulsory school attendance laws, establishment of junior high schools, creation of playgrounds and various programs for physical training, and enactment of statutes fixing minimum ages for employment all insulated young children within a narrow, age-defined category while at the same time isolating them from the newly delineated stage of adolescence. In addition, the media, philanthropic societies, the courts, and government focused increasing attention on the plight and welfare of needy children. In the 1890s and early 1900s, newspapers were filled with sensational stories of homeless, parentless waifs; tragic deaths of neglected and abandoned children; and rending custody battles.

During this period, sad and sentimental songs about children were among the most popular in the sheet music industry. Mournful ballads about poor, lost, and neglected children were common, and their lyrics reflected the vigorous attention reformers were directing toward children. "For Sale—A Baby," copyrighted in 1903, tells the tale of a mother too destitute to feed or clothe her child, so she hangs a sign in her window, "A baby in this house for sale." No one took the sign seriously, however, and the song ends with both mother and child starving to death.[31] The sheet music's cover page shows a photograph of a sad-faced but angelic, almost irresistible child of about three or four years of age, with curly, blond hair. The corner of the page contains another, smaller photograph—that of "Baby Harold," the child singer of about eight or nine who had made the song popular on the stage. All of these features—title, lyrics, sheet music cover, photograph of child performer—were calculated to pierce the emotions of a public that had become very sentimental about the need to protect the innocence of childhood.

One of the era's best-selling songs was "The Little Lost Child," a ballad about estranged parents, a missing toddler, reunion, and forgiveness. This song's melodramatic but fashionable theme and happy ending helped it sell over two million copies of sheet music. Equally important, it was the first popular song to have its performance embellished by the use of photographic slides shown on a screen behind the singer. This antecedent of the music video portrayed episodes of the ballad, including scenes of the lost child, the grieving mother, the rescuing policeman, and the final reconciliation of the parents.[32] Though also concerned with poverty and domestic disruption, this song, like "For Sale—A Baby," played upon elevated public sentiments on behalf of children.

More numerous than these lachrymose tales of suffering children were songs that emphasized the uniqueness of childhood. "Youth Is Life's Time of May" set the tone for this type of music in the 1890s, with its simple paean to childhood and its metaphor of sunny, happy times.[33] In this regard, it paralleled songs written from the perspective of an old person looking back upon the special springtime of youth. The popular hit "Toyland," from Victor Herbert's operetta of 1903,

*Babes in Toyland*, conveyed a strong image of childhood as a separate, idyllic period of life. Its well-known chorus exclaimed:

> Toyland! Toyland! Little girl and boy land.
>     While you dwell within it,
>     You are ever happy then.
>
> Childhood's Joyland, mystic merry Toyland.
>     Once you pass its borders,
>     You can ne'er return again.[34]

Sentimentality toward childhood was not new in the twentieth century, but against the background of medical, educational, and psychological age grading, songs like this one acquired added meaning. The thousands who heard, sang, and played this dreamy air knew very well at what ages those borders of childhood were crossed, and they realized that, according to normative life schedules, whether their age fell inside or outside those borders, their behavior had to conform to what society expected of them and of their age peers.

## CHANGE AND CONTINUITY IN THE 1920S AND 1930S

After World War I, the popular music industry underwent extraordinary changes as it blossomed in several new directions. The phonograph, developed in the 1890s, served as harbinger for the new era. More than sheet music, phonograph records gave more people greater access to popular songs and were responsible for the spread of new dance fads, such as the Turkey Trot, Camel Walk, and Tango. Records also made possible the popularization of ragtime and Dixieland jazz. Then, in the 1920s, came radio, and the audience for popular music enlarged dramatically.

The radio and recording industries entwined in a mutually supportive relationship; the more music that was played on the airwaves, the more records that were bought, and, in turn, the popularity of recorded music boosted the demand for it to be broadcast. Indeed, by 1930, an estimated 75 percent of radio time was filled with musical programs. In addition, technological refinements such as microphones and amplifiers made possible the star-spangled careers of soft-voiced crooners like Rudy Vallee and Bing Crosby, enabling them to compete with and surpass in popularity booming stage singers like Sophie Tucker and Al Jolson. By 1930 as well, talking motion pictures and the rise of the movie musical created new stars and a new outlet for popular songs. By the late 1930s, jukeboxes entered the field, further stimulating both record sales and composers' pens. Together, records, radios, motion pictures, and jukeboxes trampled the sheet music industry; though publishing remained an important component of the record business, the consumption of sheet music by the public declined.[35]

The various types of popular music—dances, jazz, show tunes, love ballads—and of dissemination by media—records, radio, movies—facilitated and encouraged the production of music for different audience groups, a trend that matched the age consciousness and age grading of American society. It seems logical to conclude that the intensification of age norms and accelerating institutionalization of age divisions that began in the late nineteenth century guided commercial media such as those linked to popular music in the twentieth century. Whereas songwriters and performers of the early Tin Pan Alley era (Charles K. Harris and Irving Berlin, for example) had produced music meant to appeal generally to all age groups, popular music composers and, especially, popular performers of the 1920s, 1930s, and 1940s attracted more specific kinds of fans. For example, Rudy Vallee became the idol of the collegiate set; Bing Crosby, of a somewhat older age group; and Frank Sinatra, of "bobby-soxers" (adolescent girls). Jukeboxes, which usually were located in places where young people gathered, especially met the needs of the youth culture of teenagers who wanted to jitterbug to the new swing music of Benny Goodman, Count Basie, Glenn Miller, and the Dorsey brothers. Their parents commonly preferred tamer fare broadcast on the radio, such as dance hits played by the bands of Kay Kaiser, Sammy Kay, and Guy Lombardo. The specialization was not always age-specific; the so-called "race records" of jazz recorded by black artists were produced for growing numbers of urban black consumers. But the age and peer divisions that already had rigidified throughout the society supplied ready markets for styles that matched the unique tastes of distinct peer groups.[36]

Lyrics of popular songs continued to reflect age norms and heightened age consciousness. Extending the trend exemplified by turn-of-the-century songs that mentioned explicit ages, such as "sweet sixteen," the title of and verses to "When You and I Were Seventeen," published in 1924, imply that love first strikes the average person at age seventeen.[37] Other songs treated older years in a more prescriptive way than was characteristic of lyrics in previous decades. The 1932 tune "Young and Healthy," sung by Dick Powell in the musical *42nd Street*, expressed the sentiment of an adult conscious of normative differences between stages of adulthood:

151

I'm young and healthy,
So let's be bold;
In a year or two or three,
Maybe we will be too old.[38]

Eddie Cantors's song "Keep Young and Beautiful," from the musical *Roman Scandals* of 1933, prescribed a way to avoid the decline of old age:

Old Father Time will never harm you
If your charm still remains.
After you grow old baby,
You don't have to be a cold baby:
Keep young and beautiful
It's your duty to be beautiful.[39]

And "When You're Over Sixty and You Feel Like Sweet Sixteen," written in 1933, a year after publication of the best-selling book *Life Begins at Forty*, reinforced the notion that advanced years did not have to be a period of decline, pointing out that some people get fat at age forty (an expected norm), but that staying active and romantic in middle and old age will keep one feeling young.[40]

The cult of youth, which arose before the 1920s but spread widely after World War I, found ample expression in popular songs. Lyrics not only urged retention of youthful spirit and looks, as in "Keep Young and Beautiful," and glorified the romance of youth, as in "When Hearts Are Young,"[41] but also revived nineteenth-century apprehensions about old age. The theme that something is lost when youth fades, as expressed in "Young and Healthy," was repeated in numerous songs that achieved considerable popularity. Tunes such as "While We're Young" and "When I Grow Too Old to Dream," though they were written during the Depression and probably reflected the era's general social malaise, accentuated the feeling that youth was the only time of life worth living.[42] Several songs brazenly ridiculed older people. The 1929 ditty "My Old Man" relates how at a party honoring his fiftieth birthday a father made a fool of himself by getting drunk on "Coca Cola" and dancing the "Chili con con con," ultimately driving away the embarrassed party guests.[43] In addition to its negative images of old age, this song is remarkable for its age specificity and its reference to a birthday party, neither of which had been part of either popular music or popular culture a half century earlier.[44]

While some songs were reinforcing apprehensions about growing older, others were reviving the sense of reassurance and contentment in old age that was common among lyrics in the 1860s and 1870s. Thus, ballads such as "When I First Met Mary," a 1927 composition, cloaked the dread of old age with feelings of bliss and gratitude:

> In the fall of life as we grow older,
> The world grows colder and colder each day,
> Ev'ry heart should have its share of springtime,
> It is springtime for me now so I keep saying . . .
>
> Now that we are old and gray,
> I just live and bless the day,
> When I first met Mary, my own.[45]

Sounding very much like sentimental ballads of the 1870s, a 1930 hit titled "When Your Hair Has Turned to Silver," popularized by Rudy Vallee, pledged:

> When your hair has turned to silver,
> I will love you as today.[46]

Hit tunes in the 1930s, such as Irving Berlin's "Always," Edward Heyman and Vincent Youman's "Through the Years," and Maxwell Anderson and Kurt Weill's "September Song," looked to old age as a time of love and devotion.[47] In fact, in a reversal of the usual images, "September Song" portrayed old age, rather than youth, as a time of impatience. Thus, a verse in the original song, as performed in the musical *Knickerbocker Holiday*, declared:

> But it's a long, long while from May to December,
> And the days grow short when you reach September,
> And I've lost one tooth and I walk a little lame,
> And I haven't got time for the waiting game.

And in contrast to "My Old Man," the composition "Little Old Lady," from the musical *The Show Is On*, presented a favorable though patronizing image of an old woman who, despite her advanced years, remained sweet and attractive:

> Little-old lady, passing by
> Catches ev'ryone's eye,
> You have such a charming manner,
> Sweet and shy.[48]

The variety of images of old age in songs of the 1920s and 1930s reflected growing ambivalence about the process of aging and the place of elderly people in American society. Certainly, as David Hackett

153

Fischer, Andrew Achenbaum, Carole Haber, and other historians have noted—and, as previous chapters of this book have confirmed—Americans of this era accepted old age as a separate, identifiable, age-bounded time of life, fraught with special needs and dilemmas. Indeed, increasing numbers of public and private agencies were addressing old age as a social problem. The expanding population of older people, with their intrinsic economic dependence and chronic ailments, gave younger Americans increased exposure to the distresses and debilities accompanying the aging process. Thus, the cult of youth could include fear and degradation of the elderly. Yet at the same time, reform impulses to aid old people through pensions and other insurance programs, which gained momentum through the 1920s and culminated in passage of the Social Security Act in 1935, generated sympathetic and empathetic attitudes toward old age.[49] Songwriters acknowledged and expressed these social changes. Whereas pathos often dominated images of the elderly in late-nineteenth-century popular music, alternation between apprehension and solicitude became more common in such music by the second quarter of the twentieth century.

## Trends of the Recent Past

The expansion of American popular music after World War II is too mammoth and complex to be addressed at length in these pages. In brief, the rise of rock and roll in the late 1950s, with its roots in the free, syncopated rhythms of black spiritual and jazz music and in the thematic and elemental content of folk and country and western music, not only opened vast new territory for lyricists and composers but also generated a surge in recording and live performances. The result was further fragmentation of popular music into distinct music markets, usually distinguished by age, racial, regional, or ethnic characteristics.

Both change and continuity accompanied this fragmentation. For one thing, youth and the burgeoning youth culture, fed by the postwar baby boom, received increasing attention in song lyrics. Early rock and roll tunes adopted many of the sentimental themes of previous song lyrics, and thus continued to pay homage to youthful love and spirit in songs such as the crossover country and western tune "Young Love," which declared that first love was "filled with deep devotion," and the lively hits of rhythm and blues artist Chuck Berry, who popularized "School Days" and "Sweet Little Sixteen." The latter song expressed the new values of youth culture, which asserted a teenager's ability to exude and enjoy adult-like sensuality by donning "tight dresses and lipstick," accoutrements previously denied to a sixteen-year-old female by social age norms.[50]

At the same time, composers of more traditional popular music filled the 1950s with a plethora of compositions that also emphasized the romantic, idyllic qualities of youth, reiterating themes of previous decades. These compositions included "Hello, Young Lovers," from the Rodgers and Hammerstein musical *South Pacific*; the Nat "King" Cole hit "Too Young," which argued that young people could indeed "really be in love"; "Young At Heart," which was popularized by Frank Sinatra and which claimed, like the Eddie Cantor song thirty years earlier, that when a person has a youthful spirit, "fairy tales can come true"; and "April Love," which, according to its lyrics, was "for the very young."[51] Significantly fewer songs of the era addressed the conditions of or issues relating to older people; to be young, to feel young, and to act young were the predominant values.

The recording industry, aided by the advent of vinyl plastic phonograph records, which took the form of 45 rpm "singles" and 33⅓ rpm long-playing albums ("LPs"), experienced explosive growth and reinforced the bifurcation of popular music into life-stage divisions. All the variants of rock and roll, of course, dominated youth-oriented records, which tended to be produced by independent record companies, and to be played and promoted on the radio.[52] Larger companies, such as RCA Victor, Capitol, and Decca, aiming at an older adult market, tended to record established singers and bands, as well as Broadway musicals. Thus, with the major exception of Elvis Presley, who in 1956 signed with RCA Victor, the artists on the Top Ten singles lists were performers such as Buddy Holly, Chuck Berry, and Fats Domino, who recorded for smaller companies and whose records were bought by teenagers. The best-selling LPs usually were recordings of Tin Pan Alley music; sentimental standards performed by adult-oriented singers such as Bing Crosby, Patti Page, and Nat Cole; or "mood music" bands, such as those led by Mantovani and Mitch Miller.[53] Significantly, however, the fans of some recording stars aged along with their idols, and they maintained age-graded, peer-defined cultural loyalties as they grew older. Thus, for example, Frank Sinatra, who had been the hottest star among teenagers in the late 1930s and 1940s, was most popular among young adults in the 1950s, and among middle-aged adults in the 1960s and 1970s. The people who as teenagers in the 1950s bought Elvis Presley's records by the millions were the principal consumers of his albums and attendees at his concerts in the 1960s when they—and he—were in their thirties, and they were the most nu-

155

merous mourners at his death in 1977 when he, like they, was in his forties.

Early television, the era's new popular culture marvel, also reflected the age-based divisions of popular music. Most musical broadcasts catered to audiences made up of older age groups and thus featured sedate, mellow, non-rock performers such as Perry Como, Dinah Shore, Lawrence Welk, and Liberace; Tin Pan Alley hits were promoted on programs such as "Your Hit Parade." With the exception of "The Ed Sullivan Show," which occasionally presented rock performers (Elvis Presley's first of three appearances on the show in 1956 attracted an estimated fifty-four million viewers and was a landmark in television history), the only early television musical program aimed at youth was Dick Clark's unique show, "American Bandstand." But though it was broadcast nationally by the ABC network, "American Bandstand" remained an afternoon program, not seriously considered for prime-time airing. Not until the 1960s, especially after the arrival in the United States and the rocketing to stardom of the Beatles (who premiered here on "The Ed Sullivan Show" in 1964), did television producers begin to present rock music in prime-time broadcasts on an extensive scale. Until then, the chief media disseminating popular music to young people were still records, radio, and movies.[54]

SINCE its birth, then, mass-marketed popular music has followed and reinforced other cultural developments that have institutionalized age consciousness, age norms, and age divisions in American society. Song lyrics, though consistent in their presentations of trite, sentimental themes of romance and personal introspection, have over time shifted in specific language to reflect heightened awareness of age and its importance in the general culture. Further, both the lyrics and the marketing of popular music, first through sheet music and live shows and later through phonograph records, radio, movies, jukeboxes, and television, directed appeals to specialized groups, often distinguished by age and life stage. Though in some respects songwriters and media merchants tried to find other common denominators in marketing their products, the most common denominator seemed to be age. By the early twentieth century, popular music, like many other aspects of American culture, had become age- and peer-oriented.

# · 8 ·

## CONTINUITIES AND CHANGES IN THE RECENT PAST

If one way to assess the strength of a social trend is to weigh the complaints leveled against it, then age consciousness and age grading have indeed become powerful forces in modern life. Over the past fifty years, books, newspapers, and popular and serious journals have abounded in statements decrying the age-based organization of American society.

In 1937, for example, the author of a *Forum* magazine article titled "Why I Don't Tell My Age" argued that in spite of the current obsession with age by "census takers, insurance agents, steamboat companies, ambulance chasers, obit writers, political bureaus, and other impersonal agencies," she believed "our age is nobody's business but our own."[1] "Beware of age categories," warned the title of a *Life* magazine article in 1950. Thirty years later, a *Newsweek* article tried to identify circumstances "When Age Doesn't Matter."[2] In the 1960s, perhaps the apogee of age consciousness in this country, a writer in a magazine for teenagers lamented: "I think it's a shame that American people are being more and more rigidly divided horizontally, isolating all 12-year-olds together, and all 17-year-olds, all 40ish people and all the 60-plus group and so on. I don't think this condition exists anywhere else in the world, nor has it existed before in history."[3] It seemed to many that what had once been age consciousness and age grading had developed into age stereotyping and age segregation.

On the other hand, by the 1980s some social scientists believed that the trend had reversed and that the United States was on the way to becoming an "age irrelevant society." In an interview with *Psychology Today* in 1980, Bernice Neugarten, one of the most prominent researchers in the field of age and aging, asserted her belief that "chronological age is becoming a poorer and poorer predictor of the way people live. . . . The whole internal clock I used to write about that kept us on time, the clock that tells us whether we're too young or too old to be marrying or going to school or getting a job or retiring is no longer as powerful or as compelling as it used to be."[4] Neugarten and others claimed that, unlike previous generations, contemporary Americans were more accepting of twenty-nine-year-old college presidents, fifty-year-old retirees, thirty-five-year-old newlyweds, seventy-year-old college students, and so on. Observed Neugarten, "No one says 'act your age' any more."[5]

Conclusions that American society had become "rigidly divided" by age or that it was becoming "age irrelevant" contained doses of both accuracy and overstatement, because the past half century has seen both continuity and change in age patterns. During this time, theories about age-related growth and behavior proliferated, especially with the rise of developmental psychology, which consolidated many of the concepts propounded by educators and psychologists in preceding decades. Peer association in school, at work, in recreation, and even in one's place of residence also expanded, as policymakers and personal choice continued to make age the basis of socialization. Market research on behalf of consumer-oriented industries emphasized the "demographics"—meaning age considerations—of consumer demand, and companies geared their production and advertising toward particular age groups.

As the baby boom generation matured (the movement of baby boomers through the age continuum was, analysts said, like an animal swallowed by a snake, moving as a large, visible lump through the snake's digestive tract) and as the elderly increased in disproportionate numbers to the rest of the population, all sorts of institutions became acutely aware of the pressures these age groups exerted and adjusted to meet their needs. Writers and sociologists invented new categories, such as "young urban professionals" ("Yuppies"), "young old," and "old old," which further graded society by age. And popular literature teemed with books and articles about the "midlife crisis," turning thirty, turning forty, the meaning of "old," and a person's "best age."

But at the same time, the breezes of change were blowing harder. Increased numbers of older adults among college student populations—first as a result of the GI Bill granting tuition subsidies to veterans of World War II, then of the expansion of university extension divisions, then of concerted efforts by schools to recruit older students—broadened the age mix in higher education. Movement of more women, especially married women with young children, into the labor force confounded the age norms of their life-course schedules. Liberalization of retirement provisions, intended both to expand opportunities for younger workers by encouraging older workers to retire early and to accommodate capable, willing older workers by enabling them to continue employment after age 65, partially dissolved the previously established age boundary between productive and dependent stages of life. Perhaps most important, the U.S. Congress, followed by state legislatures, passed legislation outlawing various kinds of discrimination by age, thereby undermining the importance of age as a determinant of social status. Yet all of these attempts to surmount age still did not come close to eliminating it from the public consciousness; it has remained, along with gender, race, and class, as a prime distinguishing feature in American culture and social policy.

## DEVELOPMENTAL PSYCHOLOGY AND THE BEHAVIOR OF DIFFERENT AGE GROUPS

The process of aging, which begins as soon as an individual is born, involves the interaction of two sets of factors. One set consists of the physical and psychological changes the individual undergoes as he or she grows, matures, and declines. Dentition, puberty, menopause, intellectual and emotional capacities, and certain diseases all follow schedules that are linked to human development and degeneration. But in addition to this individual history, each person is a member of a *cohort*, consisting of all others born at the same time, and each person's individual history is a component of a sociocultural environment shared with all other cohort members.

That environment, consisting of culture—the resources from which individual behavior is drawn—and society—the arena in which behavior takes place—influences the way a cohort ages by supplying external forces, such as values and events, that stamp each individual of a certain chronological age in a particular way. For example, the Vietnam War and the so-called sexual revolution of the 1960s affected twenty-year-olds of that decade much differently from the ways they affected forty-year-olds, who in turn were affected differently from seventy-year-olds. (Of course, within distinct age groupings, individuals were affected somewhat differently depending on such factors as their class and gender.)

The study of age-related biological changes has a long history, already addressed in previous chapters. The study of age-related behavioral changes also began long before 1900, but it congealed into the more rigorously defined field of developmental psychology only in the mid-twentieth century. Even more recently, sociologists and psychologists have come to focus intensively on the interrelationships between individual growth and the historical context, a process labeled life-course or life-span development. Regardless of formal labels, *development* is the key concept, and the most customary calibration of development has been age.

Though modern developmental psychology did not coalesce as a formal field of research until the twentieth century, scientists in the nineteenth century had laid the groundwork for future studies. Part of this groundwork included the systematic observation of infants' physical growth, sensory changes, motor development, and speech (these often-sentimental works have been called "baby biographies"). More important pioneering research focused on developmental characteristics of childhood and old age and was carried out by four influential individuals: Adolphe Quetelet, Sir Francis Galton, Wilhelm Preyer, and G. Stanley Hall.

Quetelet was a Belgian astronomer and mathematician who believed statistics could be applied to predict functional relationships between age and other variables such as emotional stability, muscular strength, intellectual ability, and mental illness. His book, *On Man and the Development of His Faculties*, published in Paris in 1838, anticipated research techniques used by later students of mind and behavior. Galton, a British gentleman-scientist, built upon Quetelet's methodologies in his own quantitative studies of aging. His book, *Inquiries Into Human Faculty and Its Development*, published in London in 1883, included data on age-related development, particularly in older people. Preyer, a German physiologist, is often referred to as the real founder of developmental psychology, because his book, *The Mind of the Child*, published in Leipzig in 1882, was the first fully empirical study of behavior that was arranged in age-determined sequence. Hall, whose books on *Adolescence* and *Senescence* have been discussed in previous chapters, made notable contributions from the 1880s to the 1920s, laying the foundations for the study of age groups in the United States.[6]

In the early twentieth century, Americans E. L. Thorndike and James B. Watson undertook more sophisticated experimental work on children, leading to theories of learning and behavioral modification. Also contributing to the standing of developmental psychology was the mental testing movement and establishment of the intelligence quotient (IQ) (see Chapter 4). But in the 1930s, developmental psychologists broke new ground by moving beyond the study of childhood to a view of the entire life span. A major figure in this shift was Viennese psychologist Charlotte Bühler, who identified two sets of life events, biological and biographical, that could be arranged on separate age curves. Each curve, she said, manifested age-specific regularities in activities and experiences, along with stages of transition. Later, Bühler elaborated her theories by identifying five basic life tendencies that at particular times governed a person's behavior. Dividing the life span into ten age-graded stages, she then located specific behavioral and personality patterns according to stage and basic tendency. For example, between ages twelve and eighteen, Bühler believed the tendency of "need satisfaction," particularly that of sexual needs, was dominant, while between ages twenty-five and forty-five, the major tendency was creative expression, particularly self-realization in occupation, marriage, and family (see Table 8.1).[7]

Bühler's model of psychosocial tasks and age periods was elaborated by psychoanalyst Erik Erikson, who at mid-century was the most influential theorist of personality development. Emigrating to the United States from Europe in 1938, Erikson first undertook research on child and adolescent development. But his landmark book, *Childhood and Society*, published in 1950, moved beyond his early focus and diverged from Freudian-influenced psychoanalytic theory. While Freud had concentrated on disturbances of early childhood, which he believed were key to personality formation, Erikson emphasized what he called "the development of human potential" from infancy through old age.[8] He posited eight life stages, each with its own psychosocial tasks and developmental crisis. Different tasks become salient, Erikson theorized, during different age periods, and such differences explained age variations in interests, activities, and emotions. Thus, Erikson grouped the tasks and developmental issues of children aged six to ten under the label "initiative," while he categorized those of middle adulthood, ages forty to sixty-five, under "generativity." Erikson's concepts were adopted by others, such as educational psychologist Robert J. Havighurst, who tried further to relate developmental tasks to biological changes in the human body; according to Havighurst, these changes caused the individual to adjust to new needs and opportunities and to social norms, which involved changing expectations according to the individual's age.[9]

Since World War II, developmental psychologists have continued to be concerned most intensively with childhood and old age, using computers and complex statistical procedures to supplement descriptive observation. That the field had firmly established itself was evidenced by the appearance in 1959 of its own journal, *Developmental Psychology*, followed by specialized journals such as *The Gerontologist*, which began in 1961, and *Adolescence*, first published in 1968. Work on a large segment of the life span has been undertaken by researchers using longitudinal studies; that is, social scientists are evaluating change by surveying the same people over an extended period of time rather than by making assumptions about change by examining different age groups, or cohorts, at different points in time. A longitudinal study, then, enables a researcher to follow the same subjects between, say, 1948 and 1968, by asking them to fill out questionnaires at various intervals during those twenty years, while a cohort study attempts to approximate a longitudinal effect by describing twenty-year-olds in

TABLE 8.1

Bühler's Conception of Phases and Basic Tendencies during the Life Span[a]

| Age period | Need satisfaction | Adaptive self-limitation | Creative expansion | Establishment of inner order | Self-fulfillment |
|---|---|---|---|---|---|
| | | | **Basic Tendency** | | |
| 0–1.5 yr | Trust & love, evolvement & discovery of self-sameness | | | | |
| 1.5–4 yr | | Obedience & superego ideal versus independence | | | |
| 4–8 yr | | | Autonomous, value-setting, ego-ideals aspect of task | | |
| 8–12 yr | | | | Attempts to objective self-evaluation in social roles | |
| 12–18 yr | Sex needs & problem of sexual identity | | | Review & preview of self-development (autobiographical) | Fulfillment of & detachment from childhood |
| 18–25 (30) yr | | Tentative self-determination to role in society | | | |
| 25 (30)–45 (50) yr | | | Self-realization in occupation, marriage, & own family | | |
| 45 (50)–65 (70) yr | | | | Critical self-assessment | |
| 65 (70)–80 (85) yr | | | | | Self-fulfillment |
| 80 (85)–death | Regression to predominant need satisfaction | | | | |

a *Source:* Charlotte Bühler, "Genetic Aspects of the Self," *Annals of the New York Academy of Science* 96 (1962), 755. Reproduced by permission of the publisher.

1948, thirty-year-olds in 1958, and forty-year-olds in 1968, but not necessarily the same people.

Though problems abound in both types of studies (longitudinal techniques, for example, depend on the cooperation of the subjects involved and their availability at various times), those social scientists involved in longitudinal analysis have tried to be more sensitive than cohort researchers have been to historical influences on psychological development. Their studies have shown that age is an index to historical location as well as to biological and career stages. Thus, sociologist Glen Elder, Jr., has concluded that women who were in their late teens during the Great Depression developed different attitudes toward marriage and family life from women who experienced the Depression when they were in an earlier stage of childhood.[10] While retaining age as a crucial explanatory factor, life-span analysts also have revealed greater complexities in individuals' social and behavioral patterns. In doing so, they have challenged the traditional view that only childhood experiences explain adult character—the child is father to the man— and instead assert that experiences of later life, both historical events such as wars, depressions, and epidemics and personal events such as divorce and career change, can be just as consequential. Though some proponents of life-span development theory, such as Bernice Neugarten, claim that such a viewpoint lessens the necessity for age norms, others disagree. "We have to have age norms to anchor and structure our lives," Elder has stated. "An age-irrelevant society is a rudderless society."[11]

## STRENGTHENING AND WEAKENING OF AGE NORMS

The emphasis on human development, reflected in the growing acceptance of developmental psychology, when grafted onto concepts of growth offered by educators and physicians in the nineteenth and early twentieth centuries, riveted age norms more tightly than ever before. Through the middle of the twentieth century, a wide range of authoritative, or quasi-authoritative, parties continued to voice these norms. Thus, in 1930, a Committee on Growth and Development reported to the White House Conference on Child Health and Protection that behavior, like physical growth, followed *"laws"* that were *"ordered by age"* (emphasis added). "So consistent are the laws of emergence and sequence," asserted the committee's report, "that behavior patterns may be systematically studied to elucidate the nature of mental growth. . . . Whatever intelligence scale is employed, the use of age norms can hardly be avoided."[12]

Age grading and age norms also guided new scientific interest in human sexual behavior. Freud had specified such norms in his discussions of infant sexuality, claiming in 1925, for example, that girls normally develop penis envy at the age of four.[13] More important to American culture, however, were the highly publicized studies directed by Alfred C. Kinsey, founder of the Institute for Sex Research (now known as the Kinsey Institute for Research in Sex, Gender, and Reproduction) at Indiana University. The two surveys of sexual behavior, one of American males, published in 1948, and the other of American females, published in 1953, not only arranged data according to strict age categories but also presented age norms in their analytical descriptions of the data. As the authors emphatically stated, "In the sexual history of the human male, there is no other single factor which affects frequency of outlet as much as age."[14]

In their surveys, Kinsey and his associates focused on such topics as age of first sexual activity, age of maximum sexual activity, age of first appearance of sexual characteristics, and age of first occurrence of specific activities such as masturbation, petting, homosexual contact, and coitus. Though the major revelation of the so-called Kinsey Reports was that there were significant differences in sexual behavior, and that these differences related to the educational and economic levels of the individuals surveyed, the huge variety of data could easily be read to imply age norms, even though Kinsey did not necessarily intend such an implication. Thus, if the data showed that the median age for sex play among preadolescent males was 8.59 and that nearly 50 percent of females born after 1900 had premarital sex by age 20, a reader could assume that deviants from these norms were by implication "abnormal."[15]

In addition to the sexuality of age, the physiology of age began to receive closer medical inspection in the mid-twentieth century, especially as physicians and popular writers explored more deeply the characteristics of middle age. In this context, aging and the attainment of certain ages strongly connoted transition from health and resiliency to malady and impairment. Many "experts" became obsessed with identifying various "peaks" in physical aptitude, usually attaching age norms to major biological watersheds. For example, one writer in 1954, using geriatric research, posited three principal age peaks in a woman's life: at twenty, thirty, and, most importantly, forty. Certain physiological clues, claimed the author, would enable any observer to determine a woman's approximate age. Thus, at age twenty, noticeable pores begin to appear in a woman's skin, which previously had been smooth. At thirty, he contended, a woman's previously silky, full eyelashes become dry and coarse. After forty, veins on a woman's legs become visible, vertical ridges appear on her fingernails, and the skin under her chin and ears becomes lax. The author gave no reason for why it is important to know a woman's age; his careful listing of criteria, however, assumed that age and age norms were vital public concerns.[16]

Likewise, the author of a 1954 article, "How Old Are You Really?" asserted that though different parts of the body age at different paces, "forty is probably the critical age." This is so because in men and women of forty physical strength has long since peaked and reproductive fertility, which peaked between twenty and thirty, is in sharp decline.[17] By mid-century also, a number of medical researchers were speculating that middle age was the time when susceptibility to cancer increased appreciably. For example, in an address before a symposium on aging at the Washington University Medical School in 1944, Dr. William de B. MacNider, research professor of pharmacology at the University of North Carolina, concluded that there was

> a critical period of change that has so progressed chemically between the ages of forty and fifty-five that it may with fair certainty be recognized by structural changes. . . . Of very greatest importance is the fact that at such periods or later is the time incidence for the development of cancer. . . . *The fact of cancer is intimately associated with the factor of age.* (Emphasis added.)[18]

Other medical writers focused on the shift that occurs in middle age from acute complaints, such as respiratory infections and other temporary diseases, to chronic ailments, such as urinary malfunctions, vision difficulties, hearing loss, hypertension, arthritis, and emphysema.[19]

The "midlife crisis," precipitated by the fortieth birthday, emerged out of all the attention medical researchers and psychologists in the 1960s and 1970s were devoting to the period "between the miniskirt and medicare." By 1968, the age group between forty and sixty comprised one quarter of the American population and earned over half of the national income, so its concerns and activities naturally attracted interest. Women in this age category seemed easily prone to emotional crises because of the biological changes they experienced. Menopause not only ended a woman's fertility but also supposedly induced emotional shifts that were compounded by the woman's changing status within the family. Thus, according to the popular version of midlife crisis, a woman in her forties not only begins to lose the biological function for which she was created but also begins relinquishing the social function of motherhood, as her children set out to achieve independence and ultimately leave her alone in an "empty nest."[20]

Medical treatment has greatly reduced the physical traumata of menopause, and sociological research has shown that the social and personal shocks are far less severe than many observers (mostly men) had assumed. Nevertheless, the belief in a woman's midlife crisis and a dread of age forty have persisted. Thus, a popular writer could state in 1967 that age, not marital status or any other personal characteristic, accounted for a crisis when women reached forty, because forty signals the time when a woman needs to make critical choices about her future role in life. The crisis, she insisted, *happens in some form to everyone. . . .* It is a normal aspect of growth, as natural for forty as teething is for a younger age group."[21]

Midlife crisis among males has been described as more complex but just as strong as that among females. Popular and scientific opinion has long speculated that after age forty men rapidly lose their sexual drive and capability, undergoing a kind of "male menopause." And though unlike women, midlife men do not experience acute biological changes, many seem to manifest dramatic shifts in personality. In an effort to explain these shifts, researchers such as Yale University psychologist Daniel J. Levinson and his associates pointed to age forty as a "time of horizon," when a man looks backward and forward in uncertain and melancholy ways. The middle time of life, said Levinson and his colleagues, marks a frightening division between youth and old age, hope and disappointment, accomplishment and frustration. When coupled with symptoms of physical decline, such as reduced blood circulation and lung capacity, loss of full functions in the kidneys and gastrointestinal tract, and impairment of vision and hearing, a man's questioning of his career and personal life kindles a "realization that there is not much time left."[22]

If some psychologists studying personality were, wittingly or not, reinforcing age norms for midlife changes, others studying intelligence were erasing age norms for the supposed decline in learning abilities in middle and later adult years. In the early twentieth century, tests of children undertaken by Stanford University psychology professor Lewis Terman and others seemed to show that intelligence peaked in one's teen years and remained constant at all subsequent ages.[23] Later, a different view was adopted. In 1933, N. E. Jones and H. S. Conrad published research on one thousand people, aged ten to sixty, which showed that IQ was highest among those aged eighteen to twenty-one and declined progressively at older ages.[24] This and other studies of learning, memory, and perception reinforced the view that intelligence, like physical capacity, peaked early and then declined as an individual aged, particularly after forty. Researchers at the time seldom considered how cultural factors, such as amount and quality of schooling, influenced adult IQ, just as they overlooked the effects of culture on the IQs of children.[25]

Another problem with intelligence tests was that most conclusions were drawn from cohort studies that tried to re-create individual change over time by analyzing different age groups at the same point in time. But more recent longitudinal studies, comparing the same individuals at different ages, revealed that only in tests requiring quick visual or motor response did intelligence decline with age. In other tests, intelligence among older adults remained stable or even increased. Thus, researchers such as Paul B. Baltes and K. Warner Schaie concluded that variations in intelligence scores could be attributed more to generational (cohort) differences than to chronological age; that is, when an individual was born is more important than his or her age at the time of testing.[26] Moreover, the presumed decrease in learning abilities of middle-aged and older persons was found to be better explained by greater susceptibility to physical fatigue than by decline in intelligence.

Some psychologists even questioned the concept of intelligence itself, noting that the theories supporting it and instruments used to measure it initially were developed merely to aid educators in trying to predict school performance and enhance students' learning abilities. Such definitions and tests, said critics, could well be inappropriate for gauging the potential wisdom and experience of older adults.[27] As a result of these and other revelations, some age concepts, such as mental age and stages of intelligence, have been considerably weakened.

## AGE SEGREGATION AND AGE INTEGRATION

Regardless of psychological theories and trends in age norms, many people at mid-century were bemoaning that the United States had become an age-segregated society. Such phenomena as the baby boom, the populating of suburbs by young families, the rise of retirement communities and old-age homes, the expansion of college student populations, the identification of a "generation gap" correlated to a "youth revolt," and other social trends seemed to emphasize the most drastic consequences of intentional and unintentional age grading in social organization. Within families, generational divisions sharpened as peer loyalties competed with and undermined the traditions and age integration of the family dinner. The practice of "eat and run" resulted in family members dining at different times to accommodate outside social and occupational obligations.[28] Did such age grading isolate different groups and generations from each other as much as appearances suggested? In many ways, the answer tilts toward the affirmative, but important qualifications suggest complexities that temper assumptions about broad-based age segregation.

Some demographic trends that began around the turn of the century have continued to the present, resulting in age-specific events that occur more commonly than in past eras. First, advances in medical science have generated what one observer has called "a redistribution of deaths," in which deaths occur much less frequently among very young persons and are more concentrated in later years of the life span.[29] The marked decline in infant mortality over the past one hundred years, along with the ability of drugs and medical care to cure and prevent formerly fatal diseases such as tuberculosis, pneumonia, and polio, has accustomed Americans to expect that they will evade death until they reach old age.[30] Second, the age difference between husbands and wives has continued to narrow, reinforcing the peer quality of marriage identified in Chapter 5 and strengthening expectations that one's spouse would, and should, be about the same age as oneself. In 1900, the mean age difference for American couples marrying for the first time was four years; by 1974, it was two years.[31]

Third, the life course of adolescents and young adults has become more regular and predictable, as greater proportions of the individuals in these age groups experience important transitional events—such as going to school, leaving their parents' homes, marrying, and going to work—at the same time as their age peers.[32] Though by the 1970s more young people were postponing marriage, thereby diluting the social prescription that had set proper marriage age in the early twenties, when they did marry they still tended to choose partners who were of or close to their own age. And when young adults chose to "live together" rather than officially marrying, they tended to share living quarters with age peers.

The demographic shock that has had the most dramatic effect on American age structures and age relations in the past four decades, however, has been the baby boom. In 1947, total births in this country topped 3.8 million, having been only 2.4 million in 1939 and 3.1 million in 1943, and they stayed at record high levels for the next fifteen years. As the cohort born between 1947 and 1962 aged, each transition that it made sent ripples throughout society, altering the need for elementary schools, then high schools, colleges, jobs, and housing.

By weight of numbers, the baby boom generation thus made its presence felt, intensifying society's and its own age consciousness. For example, in the 1960s, a new youth culture was created by baby boomers, whose numbers pulled down the median age of the American population to 27.9 years, the lowest it had been since early in the century. But in 1979, three decades after the baby boom began, maturing baby boomers pushed the median age beyond 30, stationing over half the population on the other side of what one observer has called the "generational Rubicon."[33] And it is no coincidence that by the mid-1980s, when the first baby boomers approached 40, popular media suddenly began focusing on women whose "biological time clocks" were running down, and on physical fitness routines to stave off the flab and degeneration of middle age.[34]

Housing policies not only responded to the baby boom but also furthered age segregation. After World War II, builders sought to capitalize on demographic trends by constructing huge numbers of suburban residences for young, growing families. The resulting communities tended to exclude single and older people who could not afford the houses and had different housing needs. As early as 1948, some social policy analysts warned that such trends were creating unhealthy age imbalances in American communities. That year, a White House Conference on Family Life stressed the need for age "mixing" in fast-growing suburbs so that old and young Americans could reap the benefits of intergenerational contact. Instead, however, the housing policies of government and financial institutions only promoted more segregation (racial as well as age and generational). Federal highway construction, insured mortgages from the Federal Housing Administration and the Veterans Administration, and the construction of huge, private suburban developments combined to encourage white families headed by parents in their late twenties and thirties to locate outside central cities. Indeed, some 80 percent of the three thousand families who first inhabited Levittown, New York, between 1958 and 1960 contained heads of household under age forty.[35]

Meanwhile, inside city limits, private builders were concentrating on apartment construction for young singles, especially in the early 1970s, as baby boomers began reaching their twenties and earning their own incomes. And at the same time, public agencies were erecting apartments for poorer, older people in central cities, often on land cleared through urban renewal, while private developers were creating new, age-segregated communities for retirees in Florida, Arizona, and California.[36]

The maturing of the baby boom generation and general aging of the population after 1970 drew increased attention to the age composition of the work force. Women in various age groups were at the center of many of the observed new trends. For example, the U.S. Department of Labor devoted a special issue of its *Monthly Labor Review* in 1975 to "Women in the Labor Force," and its analysis of this trend was organized according to age groups. The first article in the issue, "The Early Years," noted that the upsurge in women aged sixteen to twenty-four in the labor force had been one of the overlooked consequences of the baby boom. In fact, in 1974, 63 percent of all women aged twenty to twenty-four were employed, the highest rate of any female age group. (By 1985, it had risen to 72 percent.) The article's author attributed the high figure to the expanding economy of the 1960s, the opportunities generated by higher education and equal employment legislation, and the mounting pressures of inflation.[37]

The author of the second article in the issue, "The Middle Years," noted how the baby boom had also boosted the employment rate of middle-aged women—a rate that had risen from 37 percent in 1950 to 54 percent in 1974—by expanding demand for traditional female jobs in education, personal care, and medical care. Also, women's liberation, which encouraged participation in the work force by mothers with children, and demographic trends such as decline in birthrates and rise in divorce and marital separation rates, intensified women's career aspirations and economic need.[38] These same trends accelerated the employment rates of adult women after 1975 as well. The workforce participation rate of women aged twenty-five to forty-four surged from 48 percent in 1975 to 71 percent in 1985. Experts have projected that by 1995, over 80 percent of women in this age category will be employed, resulting for the first time in higher participation rates for this age group than for younger age groups.[39]

Other patterns affected employment rates of older women. According to the third article in the issue, "The Later Years," labor force participation rates among women aged fifty-five and older, which had risen from 19 percent to 25 percent between 1950 and 1970, had reversed in the early 1970s, chiefly because of changes in retirement plans and increases in social security cash benefits. (The rate has since stabilized at about 23 percent.)[40] Surveys such as those published in the *Monthly Labor Review* often were conducted from a white, middle-class perspective, failing to distinguish between women who wanted to work and women who were forced to work, between high-status and low-status jobs, and between continuous and sporadic or part-time employment. Such oversights, however, demonstrated how powerful age had become as *the* analytical criterion.[41]

Analyses of men's occupational careers seemed to be more sensitive to variations in class and status than analyses of women's. Writers tracing trends in pay, mobility, and job satisfaction were careful to distinguish between blue-collar and white-collar categories.[42] Though age necessarily continued to define the spectrum along which career trends were measured, social scientists argued that skill level, educational attainment, family and cultural background, and historical context created wide variations in career trends, even among workers of the same age. For example, in his investigation of workers' "investments" in their jobs and their expectations for success, sociologist John A. Clausen determined that careers "peaked" at different ages, depending on numerous social and economic circumstances. Yet his data (longitudinal surveys of occupational mobility and job aspirations) led him to age-based generalizations, particularly that "the forties appear to be a turning point," when most male workers begin to adapt to the realization that they have advanced occupationally as far as they can go and begin to participate more in family and recreational activities.[43]

Though age norms and patterns of age separation remained prominent in many segments of American life, in the 1960s and 1970s some trends reversed, diluting some long-held age prescriptions. Particularly notable were new patterns in higher education and parenthood. In 1970, in the wake of the explosion of youth culture on college campuses, the term "college student" still normally implied a person between eighteen and twenty-two years of age. In 1972, only 8.6 percent of all people enrolled in college degree programs were over thirty-five.[44] But as the baby boom generation passed college age, many institutions, threatened by declining enrollments, began developing programs for and encouraging matriculation of older students. Moreover, demands for technical and other specialized skills made by the changing post-industrial economy prompted many people to return to school, at least part-time, to "retool" or enhance their education.

As a result, more mature-looking individuals began to appear on college campuses. While in 1972 only one in twelve college students was thirty-five or older, by 1980 the ratio had fallen to one in nine, and by 1985 it was one in seven, or 1.66 million students out of 12.5 million. Experts project that by 1993, nearly two and one-half million college students, one-fifth of the total college population, will be thirty-five or older. Older women, particularly, have contributed to this trend; since 1980 they have outnumbered older male college students by two to one.

Many women were demonstrating changing patterns in family careers as well as in occupational and educational careers. The postwar norm of marriage at around age 20, followed by first childbirth in two years or so, gave way in the 1970s. Between 1970 and 1983, for example, the rate of first marriages per 1,000 single women aged 20 to 24 dropped by over half, from 220.1 to 106.9. In 1987, 29 percent of women aged 25 to 29 had never been married, compared with 11 percent in 1970, and 42 percent of men aged 25 to 29 had not married, compared with 19 percent in 1970. From 1970 to 1985, the percent of married women who were childless increased from 16.4 to 20.3.[45] Moreover, more women were delaying their first birth beyond their 20s and into their 30s. In 1984, the rate of first births for every 1,000 women aged 30 to 34 was 20.9, and in 1985 women in this age bracket were accounting for 25 percent of all first births, the highest these rates had been since 1964.[46] Popular women's magazines reflected this new trend, publishing increasing numbers of articles with titles such as "Having My First Baby at 40" and "Mothering After 30." In 1984, *Harper's Bazaar* presented a special section on "A Baby after 30: Are You Too Late?"

Males also participated in trends of postponed marriage and delayed childbirth. Between 1970 and 1983, men's average age at first marriage climbed from 22.5 to 24.4, and, because most husbands were around the same age as their wives, more men experienced birth of their first child later than had been the case a generation earlier. But deviations from the norms were more noticeable among women than among men, because expectations for their age at marriage and age at motherhood had always been stronger.

Trends in marriage and childbirth largely reflect changes in family careers of middle-class whites, and numerous articles in popular magazines have spoken to this limited segment of the population. Writers concerned with age and family issues often have ignored racial minorities and other disadvantaged groups, who were experiencing high rates of teenage pregnancy and illegitimate births. Certainly, social welfare experts stressed that age thirteen was "too young" for girls to become mothers, and age sixteen was "too early" for young people to marry, but their concerns reached beyond mere age norms. Nevertheless, changes in the age-related activities and needs of various population groups catalyzed new movements to examine the legal context of age-based practices and regulations. The result was significant reform in civil rights law.

## AGE DISCRIMINATION AND FEDERAL LAW

In 1945, *Business Week* magazine published an article titled "How Old Is Old?" voicing a question that, in several versions, was to be raised frequently over the succeeding decades. The article addressed the issue of whether there should be a place for older workers in the postwar labor market. Over the past fifty years, there has been a steady decline in the proportion of older workers in the labor force, as compulsory retirement plans, social security benefits, voluntary early retirement, and other pressures induced aging employees to end their work careers. During the Depression, Forty Plus Clubs had formed in almost every city in the nation to try to preserve jobs for older workers, but during World War II most of these organizations dissolved. The over-forty groups complained that employers had no incentive to utilize their members, and that they were being discriminated against.[47]

As time passed, charges of discrimination against older people intensified, and in the 1960s new voices joined the chorus against age discrimination, this time from the opposite end of the age spectrum. As the bulge of the baby boom reached the teenage and young adult years, its members, many of whom were forced to fight and die in, as well as pay taxes to support, what they believed to be a useless if not immoral and illegal war in Vietnam, began clamoring for earlier access to the rights and privileges of adulthood. They claimed that if eighteen-, nineteen-, and twenty-year olds were deemed capable of serving in the armed forces, they ought to be considered responsible enough to vote and to legally buy and consume alcoholic beverages.

These movements by old and young against perceived age discrimination not only resulted in important legislation but also stimulated the first serious considerations of the effects of age grading and age consciousness. What, people were now asking, were the real meanings of "too old" and "old enough"?

The postwar cult of youth and the popular belief—fostered by countless books and magazine articles that pinpointed a person's "peak years" as his or her 30s—that middle age ushers in a period of uselessness and decline inspired movements to counter false impressions and age discrimination, especially in employment. Demographers, social planners, and employers foresaw increasing numbers of older Americans in the decades to come and urged the establishment of policy to encourage productivity in people beyond age forty. In 1946, for example, Theodore G. Klumpp, president of Winthrop Chemical Company of New York, told the annual meeting of the American Public Health Association that by 1960, "there will be not less than 60,000,000 Americans 45 years and over and more than 21 million who are 65 and over." The social consequences implicit in these numbers, Klumpp advised, should force an end to compulsory retirement on a calendar-age basis, because physiological age is not synonymous with chronological age, and because employed older Americans would burden the country less than would hordes of retirees.[48] Over the following two decades, numerous organizations, ranging from the U.S. Department of Labor to the National Association of Manufacturers to various conferences and institutes on aging and gerontology, began to publish reports outlining the needs and advantages of "mature workers."[49]

Some discriminatory practices against older workers were not new. As in previous eras, many employers favored hiring younger employees, fearing that older job applicants would be absent from work too often, prone to accidents, slow, and inflexible. Employers also established hiring ages for new employees, barring older job seekers from even applying. But there also were new discriminatory practices, which worked against continued gainful employment among older workers. Seniority often protected those already employed, but automation and schemes encouraging early retirement—in 1956, for example, an amendment to the Social Security Act made retirement benefits first available at age sixty-two rather than at sixty-five—pushed or lured older workers out of the labor force.[50] Though unemployment rates for workers aged forty-five to sixty-five remained relatively low, once a worker in this age group lost his or her job, the length of unemployment extended much longer than that for a younger worker. Moreover, opportunities for self-employment, such as in farming and small commercial endeavors, in which artificial age barriers were less significant, were diminishing as the United States increasingly became a nation of wage and salary earners.[51]

In response to these conditions, twenty-three states by 1965 had passed laws prohibiting age discrimination in employment. Most statutes applied to persons between forty or forty-five and sixty, to employers of six or more workers, and to employment agencies that recruited and advertised for workers. Most laws also exempted family employment, domestic service, and hazardous occupations such as law enforcement and firefighting. Procedures for enforcing these laws varied, but usually they were carried out by state civil rights commissions, or departments of labor. In 1958, New York State passed one of the fullest age discrimination laws, banning employers from even asking prospective employees their age. In the law's first eight years of existence, the New York Commission for Human Rights heard 755 complaints of age discrimination, about 14 percent of all employment cases presented before it.[52]

State laws achieved some success, and their passage increased pressure on the federal government to initiate similar measures. On February 13, 1964, President Lyndon B. Johnson took the first step by issuing Executive Order 11141, which barred age discrimination in the hiring, promoting, and firing practices of those employers receiving federal contracts.[53] Shortly thereafter, Congress passed the landmark Civil Rights Act of 1964; this measure included a provision in its Title VII, which applied to employment opportunity, that directed the secretary of labor to make a study of the problem of age discrimination and report on it to Congress by June 30, 1965. That study, while finding little evidence of the kind of intolerance toward age that existed because of racial, religious, or ethnic biases, reported that there was "substantial evidence of . . . discrimination based on unsupported general assumptions about the effect of age on ability," in addition to some discrimination in "institutional arrangements which operate indirectly to restrict the employment of older workers."[54]

The report was extraordinary in its recognition of the deleterious effects of arbitrary age norms and age grading. Among its conclusions, derived from extensive surveys, were the following:

> The setting of specific age limits beyond which an employer will not consider a worker for a vacant job, regardless of ability, has become a characteristic practice in those States which do not prohibit such action . . .
>
> An unmeasured but significant proportion of the age limitations presently in effect are arbitrary in the sense that they have been established without any determination of their actual relevance to job requirements . . .
>
> The competence and work performance of older workers are, by any general measures, at least equal to those of younger workers.
>
> The private pension, health, and insurance plans which have improved the situation of employed workers are probably affecting adversely the hiring of unemployed older workers.[55]

To remedy these and other problems, the report recommended legislation "to eliminate arbitrary age discrimination in employment" and "to adjust institutional arrangements which work to the disadvantage of older workers," as well as programs to increase the availability of occupational and educational opportunities for older Americans.[56]

Congress, prodded by this report and by President Johnson's Older Americans Message of January 23, 1967, passed the Age Discrimination in Employment Act (ADEA) of 1967. This measure prohibited labor organizations and employers of fifty or more workers (the number was reduced to twenty-five a year later) from discriminating against persons aged forty to sixty-five. The Labor Department was directed to carry out the act's provisions, and enforcement was sanctioned by the Fair Labor Standards Act of 1938, under which a federal court could order that an aggrieved employee be paid damages for unpaid wages, be reinstated, or be otherwise compensated for damages incurred as a result of discrimination. Significantly, the act—as well as the state laws and executive order that preceded it—protected not those Americans in old age but those in the forty to sixty-five range who were supposedly "too old" for certain jobs. In fact, rather than addressing employment conditions of older people, a major portion of the congressional debate leading to passage of the ADEA focused on the plight of airline stewardesses and stewards who were being forced out of their jobs in their early thirties by employers' age ceilings.[57] The upper age limit for persons covered by ADEA was set at sixty-five simply because it had become the common retirement age, and legislators accepted retirement as the ordinary condition for people above that age.

As greater numbers of the elderly developed and flexed their political muscle, they forced the first real breach in the boundary between middle age and old age since the Social Security Act had rigidified it at age sixty-five. In an effort to protect older people from mandatory retirement provisions, which in 1973 affected approximately half of the private, nonagricultural work force, Congress in 1978 amended the ADEA to extend employment protection beyond age sixty-five, to age seventy for most private workers, and to remove the upper limit altogether in the federal sector. In 1986, Congress amended the ADEA even further by abolishing maximum age limitations for virtually *all* workers, except for certain personnel such as police officers and firefighters.

Several issues guided the debates leading to these amendments. First, much of the testimony centered on the idea that individual ability, rather than an arbitrary age limit, should determine whether a person qualifies for employment. Second, public opinion polls showed strong opposition to forced retirement based on age alone. Third, medical advances and greater longevity were enabling more people to remain active, productive and employable beyond age sixty-five. Fourth, medical evidence had indicated that forced retirement could have harmful physical and psychological effects on an otherwise healthy person. Fifth, in spite of pensions and insurance plans, retirement often forced people into financial difficulties.[58] It appeared that removal of age barriers to employment would help dissolve age norms and eradicate policies that isolated the elderly. However, conditions remained complicated and vexing, as the final section of this chapter will show.

At the same time that it was adjusting the mandatory age of retirement, Congress was blurring the accepted distinction between youth and adulthood, symbolized by the age at which an individual was permitted to vote. Though the original Constitution did not mention age qualifications for the franchise—the first explicit reference appeared in 1868 with the passage of the Fourteenth Amendment, which prohibited denial of the franchise to male citizens twenty-one years of age and older—the founding fathers and the legal system accepted English common law standards that set age of majority at twenty-one.

But in 1943, Representative Jennings Randolph, Democrat from Virginia, introduced a constitutional amendment to reduce the voting age to eighteen. Randolph's main justification was that because the draft age was eighteen and significant proportions of the army, navy, and marines were young men aged eighteen to twenty, the country should not be bound by any "meritless tradition"; rather, service in World War II was proving eighteen-year-olds capable of making sound judgments that should qualify them for the franchise.[59] During hearings on the amendment, several people testified not only that men old enough to fight in the war should be allowed to vote, but also that age norms had become unbalanced and arbitrary. Representative Estes Kefauver of Tennessee noted that eighteen was the age when most men and women finish high school; with civics courses and the importance of public responsibility fresh in their minds, they were capable of voting responsibly. Governor Ellis Arnall of Georgia, whose state had recently lowered the voting age to eighteen, added that at that age a person could enter a marriage contract and pay taxes and therefore should be able to vote.[60]

The amendment never passed Congress, and 150 similar proposals met with a similar fate over the next 27 years. But during the 1960s, the issue became more heated as a result of the Vietnam War and turmoil on college campuses, and in 1971 Congress passed, and the states ratified, the Twenty-Sixth Amendment to the Constitution, reducing voting age for federal elections to eighteen. Testimony during hearings on the measure for the most part repeated that of the 1940s, but there was greater emphasis on shifting age norms. For example, anthropologist Margaret Mead, called as a witness, asserted that it was no longer fair or accurate to lump together thirteen- to nineteen-year-olds under the simple label "teenagers." In the past one hundred years, she observed, the age when a person reached physical maturity had dropped by three years, and formal education, television, and computers were enabling young people to have better access to information and therefore a better understanding of their world. Children were becoming politically aware and active as early as age twelve and certainly could vote responsibly by age eighteen.[61] Other testimony supported Mead's remarks. More than half of all eighteen- to twenty-year-olds were receiving some kind of higher education, and 80 percent were high school graduates. Of nearly 11 million in that age bracket, half were married, more than 1 million had their own children, 1.4 million were in the armed forces, and over 3 million were full-time employees and taxpayers.

Action at the federal level prodded states to take similar steps. Even before Congress passed the Twenty-Sixth Amendment, nine states already had reduced voting age for state and local elections. Between 1971 and 1973, thirty-nine states granted at least some other rights of adulthood to eighteen- to twenty-year-olds, including the legal ability to own and dispose of property, make wills, sign binding contracts (including those calling for installment payments), sue and be sued, marry without parental consent, and undergo serious medical treatment without parents' consent. In addition, eighteen states used the reasoning "old enough to vote, old enough to drink" to lower the legal age for purchasing and consuming liquor. But then teenage alcoholism and liquor-related traffic accidents rose sharply, and by 1979 these states had begun to reverse themselves and raise the drinking age back toward twenty-one. As had older adults, youths had begun to break down and alter long-standing age norms, but society and governments remained conscious of age and uncertain of how much protection to afford certain age groups.

## THE GRAYING OF AMERICA

As the youth rebellion of the 1960s calmed, older Americans, now the fastest-growing segment of the population, attracted more popular and scholarly attention than ever before. In 1940, Americans aged 65 and over numbered 9 million, or 6.8 percent of the total population. By 1970, their numbers had more than doubled to 20.2 million, and they constituted nearly 10 percent of the population. By 1985, the figure had swelled to 28.5 million, or 11.9 percent of the population, and demographers projected that by 2000, some 35 million Americans, or 17 percent of the population, would be 65 or older.[62] More important than the figures themselves was what this "graying of America" meant. In spite of measures such as the ADEA, most economists predicted severe pressures on all segments of society because so many Americans would be retired or otherwise not contributing to the national income. In 1977, the dependency ratio—the proportion of people between ages 16 and 64 to those below 16 and over 64—stood at 4 to 1, meaning that there were 4 people normally able to sustain themselves for every person normally dependent for support on someone else. By the 1990s, largely because of huge increases in the number of elderly people, the ratio is predicted to drop to 1 to 1, meaning that those in their productive years will have to work much harder to support dependent age groups. Similarly, in 1945, the ratio of wage earners to social security recipients was 35 to 1; in 1977, it had fallen to 3.2 to 1, and it is expected to drop to 2 to 1 after 2000, putting enormous financial burdens on taxpayers.[63] Predictions such as these have heightened consciousness among the media, lawmakers, and taxpayers of the public effects of old age and aging.

During much of the recent past, amateur advisers and helping professionals have taken two related approaches to old age. The first is a patronizing attempt to help people "grow old gracefully," so that they can accept their decline and "disengagement" from active life without undergoing psychological harm. The second is also patronizing—the attitude that old age is an economic "problem" requiring public intervention. There were exceptions to these approaches, such as the program advanced in the 1930s by Dr. Francis Townsend, a retired California physician who mustered millions of older people behind a scheme that would boost the sagging economy by granting a government-funded old-age pension of $200 per month to all persons over age sixty, provided that they spent the money within the month it was awarded.[64] But for the most part, private and public agencies sponsored research to define the elderly's needs and desires, and this research involved older people only to the extent that they were objects of study. In 1940, the National Institutes of Health began centralizing these studies, and the next year the Public Health Service sponsored a conference on mental health in old age. In 1942, medical interests organized the American Geriatrics Society, and in 1945, a number of scholars interested in social issues related to old age formed the Gerontological Society. Their own *Journal of Gerontology* began publication in 1946.[65]

But as the numbers of elderly increased, so too did their desire to engage actively in affairs of society and in their own interest. A major shift occurred in the late 1950s with the founding of organizations such as the American Association of Retired Persons (AARP) and the National Retired Teachers Association (NRTA), which claimed nearly ten million members by 1978. The AARP, NRTA, National Council of Senior Citizens, Gray Panthers, and other so-called senior organizations have exploited consciousness of, and sympathy toward, old age to lobby with varying degrees of militancy for rights, such as fair em-

179

ployment and access to housing and social welfare, and for privileges, such as discounts on bus fares, hotel rooms, and other goods and services.[66]

In 1965, public recognition of the elderly's needs and demands resulted in the most significant old-age legislation in thirty years. In July of that year, Congress created Medicare, which provided hospital insurance benefits for social security recipients, coverage of nursing home care for all persons over sixty-five, and low-cost voluntary insurance for all elderly persons to cover costs of physicians' services, diagnostic tests, and some medical devices. That same year, Congress passed, and President Johnson signed, the Older Americans Act, which established an Administration of Aging to fund and coordinate programs pertaining to older people's health, housing, economic needs, and legal status.[67] Amendments to the Older Americans Act subsequently expanded programs and funding, especially in the areas of health care and nutrition. Another significant plateau in age-oriented legislation was reached in 1975, with passage of the Age Discrimination Act (ADA). A complement to the ADEA and to the 1964 Civil Rights Act, the ADA outlawed discrimination based on age in all programs and institutions receiving federal funds, unless the program was designed for a specific age group at its inception.[68]

As public agencies were establishing programs and legislation exclusively for the elderly, residential patterns were showing increased isolation of older people from other age groups. Earlier chapters have noted how health care and social welfare professionals wished to confine sick and declining older people to institutions. This practice continued into the late twentieth century, particularly as nursing and convalescent homes were built to house superannuated persons who could not care for themselves and whose families were unable or unwilling to care for them. Once Medicare began providing aid for nursing home care for all needy persons over sixty-five, residents in these institutions increased by 36 percent, from 1.1 million in 1971 to 1.5 million in 1982.[69]

But even more older people, usually affluent, have segregated themselves into retirement communities where they purposely choose to live only with age peers. Places like Sun City, Arizona, and Sun City Center, Florida, exclude younger age groups, prohibiting anyone under fifty from buying or renting in the settlement and refusing residence to people with school-age children.[70] Though for some residents these communities represent "well-manicured way stations on the way to the cemetery," for others they offer pleasant and safe havens where they can enjoy the company of and activities with peers who share their interests and needs.[71] Indeed, the huge expansion in the number of older Americans involved in senior organizations and retirement communities not only results from the increased numbers of elderly in the population generally, as well as the increased attention paid to them, but also may reflect the continuing habit of peer association carried throughout the lives of people born after 1900, a habit that was less common among people born before 1900.

Continued age segregation of the elderly—either in new suburban retirement communities, in old-age institutions, or, most often, in the deteriorated neighborhoods of central cities—in addition to extended life expectancies resulting from better medical care, has created new age grades in the social structure. Just as youth and adulthood have been subdivided into age categories, so too has old age. Some experts now recognize at least two categories: the "young old," consisting of retired but vigorous people between fifty-five and seventy-five, and the "old old," who are over seventy-five and more likely to be sick, feeble, poor, and isolated.[72] Some observers even have offered three divisions of old age: "young," consisting of those between fifty-five and seventy, who are vigorous, actively engaged in society, and, at least among people in their fifties and early sixties, likely to have a living parent; "middle," consisting of those aged seventy to eighty or eighty-five, who are most likely retired, partly active, and just beginning to suffer from physical decline; and "old," consisting of those over eighty or eighty-five, the fastest growing group and that most in need of health and social services. Ronald Reagan, at seventy-seven active in his last year as president, helped gain the "middle" old—and older people generally—new respect. (Critics, of course, scoffed that Reagan's age made him too old for effective leadership, and that his performance proved the point.) But increasing media attention on incurable, chronic ailments such as Alzheimer's disease, which normally afflict people over seventy-five, helped shift the most negative and pathetic stereotypes of old age from elderly people in general to those in the "old old" category.

Whatever the categories, Americans in their advanced years have been most responsible for keeping the terms *age* and *aging* before the public in the past three decades. Countless geriatric and gerontological studies, many of them sponsored by the Institute on Aging of the National Institutes of Health, have filled scholarly journals and served as the inspiration for frequent popular magazine and newspaper articles that focus on problems and prospects of old age. Most newspapers now contain regular columns explicitly aimed at senior citizens, and magazines for the elderly, such as *Harvest Years*, founded in 1972,

*Modern Maturity*, the magazine of AARP, and *50 Plus*, have multiplied. To be sure, legal and institutional changes have confounded the age norms for old age. There is less certainty now than there was a generation ago exactly when a person becomes "old."

BY THE latter part of the twentieth century, Americans had become more sensitive to the consequences of using age as a criterion for social status and as a norm for behavioral expectations. The entry of the term *ageism* into the common vocabulary signals recognition of widespread stereotyping of and discrimination against people because of their chronological age. Perhaps, as with racism and sexism, this recognition also represents the peak of age consciousness in the course of American cultural history. It also may signal the denouement in age grading: a new attitude—that age does not matter as much as it has in the past century—may characterize future decades. On the other hand, confirmation of the existence of ageism may simply mean that social and legal adjustments need to be made in order that the natural and necessary utilization of age norms and age categories may effectively continue.

# CONCLUSION

In 1983, zoologist Desmond Morris published *The Book of Ages*, a volume that epitomizes the current obsession with age. His purpose, he said, was to show that "every age has something to offer, if we accept it for what it is." Drawing upon biographies, social science research, and his own knowledge of biological processes, Morris presented an overview of every discrete age from zero to one hundred, outlining in two pages for each age what is "normal" in a human's physical and intellectual development, and listing accomplishments that famous personages had achieved at that age. Thus, he declared, at age four "the child begins to assert itself as an individual" and reaches 60 percent of adult height; four is also the age at which Gustave Mahler began composing and Adam Smith was carried off by gypsies. Age twenty-seven, according to Morris, "is the ideal age for becoming a mother"; it is also the age at which Yury Gagarin became the first human space traveler and at which jazz legend Bix Beiderbecke died. Seventy-five marks the start of "confirmed senescence or primary old age" and the end of "quiescent pre-senescence"; it is also the age at which "Foxy Grandpa" Ed Delano bicycled from California to Massachusetts in thirty-three and one-half days.

Morris recognized that his book presented two different messages. First, he emphasized that "there are typical features of each age. As members of the human species we are *likely* to behave in certain predictable ways as we pass, each year, from birth to death." Second, "there are always exceptions to the rule—individuals who break the pattern, being either unusually early or unusually late in their progress from childhood to old age."[1] These two messages echo the major theme of the preceding chapters: Americans have come to accept the belief that there are distinct norms—"typical features," as Morris called them—for every discrete age; and by identifying what is "unusually early or unusually late," we measure ourselves against other people in highly age-conscious ways. These attitudes, and the age-graded institutions that have generated and reflected them, have shaped a significant component of American social and cultural history for the past century.

The rise of age consciousness and age grading provokes a number of questions, not the least of which is: In a modern, bureaucratic society, was and is there any alternative to age as an organizing determinant of the kinds of roles, activities, and institutions that are germane to modern organization and that this book has examined? Probably not. Certainly, gender, race, and ethnicity, which like age are universal characteristics, frequently are used to determine roles and rewards in society, but with more discriminatory effects than age produces, as recent social movements have proven with increasing and discomforting frequency. Economic need also could and often does determine an individual's status and a society's allocation of resources. But need must be defined and therefore requires assessment procedures that can become the subject of considerable dispute.[2]

Chronological age is what sociologists call an ascriptive trait, in that it belongs to everyone and cannot be influenced by one's achievements: when you are twenty-five, you are twenty-five regardless of whether you are a prisoner, a graduate student, or a corporation president. But unlike other ascriptive qualities, including gender and race, age is not stable; it follows an ordered sequence of change. Because this sequence is uniform and easily measured, age offers a handy framework for representing social and cultural expectations for individual experiences and roles. Thus, although one's accomplishments cannot change his or her age, one's age has become a gauge by which to assess his or her accomplishments. Over the past one hundred years, various experts have explicitly advised that one *should* have finished third grade by age eight, *should* have married by age twenty-five, *should* retire at age sixty-five, and so on. More recently, the prescriptions have become even more internalized: for instance, one *normally* can expect to experience emotional crises at ages thirty, forty, and fifty.

What specific factors underlie the increasing importance of age in modern society? The German sociologist Martin Kohli has identified four issues that have propelled the process of age grading.[3] Though Kohli has constructed his scheme in relation to economic activity, it can be applied in a general way to American society since the late nineteenth century. First, age grading has resulted from the urge for rationalization. A modern, industrial society needs an orderly, calculable means of organization, a way of making all forms of activity sensible, uniform, predictable. In such a society, where time has become the critical measure of almost all activity, age operates in a personal sense as a means of assessing "time passed and time still to go," as a means of making logical decisions and understanding the "meanings of life." It also helps individuals perceive and understand others more fully. Looks can be deceiving, but age involves certain expectations that, when measured against past experiences and future expectations, allow individuals to type themselves and others.

Second, age grading has provided the organizing principle for social control. Family and community sanctions no longer suffice in a world of large-scale industrial production and heterogeneous cities. Proponents and administrators of institutions, such as schools and social welfare systems, have needed standards to guide the establishment and operation of those institutions. As previous chapters have shown, age filled that need.

Third, age has replaced more informal mechanisms for determining access to certain positions. In previous eras, people succeeded to certain ranks when they were "ready"—that is, had mastered a skill or acquired the requisite physical strength or biological capacities (such as childbearing)—or when a position became vacant through death or other forms of removal. The complexities of modern life require more regular systems; though competition survives, age norms and rules of seniority often prevail.

Finally, age has functioned as a method of integrating the multiple roles and responsibilities individuals assume in modern society. In preindustrial times, individual, family, and work roles intertwined. Children worked at home when they were able and worked for someone else or went to school when their parents did not need them. People married when they could support a household; they retired when they no longer could work. Eventually, however, as individual needs came to prevail over group needs and as dimensions of people's lives—school career, work career, family career, peer associations, leisure time, organizational activities—separated and increased, more explicit guidelines were needed for *when* transitions should be made within each dimension. Synchronization of roles and responsibilities became a more pressing concern.[4] Age norms and age grading facilitated that synchronization.

WHAT further consequences have resulted from the age consciousness and age grading of American culture and society? Some undoubtedly have been salutary. Given that modern society often stresses meeting the needs of the individual—a process that social scientists call "individualization"—rather than those of the kin, residential, or other group of which the individual is a member,[5] age consciousness and age grading promote appreciation of the individual, giving each person a more discrete identity. Being thirteen or seventy-three means more than being a "youth" or an "elder." Age grading has helped policymakers identify particular age groups—infants, teenagers, middle-agers, old old—as "problems" in need of particular resources to help individuals within these groups adapt to their environment and aid others in adapting to them. For example, during the past few decades, a broad range of people, including politicians, social workers, corporate executives, advertising and marketing experts, and others, have worked to create a more positive image of old age and provide greater intellectual and social opportunities for older people. These efforts stem from idealistic as well as self-interested motives, but they also reflect a sanguine recognition of age and aging.[6]

The rationalization of social and economic organization and its accompanying centralization of power in the hands of government have supplanted the family and other associations that traditionally held an intermediate position between the individual and the state.[7] The result, analysts say, has been a more anonymous and powerless position for the individual. Yet age-based peer groups, whose organization and influence have been generated by the rationalization process, have enabled people to reestablish meaning to their individuality and find group support in adapting to rationalization and centralization. Thus, the peer relationships, discussed in Chapters 5 through 8, that formed in the contexts of school, work, and leisure provided new and vital means for individuals to recapture a fading sense of identity.

Moreover, it might be possible that individuals in a peer-based society, one created by age consciousness and age grading, can achieve more than they could if they acted outside of peer contexts. For decades, crowd psychologists have pointed to the positive as well as negative effects of group organization on individuals. In the 1920s, for example, Paul Hanley Furfey, who wrote about youth gangs, cited studies showing that boys could accomplish individual tasks, such as schoolwork, faster and more accurately when working in a same-age peer group than when they were alone.[8] Furfey and others concluded that the influences exerted by inspiration and competition seemed to be strengthened by association with age peers. If, as previous chapters have asserted, twentieth-century Americans have become accustomed to socialization and association within peer groups, rather than in groups in which ages are mixed, is it possible to hypothesize that accomplishments broader than those noted by Furfey, such as in science and technology, likewise have resulted from peer inspiration and competition? Answers are elusive and lie beyond the scope of this book but may shed further light on recent American culture.

Age consciousness and age grading also have produced deleterious consequences, some obvious, others less so. Since the 1960s, ageism has attracted increasing attention from those concerned with discrimination in American society and has become a topic of both serious and casual public discourse. As noted throughout this book, Americans have come to consider age a proxy for, or predictor of, many characteristics thought to be related to age—characteristics such as physical or emotional maturity, readiness to assume certain responsibilities, employability, and likelihood of experiencing certain medical or social problems.[9] Such assumptions frequently involve treating one age or age group differently from another and even excluding one or more age groups from certain benefits, such as employment, rights and privileges (for example, voting and buying beer), and education programs. Such actions may, and do, result in injustice for those disadvantaged by them, because age may not be a true criterion for determining qualification for a certain benefit.

The virtue of age, its ascriptive quality, is also the vice that creates ageism. Like gender and race, age cannot be changed. To disadvantage individuals merely because they possess a particular characteristic, one for which they cannot be held morally responsible, offends traditional American sensibilities of fairness. Moreover, as histories of racial and ethnic minorities in America have proven, treatment of individuals on the bases of these unchangeable traits can create and reinforce negative stereotypes derived from faulty generalizations. Such stereotypes not only promote self-fulfilling expectations about a group but also undermine the ideal of respect for individual uniqueness. Only recently have social scientists begun to question whether changes or characteristics that seem to occur in all individuals when they attain a certain age reflect "true" age changes—that is, whether they really relate to chronological age—or whether they occur as a result of other factors linked only peripherally with age. For example, sociologist Glen Elder's conclusion that youngsters whose families were economically deprived during the Great Depression followed different life careers than those whose families were not deprived suggests that a specific historical event can create different patterns among people of different ages, depending on when in their lives and under what economic circumstances they experienced the event.[10]

Improvements in diet, housing, and general health care have created what one writer has called "mass longevity," a condition in which, unlike in previous eras of history, most people live to advanced age.[11] The social consequences of mass longevity have been likened to the class formation and tensions resulting from industrialization and mass production, because contemporary American society now contains large numbers of elderly people who make up a highly recognizable group and who are conscious of their numbers. This age group holds

187

and competes for resources—housing, political power, jobs—in ways that prompt some analysts to believe that there is potential for new class struggle, not between socioeconomic classes but between age classes. More importantly, mass longevity has stretched the life cycle so that more people than in previous eras are personally concerned with the aging process and with what "growth" and "age" mean as one becomes older. Increases in life expectancy and survival rates mean that individuals have more company as they grow older, making them more aware of their age peers and the demands they can make on society to address their problems. Such a political process provides the support for efforts of people like octogenarian Congressman Claude Pepper of Florida, who has been a leading force in establishing legislative measures to protect—some would say advantage—older people.

But to some extent, efforts to remedy perceived unequal treatment stemming from age discrimination can create unexpected discriminatory consequences. Most Americans would agree that if one age group was considered equal to other age groups but was treated unequally, that would constitute unjust discrimination. Legislators used such an argument to abolish compulsory retirement, their reasoning being that older persons (or at least many of them) were unfairly being pushed out of their jobs because of their age alone, when in fact they were as capable of performing those jobs as younger workers. But if age is removed as a reason for discriminating negatively against people, should it remain a reason for discriminating in their favor? Should older people who, as a result of legislative reform, receive equal treatment in employment also receive, by virtue of their age, unequal treatment in the form of reduced transit fares, merchandise and entertainment discounts, free or subsidized medical and social services, and other benefits? Much of national policy as it has developed over the past century is based on the assumption that older people and juveniles are not equal to adults and thus are in need of special protection and legal status. Can an age group be considered equal and unequal at the same time?

A vexing challenge to age-based resource allocation recently has been raised by Daniel Callahan, director of the respected biomedical ethics institute, The Hastings Center, in Hastings-on-Hudson, New York. In his controverisal book, *Setting Limits: Medical Goals in an Aging Society* (1987), Callahan asks whether too much public and private money is being devoted to heroic methods of keeping alive elderly people whose lives have extended beyond the natural limits of quality existence. Callahan is skeptical, asserting that the battle against disease and death pushes individuals and governments that fund the battle into a bottomless financial pit. And in spite of all efforts and billions of dollars, people still die. Callahan bluntly suggests that programs such as Medicare should stop paying for expensive medical procedures for people eighty and older. Instead, government should spend more money on making qualitative improvements in older people's lives, such as providing better home care service and higher social security benefits. In return, he proposes, the elderly and their families should agree not to prolong an already full life if such prolongation means depriving younger people of resources that could save their lives until they reached old age.[12]

Similarly, Sheldon Danzinger and Eugene Smolensky, economists at the University of Wisconsin, have asserted that policies dealing with poverty relief have been overly and deleteriously age-conscious. These policies and the agencies that administer them, say Danzinger and Smolensky, oversimplify when they assume that those most in need of relief are young age groups and old age groups, with the result that others in need have been overlooked, and that some children and elderly have undeservedly received relief.[13]

Questions concerning age discrimination and access to resources arise because, as a means of characterizing a person, formal age, which is determined by an event, usually a birthday, has replaced functional age, which is determined by ability or change in ability. Formally, a person reaches adulthood at twenty-one and old age at sixty-five; functionally, those statuses can be influenced by a range of physical, psychological, and intellectual factors. If characteristics associated with functional age were made more important than those associated with formal age, then seventy-year-olds could contest compulsory retirement at sixty-five on the grounds that if they were under sixty-five, they would not be subject to such retirement, and therefore the standard is discriminatory. But then sixteen-year-olds wishing to vote or purchase liquor could make similar charges against laws imposing age restrictions in those areas. Moreover, by the same reasoning, fifty-year-old commuters could refuse to pay full bus fare, claiming discounts are unfairly available to older persons, and thirty-year-old criminals could demand the leniency that juvenile courts allow offenders of minor age.[14]

These examples are perhaps extreme, but the point is that though the age grading and age standards that have pervaded American society since the late nineteenth century may have made us overly age-conscious and age-segregated, tinkering with or removing these standards can create thorny problems. The history of age grading shows that in a bureaucratized society, age has considerable practical advantages as an administrative and normative gauge. It is an easily measured, inescapable attribute and a quality that everyone has experienced or will experience. Unlike other characteristics, such as income or educational credentials, it cannot be readily manipulated. Nor is it susceptible to subjective definition by impersonal agencies, such as government departments or business firms. We are a society that craves order, and age lends a sense of order to life. In sum, we can respond to age consciousness and age grading in the same way that French entertainer Maurice Chevalier responded to a query about how it felt to be old: "It isn't bad when you consider the alternative."

# NOTES

## Introduction

1. My use of the concept of norms is influenced by the work of sociologists George Homans and Francesca Cancian. Homans defined a norm as "an idea in the minds of the members of a group, an idea that can be put in the form of a statement specifying what the members or other men should do, ought to do, are expected to do, under given circumstances." Cancian has refined the definition, asserting that norms "are shared beliefs about what actions and attributes bring respect and approval from oneself and others." Though norms are not behavior itself, they are, according to Homans, "what people think behavior ought to be." See Homans, *The Human Group* (New York: Harcourt Brace and World, 1950), p. 124, and Cancian, *What Are Norms? A Study of Beliefs and Actions in a Maya Community* (London and New York: Cambridge University Press, 1975), p. 6.

2. Anne Foner, "Age Stratification and the Changing Family," in John Demos and Sarane Spence Boocock, eds., *Turning Points: Historical and Sociological Essays on the Family*, in *American Journal of Sociology* 84, supplement (Chicago: University of Chicago Press, 1978), pp. 340–65; Thomas P. Monahan, *The Pattern of Age at Marriage in the United States* (Philadelphia: Stephenson Brothers, 1951), p. 37.

3. See Bernice L. Neugarten and Joan W. Moore, "The Changing Age Status System," in Bernice L. Neugarten, ed., *Middle Age and Aging: A Reader in Social Psychology* (Chicago and London: The University of Chicago Press, 1968), pp. 5–21.

4. Warren I. Susman, *Culture and History: The Transformation of American Society in the Twentieth Century* (New York: Pantheon Books, 1984), pp. xix–xxx.

## Chapter 1

1. Robert Kempt, ed., *The American Joe Miller: A Collection of Yankee Wit and Humor* (London: Adams and Francis, 1865), p. 141.

2. For a cogent theory of modern age stratification, see Anne Foner, "Age Stratification and the Changing Family," in John Demos and Sarane Spence Boocock, eds., *Turning Points: Historical and Sociological Essays on the Family*, in *American Journal of Sociology* 84, supplement (Chicago: University of Chicago Press, 1978), pp. 340–43.

3. The French, German, and Irish equivalents of *boy—garçon*, *knabe*, and *lad*—all had double meanings and, to some extent, still do. See John R. Gillis,

*Youth and History: Traditions and Changes in European Age Relations, 1770–Present* (New York: Academic Press, 1974), p. 1.

4. Philippe Ariès, *Centuries of Childhood: A Social History of Family Life*, trans. Robert Baldick (New York: Knopf, 1962), pp. 15–32.

5. Carroll D. Wright, *A Report on Marriage and Divorce in the United States, 1867–1886* (Washington, D.C.: Government Printing Office, 1889), pp. 29–31; Joseph F. Kett, *Rites of Passage: Adolescence in America, 1790 to the Present* (New York: Basic Books, 1977), pp. 39–40.

6. Much of the information in this chapter has been culled from secondary sources and is presented as background to the succeeding chapters, which analyze the shift to the more profound consciousness of, and intense stratification by, age—a shift that accelerated in the late nineteenth century.

7. On gender differentiation in rural work in the nineteenth century, see Nancy Grey Osterud, "Strategies of Mutuality: Relations Among Women and Men in an Agricultural Community" (Ph.D. diss., American Civilization Program, Brown University, 1984).

8. See, for example, Alan Dawley, *Class and Community: The Industrial Revolution in Lynn* (Cambridge, Mass.: Harvard University Press, 1976), and Susan E. Hirsch, *Roots of the American Working Class: The Industrialization of Crafts in Newark, 1800–1860* (Philadelphia: University of Pennsylvania Press, 1978).

9. John Demos, *A Little Commonwealth: Family Life in Plymouth Colony* (New York: Oxford University Press, 1970); Philip T. Greven, Jr., *Four Generations: Population, Land and Family in Colonial Andover, Massachusetts* (Ithaca: Cornell University Press, 1970); Robert V. Wells, *Revolutions in Their Lives: A Demographic Perspective on the History of Americans, Their Families, and Their Society* (Westport, Conn.: Greenwood Press, 1982), pp. 49–50.

10. On household size, see Wells, *Revolutions in Their Lives*, pp. 151–57.

11. The information presented in the following discussion has been taken from Darrett B. and Anita H. Rutman, *A Place in Time: Middlesex County, Virginia, 1650–1750* (New York: W. W. Norton, 1984), esp. pp. 108–10 and 113–14.

12. Wells, *Revolutions in Their Lives*, pp. 43–44.

13. Ibid., pp. 55–56.

14. See Paul C. Glick, "The Life Cycle of the Family," *Marriage and Family Living* 18 (1955), 3–9; Paul C. Glick and Robert Parke, Jr., "New Approaches in Studying the Life Cycle of the Family," *Demography* 2 (1965), 187–212; and Peter Uhlenberg, "Cohort Variations in Family Life Cycle Experiences of U.S. Females," *Journal of Marriage and the Family* 34 (1974), 284–92.

15. Thomas E. Cone, *History of American Pediatrics* (Boston: Little, Brown, 1979), pp. 25–26; John Demos, "The American Family in Past Time," *American Scholar* 43 (1974), 428.

16. Lorena S. Walsh, " 'Till Death Do Us Part': Marriage and Family in Seventeenth-Century Maryland," in Thad W. Tate and David L. Ammerman,

eds., *The Chesapeake in the Seventeenth Century: Essays on Anglo-American Society* (Chapel Hill: University of North Carolina Press, 1979), p. 149.

17. Greven, *Four Generations*, chap. 4; Wells, *Revolutions in Their Lives*, pp. 56–57; Kett, *Rites of Passage*, pp. 14–36; Edward Shorter, *The Making of the Modern Family* (New York: Basic Books, 1975), pp. 23–27.

18. Greven, *Four Generations*, p. 189; Maris A. Vinovskis, "Mortality Rates and Trends for Massachusetts Before 1860," *Journal of Economic History* 32 (March 1972), 184–213.

19. Noah Webster, "Number of Deaths, In the Episcopal Church in New York, in each month for ten years—from January 1, 1786 to December 31, 1795," *Memoirs of the Connecticut Academy of Arts and Sciences* 1, pt. 1 (New Haven, 1810), pp. 97–98; table presented in Wells, *Revolutions in Their Lives*, p. 34.

20. Vinovskis, "Mortality Rates and Trends," pp. 191–99.

21. Wells, *Revolutions in Their Lives*, pp. 80–83.

22. Donald J. Bogue, *The Population of the United States* (Glencoe, Ill.: The Free Press, 1959), pp. 102–3.

23. Demos, *A Little Commonwealth*, pp. 24–36; Wells, *Revolutions in Their Lives*, p. 53.

24. Greven, *Four Generations*, pp. 143–47.

25. David L. Angus, Jeffrey E. Mirel, and Maris A. Vinovskis, "Historical Development of Age-Stratification in Schooling" (unpublished typescript, 1988), pp. 2–3; Ross W. Beales, Jr., "In Search of the Historical Child: Miniature Adulthood and Youth in Colonial America," *American Quarterly* 27 (1975), 379–98.

26. See Thomas Dublin, *Women at Work: The Transformation of Work and Community in Lowell, Massachusetts, 1820–1860* (New York: Columbia University Press, 1979).

27. The information on early patterns of American education is drawn from Lawrence Cremin, *American Education: The National Experience, 1783–1876* (New York: Harper and Row, 1980).

28. Gerald F. Moran and Maris A. Vinovskis, "The Great Care of Godly Parents: Early Childhood in Puritan New England," in John Hagen and Alice Smuts, eds., *History and Research in Child Development* (Chicago: University of Chicago Press, 1986), pp. 24–37.

29. Angus, Mirel, and Vinovskis, "Historical Development of Age-Stratification in Schooling," pp. 4, 9.

30. See Millard Fillmore Kennedy and Alvin F. Harlow, *Schoolmaster of Yesterday* (New York: McGraw-Hill, 1940).

31. Cremin, *American Education*, pp. 406–9; Kett, *Rites of Passage*, p. 55; David F. Allmendinger, Jr., "The Dangers of Ante-Bellum Student Life," *Journal of Social History* 7 (Fall 1973), 75–83; John Rickard Betts, *America's Sporting Heritage: 1850–1950* (Reading, Mass.: Addison-Wesley, 1974), p. 37.

32. Kett, *Rites of Passage*, pp. 42–43.

33. For information on early temperance societies, see David I. Macleod, *Building Character in the American Boy: The Boy Scouts, YMCA, and Their Forerunners, 1870–1920* (Madison: University of Wisconsin Press, 1983), p. 84.

34. Richard C. Morse, *History of the North American Young Men's Christian Association* (New York: Association Press, 1913), p. 2.

35. Osterud, "Strategies of Mutuality," p. 378.

36. Theodore Raph, *The Songs We Sang: A Treasury of American Popular Music* (New York: A. S. Barnes, 1964), p. 75.

37. Walter I. Trattner, *Crusade for the Children: A History of the National Child Labor Committee and Child Labor Reform in America* (Chicago: Quadrangle Books, 1970), p. 30; Thomas Patrick Monahan, *The Pattern of Age at Marriage in the United States*, vol. 1 (Philadelphia: Stephenson Brothers, 1951), p. 29.

38. Carole Haber, *Beyond Sixty-Five: The Dilemma of Old Age in America's Past* (Cambridge, England: Cambridge University Press, 1983), pp. 35–36; David J. Rothman, *The Discovery of the Asylum: Social Order and Disorder in the New Republic* (Boston: Little, Brown, 1971), pp. 32–41; Gary B. Nash, "Poverty and Poor Relief in Pre-Revolutionary Philadelphia," *William and Mary Quarterly* 3d ser., 33 (January 1979).

39. Hirsch, *Roots of the American Working Class*, pp. 21, 41–42. See also Paul G. Faler, *Mechanics and Manufacturers in the Early Industrial Revolution in Lynn* (Albany: State University of New York Press, 1981), chap. 3; Dawley, *Class and Community*, chap. 1.

40. Dawley, *Class and Community*, p. 18.

41. Hirsch, *Roots of the American Working Class*, chap. 1.

42. Ibid., pp. 42–44.

43. Faler, *Mechanics and Manufacturers*, pp. 94–97.

44. Hirsch, *Roots of the American Working Class*, pp. 42–43.

45. Charles William Day, *Hints on Etiquette and the Usages of Society: with a Glance at Bad Habits* (Boston: Otis, Broaders, 1844), p. 32.

46. Anon., *Etiquette for Ladies* (Philadelphia: Lindsay and Blakiston, n.d.), pp. 53, 66.

47. Ibid., p. 53.

48. Harvey Newcomb, *How To Be a Lady: A Book for Girls* (Boston: Gould and Lincoln, 1853).

49. Ibid., p. 3.

50. The absence of age specificity might suggest, of course, that everyone already knew the ages at which these prescriptions were directed. Nevertheless, it is the lack of precision, as contrasted with later expressions of age norms, that is important.

51. Joel Hawes, *Lectures to Young Men on the Formation of Character*, 5th ed. (Hartford, Conn.: Cooke, 1831), pp. 8ff.

52. Ibid., p. 19.

53. Ibid., pp. 35–36.

54. Kett, *Rites of Passage*, p. 14.

55. *The Well-Bred Boy and Girl* (Boston: B. B. Massey, 1852), chaps. 1, 4.

56. See John Angell James, *The Young Man From Home* (New York: American Tract Society, 1839); Daniel Clarke Eddy, *The Young Man's Friend* (Boston: Gould, Kendall, and Lincoln, 1850); Daniel Wise, *The Young Man's Counsellor* (New York: Carlton and Porter, 1850); Timothy Titcomb, *Titcomb's Letters to Young People, Single and Married* (New York: Charles Scribner, 1858); and Horace Mann, "A Few Thoughts for a Young Man," a lecture delivered before the Boston Mercantile Library Association, on its 29th anniversary (Boston: Ticknor, Reed and Fields, 1877).

57. Titcomb, *Titcomb's Letters to Young People*, pp. 98–99.

58. Ibid., p. 28. See also The Right Honorable Countess of * * * * *, *Mixing in Society: A Complete Manual of Manners* (New York: George Routledge and Sons, 1874), chap. 12.

59. Jean Dubois, *Marriage, Physiologically Discussed*, 2d ed., trans. William Greenfield (New York: n.p., 1839), p. 38.

60. Titcomb, *Titcomb's Letters to Young People*, pp. 167–251.

61. William A. Alcott, *The House I Live In: The Human Body, for the Use of Families and Schools* (Boston: Waitt, Peirce, 1844), p. 39.

62. Ibid., p. 94.

63. John Putnam Demos, *Entertaining Satan: Witchcraft and the Culture of Early New England* (New York: Oxford University Press, 1982), pp. 66–68.

64. David Hackett Fischer, *Growing Old in America* (New York: Oxford University Press, 1977), pp. 26–37.

65. Increase Mather, *The Dignity and Duty of Aged Servants of the Lord* (Boston: n.p., 1716), pp. 52, 63; quoted in Fischer, *Growing Old in America*, p. 33.

66. Fischer, *Growing Old in America*, pp. 86–99.

67. Ibid., pp. 47–48.

68. Jane Range and Maris Vinovskis, "Images of the Elderly in Popular Magazines," *Social Science History* 3 (Spring 1981), 123–70.

69. Osterud, "Strategies of Mutuality," pp. 174–75.

70. Rebecca Burlend (attributed author), *A Picture of True Emigration* (Chicago: The Lakeside Press, 1936), p. 9.

71. Mary Custis Lee deButts, ed., *Growing Up in the 1850s: The Journal of Agnes Lee* (Chapel Hill: University of North Carolina Press, 1984), p. 37.

72. Ibid., p. 31.

73. Matilda White Riley, Marilyn Johnson, and Anne Foner, *Aging and Society. Volume 3: A Sociology of Age Stratification* (New York: Russell Sage Foundation, 1972); John Modell, Frank Furstenberg, and Theodore Hershberg, "Social Change and Transitions to Adulthood in Historical Perspective," *Journal of Family History* 1 (Autumn 1976), 7–33.

CHAPTER 2

1. Philippe Ariès, *Centuries of Childhood: A Social History of Family Life*, trans. Robert Baldick (New York: Knopf, 1962), p. 412.

2. See Lawrence A. Cremin, *American Education: The Colonial Experience, 1607–1783* (New York: Harper and Row, 1970); Cremin, *American Education: The National Experience, 1783–1876* (New York: Harper and Row, 1980); Michael B. Katz, *The Irony of Early School Reform: Education Innovation in Mid-Nineteenth Century Massachusetts* (Cambridge: Harvard University Press, 1968); Katz, *Class, Bureaucracy, and the Schools: The Illusion of Educational Change in America* (New York: Praeger, 1971); Carl F. Kaestle, *The Evolution of an Urban School System: New York City, 1750–1850* (Cambridge: Harvard University Press, 1973); Stanley K. Schultz, *The Culture Factory: Boston Public Schools, 1789–1860* (New York: Oxford University Press, 1973); and Selwyn K. Troen, *The Public and the Schools: Shaping the St. Louis System, 1835–1920* (Columbia: University of Missouri Press, 1975).

3. Thomas E. Cone, Jr., *History of American Pediatrics* (Boston: Little, Brown, 1979), pp. viii, 5–6.

4. Simon Somerville Laurie, *Historical Survey of Pre-Christian Education*, 2d ed. (New York: Longman, Greens, 1895), chaps. 2–3; Frank Forest Bunker, *Reorganization of the Public School System*, U.S. Bureau of Education, Bulletin No. 8 (Washington, D.C.: Government Printing Office, 1916), p. 41.

5. Bunker, *Reorganization*, pp. 41–42.

6. Frank Forest Bunker, "The Rise of the Graded School," in Bunker, *The Junior High School Movement—Its Beginnings* (Washington, D.C.: W. F. Roberts, 1935), p. 108.

7. See Ellwood P. Cubberly, *Public Education in the United States*, rev. ed. (Boston: Houghton Mifflin, 1934), pp. 347–49.

8. Carl F. Kaestle, ed., *Joseph Lancaster and the Monitorial School Movement: A Documentary History* (New York: Teachers College Press, 1973); Cubberly, *Public Education*, pp. 125–33.

9. Samuel Harrison Smith, "Remarks on Education: Illustrating the Close Connection Between Virtue and Wisdom," in Frederick Rudolph, ed., *Essays on Education in the Early Republic* (Cambridge: Belknap Press of Harvard University Press, 1965), pp. 169–223. See also Cremin, *American Education: The National Experience*, p. 123.

10. Cubberly, *Public Education*, pp. 138–41; Cremin, *American Education: The National Experience*, pp. 389–90; Dean May and Maris A. Vinovskis, "A Ray of Millennial Light: Early Education and Social Reform in the Infant School Movement in Massachusetts, 1826–1840," in Tamara K. Hareven, ed., *Family and Kin in American Urban Communities, 1800–1940* (New York: New Viewpoints, 1976), pp. 62–69.

11. For objections to the education of young children, see William Woodbridge, "Infant Education," *American Annals of Education* 1 (August 1830), 355–56; J.V.C. Smith, "The Infantile Frame," *American Annals of Education and Instruction for the Year 1834* 4 (February 1834), 75; Amariah Brigham,

*Remarks on the Influence of Mental Cultivation and Mental Excitement Upon Health*, 2d ed. (Boston: March, Capen and Lyon, 1833); Samuel B. Woodward to Horace Mann, December 7, 1840, in Massachusetts Board of Education, *Fourth Annual Report* (1840), appendix; and Heman Humphrey, *Domestic Education* (Amherst, Mass.: J. S. and C. Adams, 1840), pp. 11–12. See also Carl F. Kaestle and Maris A. Vinovskis, *Education and Social Change in Nineteenth Century Massachusetts* (Cambridge and New York: Cambridge University Press, 1980), pp. 56–61; Cremin, *American Education: The National Experience*, p. 389; and Joseph F. Kett, *Rites of Passage: Adolescence in America, 1790 to the Present* (New York: Basic Books, 1977), p. 124.

12. See William J. Shearer, *The Grading of Schools*, 2d ed. (New York: H. P. Smith, 1898), pp. 17–19; David B. Tyack, *The One Best System: A History of American Urban Education* (Cambridge: Harvard University Press, 1974), p. 44; and Kett, *Rites of Passage*, pp. 124–25.

13. Cubberly, *Public Education*, pp. 300–312.

14. Quoted in Katz, *Class, Bureaucracy, and Schools*, p. 35.

15. See Lawrence A. Cremin, ed., *The Republic and the School: Horace Mann on the Education of Free Man* (New York: Bureau of Publications, Teachers College, Columbia University, 1957), pp. 16–17, 54–56; Cremin, *American Education: The National Experience*, pp. 155–56; Cubberly, *Public Education*, p. 311; and "History of Age Grouping in America," in *Youth: Transition to Adulthood. Report of the Panel of Youth of the President's Advisory Committee* (Chicago and London: University of Chicago Press, 1974), pp. 9–29.

16. Bunker, "The Rise of the Graded School"; Tyack, *The One Best System*, p. 44; Cubberly, *Public Education*, pp. 311–12.

17. Cremin, *American Education: The National Experience*, pp. 178–79.

18. Quoted in Troen, *The Public and the Schools*, pp. 150–51.

19. Kett, *Rites of Passage*, p. 291.

20. John R. Gillis, *Youth and History: Traditions and Changes in European Age Relations, 1770–Present* (New York: Academic Press, 1974), p. 102.

21. Brown University, Records of Admission, 1850 and 1880.

22. Gillis, *Youth and History*, pp. 102–3.

23. Ibid., pp. 70, 390–91.

24. See, for example, G. P. Quackenboss, *Elementary History of the United States* (New York: D. Appleton, 1860); A. B. Berard, *School History of the United States*, rev. ed. (Philadelphia: Cowperthwaite, 1867); John A. Andrews, *Pictorial School History of the United States* (New York: Clark and Maynard, 1868); L. J. Campbell, *A Concise School History of the United States* (Boston: Brewer and Tilston, 1874); and Thomas Wentworth Higginson, *Young Folks' History of the United States* (Boston: Lee and Shepard, 1875).

25. See also Oscar Gerson, *History Primer* (Philadelphia and New York: Hinds, Noble, and Eldredge, 1906), which specifies that it is for the "third and fourth grades"; Henry E. Bourne and Elbert J. Benton, *Introductory American*

*History* (Boston: D. C. Heath, 1912), "recommended for the sixth grade"; and Bourne and Benton, *A History of the United States* (Boston: D. C. Heath, 1913), written specially for the "seventh and eighth grades."

26. Alexander E. Frye, *The Child and Nature: Geography Teaching with Sand Modeling* (Hyde Park, Mass.: Bay State Publishing Company, 1888), p. 201.

27. George William Myers, *Myers Arithmetic*, vol. 1 (Chicago: Scott, Foresman, 1898), p. iii.

28. Frank Glenn Lankard, *A History of the American Sunday School Curriculum* (New York: The Abingdon Press, 1927), pp. 62–63.

29. Ibid., pp. 74–88, 95–98.

30. Ibid., pp. 128–52.

31. John H. Vincent, *Two Years With Jesus* (New York: Carter and Porter, 1867).

32. Lankard, *A History of the American Sunday School Curriculum*, pp. 233–36, 261–65.

33. Cone, *History of American Pediatrics*, p. 30. Cone points out that most sick people, including children, were treated at home by their families, and they probably were better off than those treated professionally, because they escaped the severe and dangerous treatments applied by physicians.

34. Ibid., p. 64.

35. Ibid., p. 65.

36. Ibid., pp. 71–72.

37. Richard T. Evanson and Henry Maunsell, *Practical Treatise on the Management and Diseases of Children*, 4th ed. (Dublin: Thomas I. White, 1842), pp. 14–16.

38. Ibid., pp. 18–19.

39. Cone, *History of American Pediatrics*, pp. 69–70.

40. *New York Times*, April 10, 1874, p. 8.

41. Cone, *History of American Pediatrics*, p. 100.

42. Ibid., pp. 99–101.

43. Ibid., p. 70.

44. Abraham Jacobi, "Relations of Pediatrics to General Medicine," *Transactions of the American Pediatric Society* 1 (1889), 8, 15.

45. Henry Ingersoll Bowditch, "Relation Between Growth and Disease," *Boston Medical and Surgical Journal* 104 (May 19, 1881), 469.

46. For historical material on the early YMCA in England, France, and the United States, see Richard C. Morse, *History of the North American Young Men's Christian Association* (New York: Association Press, 1913), pp. 11, 17, 40–41, 76; David I. Macleod, *Building Character in the American Boy: The Boy Scouts, YMCA, and Their Forerunners, 1870–1920* (Madison: University of Wisconsin Press, 1983), pp. 72–74; and Paul Boyer, *Urban Masses and Moral Order in America, 1820–1920* (Cambridge: Harvard University Press, 1978), pp. 112–20.

47. Macleod, *Building Character*, p. 77.

48. Morse, *History of the North American Young Men's Christian Association*, pp. 146, 170, 235–36; Macleod, *Building Character*, pp. 77–80.

49. Frank Luther Mott, *A History of American Magazines, Vol. 3: 1865–1885* (Cambridge: Harvard University Press, 1938), p. 174.

50. Ibid., p. 6.

51. Ibid., pp. 174–80; R. Gordon Kelly, ed., *Children's Periodicals of the United States* (Westport, Conn.: Greenwood Press, 1984), p. 155.

## CHAPTER 3

1. Daniel T. Rodgers, *The Work Ethic in Industrial America, 1850–1920* (Chicago: University of Chicago Press, 1974), pp. 17–18.

2. Stephen Kern, *The Culture of Time and Space, 1880–1918* (Cambridge: Harvard University Press, 1983), p. 12.

3. "Recording Time for Employers," *Scientific American* 63 (August 12, 1890), 74. See also Daniel J. Boorstin, *The Americans: The Democratic Experience* (New York: Random House, 1973), pp. 363–69; T. J. Jackson Lears, *No Place for Grace: Antimodernism and the Transformation of American Culture, 1880–1920* (New York: Pantheon Books, 1981), pp. 10–11; Alfred D. Chandler, *The Visible Hand: The Managerial Revolution in American Business* (Cambridge, Mass.: Belknap Press, 1977), pp. 281–83; and Rodgers, *The Work Ethic in Industrial America*, pp. 24, 53–55.

4. George M. Beard, *American Nervousness* (New York: G. P. Putnam's Sons, 1881), p. 103. See also Kern, *The Culture of Time and Space*, p. 15.

5. E. P. Thompson, "Time, Work, Discipline, and Industrial Capitalism," *Past and Present* 38 (February, 1968), 5–16; Kern, *The Culture of Time and Space*, p. 13.

6. Theodore M. Porter, *The Rise of Statistical Thinking, 1820–1900* (Princeton, N.J.: Princeton University Press, 1986), pp. 5–6.

7. Frances Willard, *How to Win: A Book for Girls* (New York: Funk and Wagnalls, 1889), pp. 117–22.

8. *Godey's Ladies Book and Magazine* (October 1867), 318.

9. James D. McCabe, "Etiquette of Courtship and Marriage," in *The Household Encyclopedia of Business and Social Forms* (Philadelphia: Standard Publishing Company, 1880), p. 456.

10. The most explicit age norms I was able to find in advice literature published before 1889 was in an 1856 publication titled *The Physiology of Marriage*. The author of one piece in this collection of anonymous articles presented the common nineteenth-century argument that the release of sexual energy contributes to the deterioration of the bodily fabric, thereby reducing the power to survive. Thus, he warned, no person should consummate marriage until his or her body has reached physical maturity. "On the whole," the author recommended, "the female should be, at least, twenty-one [before she marries] and the male twenty-eight." Moreover, the author cites a study which concluded that for every year a female marries below the age of twenty-one, she will suffer on average three years of premature physical decay. Such advice,

of course, expresses strong age norms, but it is the exception; most writers were not nearly so conscious of specific ages. See "An Old Physician," in *The Physiology of Marriage* (Boston: John P. Jewett, 1856), pp. 20–22.

11. "Who Shall Be Younger?" in "Side Talks With Girls," *Ladies Home Journal* 7 (September 1890), 10.

12. Ibid.

13. Cyrus Edson, "The Evils of Early Marriage," *North American Review* 157 (February 1894), 230–34.

14. Louis Starr, ed., *An American Textbook on the Diseases of Children* (Philadelphia: W. B. Saunders, 1894), pp. 12–13.

15. Ibid., pp. 11, 30–35, 117–18, 183, 362.

16. See L. Emmet Holt, *The Diseases of Infancy and Childhood*, 6th ed. (New York and London: D. Appleton, 1914), pp. 15–21.

17. L. Emmet Holt, *Food, Health, and Growth: A Discussion of the Nutrition of Children* (New York: Macmillan, 1930), pp. 23–30.

18. James Foster Scott, *The Sexual Instinct: Its Use and Dangers as Affecting Heredity and Morals* (New York: E. B. Treat, 1898), p. 47.

19. Carole Haber, *Beyond Sixty-Five: The Dilemma of Old Age in America's Past* (Cambridge, England: Cambridge University Press, 1983), pp. 47–48.

20. Scott, *The Sexual Instinct*, p. 70.

21. See W. Andrew Achenbaum, *Old Age in the New Land: The American Experience Since 1790* (Baltimore: The Johns Hopkins University Press, 1978), and Haber, *Beyond Sixty-Five*. Though their theses differ, both authors refute the theory advanced by David Hackett Fischer in *Growing Old in America* (New York: Oxford University Press, 1977) that American attitudes toward old age actually changed most dramatically between 1780 and 1820. I find Achenbaum's and Haber's books more convincing than Fischer's on this issue.

22. See Tamara K. Hareven, "The Last Stage: Historical Adulthood and Old Age," *Daedalus* 104 (Fall 1976), 13–27; Howard P. Chudacoff and Tamara K. Hareven, "Family Transitions to Old Age," in Tamara K. Hareven, ed., *Transitions: The Family and Life Course in Historical Perspective* (New York: Academic Press, 1978), pp. 217–43; and Howard P. Chudacoff and Tamara K. Hareven, "From Empty Nest to Family Dissolution: Life Course Transitions into Old Age," *Journal of Family History* 4 (Spring 1979), 69–83.

23. Haber, *Beyond Sixty-Five*, pp. 49–57.

24. Jean M. Charcot and Alfred Loomis, *Clinical Lectures on the Diseases of Old Age* (New York: William Wood, 1881), pp. 74–75; quoted in Haber, *Beyond Sixty-Five*, p. 60.

25. Haber, *Beyond Sixty-Five*, pp. 58–61.

26. W. Bevan Lewis, "Insanity at the Puerperal, Climacteric, and Lactational Periods," *Wood's Medical and Surgical Monographs* 6 (1890), 341.

27. Haber, *Beyond Sixty-Five*, p. 70; T. S. Clouston, *Clinical Lectures on*

*Mental Disease* (Philadelphia: Henry C. Lea's Sons, 1884), p. 388; Charles Mercier, *Sanity and Insanity* (New York: Scribner and Welford, 1890), p. 309.

28. *Oxford English Dictionary* (Oxford: Clarendon Press, 1961), p. 454; quoted in Haber, *Beyond Sixty-Five*, p. 74.

29. Haber, *Beyond Sixty-Five*, pp. 72–75; Achenbaum, *Old Age in the New Land*, pp. 43–44. See also E. N. Leake, "At What Period of Life Does Old Age Begin?" *The Medical Examiner* 6, no. 10 (October 1896), 191, and S. Newton Leo, "A Consideration of the Senile State and its Treatment," *New York Medical Journal* 84, no. 25 (October 1894), 757.

30. Mercier, *Sanity and Insanity*, p. 305. See also B. Furneaux Jordan, "Pathological and Clinical Notes with Especial Reference to Diseases in the Aged," *The Birmingham Medical Review* 32 (July 1892), 7; Julius Althaus, "Old Age and Rejuvenescence," *The Lancet* 1 (January 1899), 150; and Haber, *Beyond Sixty-Five*, pp. 74–76.

31. See, for example, Althaus, "Old Age and Rejuvenescence," pp. 150–51; Colin A. Scott, "Old Age and Death," *The American Journal of Psychology* 8, no. 1 (October 1896), 67; and Haber, *Beyond Sixty-Five*, p. 77.

32. Quoted in Haber, *Beyond Sixty-Five*, p. 91.

33. Ibid.; Morris J. Vogel, *The Invention of the Modern Hospital: Boston, 1870–1930* (Chicago: University of Chicago Press, 1980), p. 73.

34. Vogel, *Invention of the Modern Hospital*, chap. 4.

35. Haber, *Beyond Sixty-Five*, chap. 5.

36. Celia Parker Woolley, *The Western Slope* (Evanston, Ill.: W. S. Lord, 1903), quoted in Gail Bederman, "A New Time of Life: Middle Age and Images of Middle-Aged Women in Magazine Fiction, 1870–1940" (unpublished seminar paper, Brown University, 1984), p. 10. See Lois Banner, *American Beauty* (New York: Knopf, 1983), pp. 219–25.

37. Charles W. Eliot, *Educational Reform: Essays and Addresses* (New York: The Century Company 1898), p. 152. See also Andrew D. White, "The Future of American Universities," *North American Review* 151 (October 1890), 443–52. White, who was president of Cornell University, wanted students to begin college at age thirteen or fourteen so that they would not waste their productive years. Echoing Eliot, White observed, "The student is on the average seventeen or eighteen years of age when he enters college, is graduated at twenty-one or twenty-two, and then takes two or three years more in a professional school, bringing him not infrequently up to his twenty-fifth or twenty-sixth year when he goes out into the world."

38. Eliot, *Educational Reform*, pp. 151–76.

39. National Education Association, *Report of the Committee of Ten* (New York: National Education Association, 1893), p. 61. See also Frank Forest Bunker, *Reorganization of the Public School System*, U.S. Bureau of Education, Bulletin No. 8 (Washington, D.C.: Government Printing Office, 1916), pp. 47–48.

40. *Report of the Committee of Ten*, pp. 85, 96.

41. Bunker, *Reorganization*, p. 53.

42. Nicholas Murray Butler, "The Scope and Function of Secondary Education," *Educational Review* 16 (1898), 21.

43. William J. Shearer, *The Grading of Schools*, 2d ed. (New York: H. P. Smith, 1898), pp. 22–31.

44. Thus, University of Chicago President William Rainey Harper, in urging greater coordination between secondary schools and institutions of higher learning, could blandly observe in 1902, "It has now come to be generally recognized that the ideal high school must have a curriculum of four years." See Harper, "The Trend of University and College Education in the United States," *North American Review* 174 (April 1902), 457–65.

45. Duncan Emrich, *Folklore on the American Land* (Boston: Little, Brown, 1972), pp. 190–91, 199.

46. Anon., *Maidenhead Stories, Told By a Set of Joyous Students* (New York: Erotica Biblion Society, 1897).

47. Flo V. Menninger, *Days of My Life: Memories of a Kansas Mother and Teacher* (New York: Richard R. Smith, 1939), pp. 59–60.

48. David J. Hill, "The Emancipation of Women," *Cosmopolitan* 1 (April 1886), 96–99. See also Erma J. Babcock, "Home Duties First," *Cosmopolitan* 1 (May 1886), 196–97.

49. Belva Lockwood, "The Present Phase of the Women Question," *Cosmopolitan* 4 (October 1888), 467–70. See also Mona Caird, "The Emancipation of the Family," *North American Review* 151 (July 1890), 22–37.

## Chapter 4

1. U.S. Bureau of the Census, *Bulletin 13: A Discussion of Age Statistics* (Washington, D.C.: Government Printing Office, 1904), p. 9.

2. Dorothy Ross, *G. Stanley Hall: The Psychologist as Prophet* (Chicago: University of Chicago Press, 1972), pp. 81–133. See also Stephen Kern, *The Culture of Time and Space, 1880–1915* (Cambridge: Harvard University Press, 1983), p. 41, for a brief discussion of Preyer's influence on early child psychology.

3. G. Stanley Hall, *Adolescence: Its Psychology and Its Relations to Physiology, Anthropology, Sociology, Sex, Crime, Religion, and Education* (New York: D. Appleton, 1904). See also Hall, "Child Study and Its Relation to Education," *The Forum* 29 (1900), 688–702; Sara Carolyn Fisher, "The Psychological and Educational Work of Granville Stanley Hall," *American Journal of Psychology* 36 (1925), 1–52; Lawrence A. Cremin, *The Transformation of the School: Progressivism in American Education, 1876–1957* (New York: Random House, 1961), pp. 100–102; and Ross, *G. Stanley Hall*, chaps. 3–4.

4. G. Stanley Hall, *Youth: Its Education, Regimen, and Hygiene* (New York: D. Appleton, 1907), p. 135. See also Fisher, "Psychological and Educational Work," pp. 41–43; Dominick Cavallo, *Muscles and Morals: Organized Playgrounds and Urban Reform, 1880–1920* (Philadelphia: University of Pennsylvania Press, 1981), pp. 55–60; and David I. Macleod, *Building Char-*

*acter in the American Boy: The Boy Scouts, YMCA, and Their Forerunners, 1870–1920* (Madison: University of Wisconsin Press, 1983), pp. 99–100.

5. "Report of the Commission of Twenty-One," *School Review* 13 (1905), 23–25.

6. Quoted in Frank Forest Bunker, *Reorganization of the Public School System*, U.S. Bureau of Education, Bulletin No. 8 (Washington, D.C.: Government Printing Office, 1916), p. 63.

7. Ibid., pp. 63–64.

8. Frank Glenn Lankard, *A History of the American Sunday School Curriculum* (New York: The Abingdon Press, 1927), pp. 272–303.

9. David L. Angus, Jeffrey E. Mirel, and Maris A. Vinovskis, "Historical Development of Age-Stratification in Schooling," (unpublished typescript, 1988), p. 14.

10. Leonard P. Ayers, *Laggards in Our Schools: A Study of Retardation and Elimination in City School Systems* (New York: Charities Publication Committee, 1909). See also David B. Tyack, *The One Best System: A History of American Urban Education* (Cambridge: Harvard University Press, 1974), pp. 199–201.

11. Lightner Witmer, "What Is Meant by Retardation," *The Psychological Clinic* 4 (1910), p. 124.

12. George Dayton Strayer, *Age and Grade Census of Schools and Colleges*, U.S. Bureau of Education, Bulletin no. 5 (Washington, D.C.: Government Printing Office, 1911), pp. 103–4.

13. Quoted in Bunker, *Reorganization of the Public School System*, pp. 87–89.

14. Ibid., pp. 101–2.

15. Ellwood P. Cubberly, *Public Education in the United States*, rev. ed. (Boston: Houghton Mifflin, 1934), p. 555.

16. U.S. Bureau of the Census, *Fourteenth Census of the United States. Volume I: Population* (Washington, D.C.: Government Printing Office, 1922), pt. 2, pp. 1041, 1045; U. S. Bureau of the Census, *Statistical History of the United States* (Washington, D.C.: Government Printing Office, 1975), pp. 368–69. Significantly, these figures contrast with those for England, where as late as 1909 only 1.5 percent of youths between ages fifteen and eighteen attended secondary schools. The concept of adolescence as a peculiar life stage had deeper roots in England than in the United States. In fact, the origin of the modern concept of adolescence has been traced to the reforms of Thomas Arnold, who as headmaster of Rugby School between 1827 and 1839 attempted to instill intellectual, moral, and spiritual virtues in young men by cloistering them in a boarding school away from, but imitative of, adult society. Yet only much later did the link between secondary schooling and adolescence strengthen—and with it, the distinctiveness of age-graded peer grouping—leading to the conclusion that age norms for youths were more pervasive and highly developed in America earlier than they were in England. See John R.

Gillis, *Youth and History: Tradition and Change in European Age Relations, 1770–Present* (New York: Academic Press, 1974), pp. 118–19.

17. Joseph F. Kett, *Rites of Passage: Adolescence in America, 1790 to the Present* (New York: Basic Books, 1977), pp. 133, 183–86; Macleod, *Building Character*, pp. 24–28; John Modell et al., "Social Change and Transitions to Adulthood in Historical Perspective," *Journal of Family History* 1 (Autumn 1976), 7–32; Joseph F. Kett, "History of Age Grouping in America," in James S. Coleman et al., eds., *Youth: Transition to Adulthood* (Chicago: University of Chicago Press, 1974), pp. 19–24.

18. Joseph Green Cogswell and George Bancroft, *Prospectus of a School to be Established at Round Hill, Northampton, Massachusetts* (Cambridge, Mass.: Hilliard and Metcalf, 1823), p. 17, quoted in Betty Spears and Richard A. Swanson, *History of Sport and Physical Activity in the United States* (Dubuque, Ia.: Wm. C. Brown, 1978), pp. 80–81.

19. Spears and Swanson, *History of Sport*, pp. 119–24.

20. Cubberly, *Public Education*, pp. 606–7.

21. Luther Halsey Gulick, "Psychological, Pedagogical, and Religious Aspects of Group Games," *Pedagogical Seminary* 6 (March 1899), 135–51.

22. Luther Halsey Gulick, "The Policy of the Open Door," *Pratt Institute Monthly* 10 (June 1902), 220.

23. Luther Halsey Gulick, "Activities of the Boys' Branch of the P.S.A.L. of New York City," *The Playground Association of America Proceedings* 2 (1908), 412.

24. Ethel Josephine Dorgan, *Luther Halsey Gulick, 1865–1918* (New York: Bureau of Publications, Teachers College, Columbia University, 1934), pp. 79–82.

25. Jessie Hubbell Bancroft, *Rules for Games* (New York: American Sports Publishing Company, 1903).

26. Jessie Hubbell Bancroft, *Games for the Playground, Home, School, and Gymnasium* (New York: Macmillan, 1920), pp. 12–13.

27. Ibid., p. 15.

28. Ibid., pp. 13–14.

29. Clarence E. Rainwater, *The Play Movement in the United States: A Study of Community Recreation* (Chicago: University of Chicago Press, 1922), pp. 8–11, 192–200; John Collier and Edward M. Barrows, *The City Where Crime Is Play* (New York: Peoples Institute, 1916); Henry S. Curtis, *The Play Movement and Its Significance* (New York: Macmillan, 1917); Joseph Lee, "Restoring Their Play Inheritance to Our City Children," *The Craftsman* 25 (March 1914), 545–55; Spears and Swanson, *History of Sport*, pp. 171–73; Cavallo, *Muscles and Morals*, chaps. 1, 3.

30. Rainwater, *The Play Movement*, pp. 192–200.

31. George Ellsworth Johnson, *Education By Play and Games* (Boston: Ginn, 1907), pp. 8, 16–17. Johnson gives no explicit reason for using age fifteen as the upper bound of his developmental scheme; he only implies that

because most of one's physical maturing is completed by age sixteen, a child's play by that age no longer requires special attention.

32. Macleod, *Building Character*, pp. 24–28; Benjamin G. Rader, *American Sport: From the Age of Folk Games to the Age of the Spectator* (Englewood Cliffs, N.J.: Prentice-Hall, 1983), pp. 146–49.

33. See J. McKeon Cattell, "Mental Tests and Measurement," *Mind* 15 (1890), 373–81; J. McKeon Cattell and Livingston Farrand, "Physical and Mental Measurements of the Students of Columbia University," *Psychological Review* 3 (1896), 618–48; Thaddeus L. Bolton, "The Growth of Memory in Schoolchildren," *American Journal of Psychology* 4 (April 1891), 362–80; Joseph Jastrow, "Some Anthropological and Psychological Tests on College Students: A Preliminary Survey," *American Journal of Psychology* 4 (December 1891) 902–10; J. Allen Gilbert, "Research on Mental and Physical Development of School Children," *Studies of the Yale Psychological Laboratory* 2 (1894), 40–100; and Don C. Charles, "Historical Antecedents of Life-Span Developmental Psychology," in L. R. Goulet and Paul B. Baltes, eds., *Life-Span Developmental Psychology: Research and Theory* (New York and London: Academic Press, 1970), p. 32.

34. See the entry on Alfred Binet by Pierre Pichot in the *International Encyclopedia of the Social Sciences*, vol. 2 (New York: Macmillan, 1968), pp. 74–78; Joseph Peterson, *Early Conceptions and Tests of Intelligence* (Yonkers, N.Y.: World Book Company, 1925), chaps. 5–10; Lawrence A. Cremin, *The Transformation of the School: Progressivism in American Education, 1876–1956* (New York: Vintage Books, 1964), p. 186; and Charles, "Historical Antecedents of Life-Span Developmental Psychology," p. 33.

35. Charles, "Historical Antecedents of Life-Span Developmental Psychology," p. 33.

36. See Lewis M. Terman, *The Measurement of Intelligence* (Boston: Houghton Mifflin, 1916).

37. See, for example, Ronald D. Cohen, "Child Saving and Progressivism, 1885–1915," in Joseph M. Hawes and N. Ray Hiner, eds., *American Childhood: A Research Guide and Historical Handbook* (Westport, Conn.: Greenwood Press, 1985), pp. 289–90.

38. See Harlan C. Hines, *A Guide to Educational Measurements* (Houghton Mifflin, 1924).

39. Lewis M. Terman, *The Intelligence of School Children: How Children Differ in Ability, the Use of Mental Tests in School Grading, and the Proper Education of Exceptional Children* (Boston: Houghton Mifflin, 1919), pp. 28–29.

40. Cremin, *The Transformation of the School*, pp. 138–40; David John Hogan, *Class and Reform: School and Society in Chicago, 1880–1930* (Philadelphia: University of Pennsylvania Press, 1985), pp. 86–89.

41. *People ex. rel. Sinclair v. Sinclair*, 95 N.Y. Supp. 861 (1905). See also *People ex. rel. Sinclair v. Sinclair*, 91 App. Div. 322, 86 N.Y. Supp. 539 (1904).

42. *People ex. rel. Barry v. Mercein*, 38 Am. Dec. 644 (1842).

43. Benjamin B. Lindsey, "The Bad Boy: How to Save Him," *Leslie's Monthly Magazine* 60 (June 1905), 169–70. See also Anthony M. Platt, *The Child Savers: The Invention of Delinquency* (Chicago: University of Chicago Press, 1969), esp. chaps. 5 and 6, and Hogan, *Class and Reform*, pp. 60–65.

44. Lindsey, "The Bad Boy," p. 170.

45. Kett, *Rites of Passage*, p. 255; Hastings H. Hart, ed., *Juvenile Court Laws in the United States* (New York: Charities Publication Committee of the Russell Sage Foundation, 1910), pp. 1–118; Gilbert Cosulich, *Juvenile Court Laws of the United States*, 2d ed. (New York: National Probation Association, 1939), pp. 20–29, 58–61; Grace Abbott, *The Child and the State* (Chicago: University of Chicago Press, 1938), pp. 392–428. The exceptions to states that used age fourteen were Illinois, which set the age at twelve, and New Hampshire, which used age seventeen.

46. Carroll D. Wright, *A Report on Marriage and Divorce in the United States, 1867 to 1886* (Washington, D.C.: Government Printing Office, 1887), pp. 28–31.

47. U.S. Bureau of the Census, *Special Reports: Marriage and Divorce, 1867–1906. Part I: Summary, Laws, Foreign Statistics* (Washington, D.C.: Government Printing Office, 1909), pp. 184–89. A few southern states plus New Hampshire retained lower age limits; in these states, males as young as fourteen and females as young as twelve could marry with parental consent. But higher minimum ages were becoming standardized almost everywhere else.

48. Ibid., p. 185. In New Jersey, a license was required of all nonresidents marrying in that state, and New York had already passed a license requirement law that was to become effective as of January 1, 1908.

49. Anna Garlin Spencer, "The Age of Consent and Its Significance," *Forum* 49 (1913), 408.

50. See Edith Houghton Hooker, *The Laws of Sex* (Boston: Richard B. Badger, The Gorham Press, 1921).

51. Walter I. Trattner, *Crusade for the Children: A History of the National Child Labor Committee and Child Labor Reform in America* (Chicago: Quadrangle Books, 1970), p. 30.

52. Ibid., pp. 33–35; Hogan, *Class and Reform*, pp. 52–60.

53. Felix Adler, "Child Labor in the United States and Its Attendant Evils," *Annals of the American Academy of Political and Social Science* 25 (May 1905), 425.

54. Madeleine Wallin Sikes and Josephine C. Goldmark, *Child Labor Legislation* (New York: National Consumers' League, 1904).

55. "Standard Child Labor Law," *Annals of the American Academy of Political and Social Science* 31 (May 1908), 56–62.

56. Albert H. Freiberg, "Some of the Ultimate Effects of Premature Toil," *Annals of the American Academy of Political and Social Science* 29 (January 1907), 21–22; Owen R. Lovejoy, "Some Unsettled Questions about Child Labor," in *The Child Workers of the Nation: Proceedings of the Fifth Annual*

*Conference of the National Child Labor Committee* (New York: National Child Labor Committee, 1909), pp. 50–51. See also Abbott, *The Child and the State*, pp. 259–404, 461–545.

57. *The Employment of Young Persons in the United States* (New York: National Industrial Conference Board, 1925), pp. 67–68.

58. *Hammer v. Dagenhart* 247 United States Reports 251, 268 (June 1918).

59. *Bailey, Collector of Internal Revenue v. Drexel Furniture Company* 259 United States Reports 20, 34–44 (1922). See also *The Employment of Young Persons in the United States*, p. 68, and Trattner, *Crusade for the Children*, pp. 119–42.

60. Richard Meckel, "The Awful Responsibility of Motherhood: American Health Reform and the Prevention of Infant and Child Mortality Before 1913" (Ph.D. diss., Department of American Studies, University of Michigan, 1980), p. 344.

## CHAPTER 5

1. Paul Hanley Furfey, *The Gang Age: A Study of the Preadolescent Boy and His Recreational Needs* (New York: Macmillan, 1928), pp. 131, 137.

2. S. N. Eisenstadt, whose writings constitute one of the most definitive bases for studying peer groups, has used the term *peer group* interchangeably with *age group* and with *age homogeneous group*. See Eisenstadt, *Generation to Generation: Age Groups and Social Structure* (Glencoe, Ill.: The Free Press, 1956), pp. 50–55, 174.

3. For example, Paula Fass, in *The Damned and the Beautiful: American Youth in the 1920s* (New York: Oxford University Press, 1977), argues that the concepts of peer group and peer relations apply more directly to college students, at least to college students in the 1920s, than to adolescents or children, because of the intensity of interaction between peers that the college environment fosters. See her chapters 3–5.

4. Eisenstadt, *Generation to Generation*, pp. 50–55, 182–87, 271–94. See also David I. Macleod, *Building Character in the American Boy: The Boy Scouts, YMCA, and Their Forerunners, 1870–1920* (Madison: University of Wisconsin Press, 1983), p. 104, and Fass, *The Damned and the Beautiful*, pp. 121–22.

5. Fass, *The Damned and the Beautiful*, pp. 369–72.

6. Eisenstadt viewed peer relationships as vital and confined to adolescents making the transition from family to community in modern societies. Once youths became integrated into the adult world, he claimed, the need for peer group identity and support faded. See Eisenstadt, *Generation to Generation*, pp. 299–306. I contend, however, that historical evidence in the twentieth century shows peer relationships to extend through all stages of life.

7. John R. Gillis, *Youth and History: Tradition and Change in European Age Relations, 1770–Present* (New York: Academic Press, 1974); Philip T.

Greven, Jr., *Four Generations: Population, Land and Family in Colonial An-dover, Massachusetts* (Ithaca: Cornell University Press, 1970).

8. Joseph F. Kett, *Rites of Passage: Adolescence in America, 1790 to the Present* (New York: Basic Books, 1977), chap. 1.

9. See, for example, Greven, *Four Generations*, p. 34, who shows that in the last decades of the seventeenth century in Andover, Massachusetts, 60.5 percent of males married at ages twenty-five and older, while 75.3 percent of women married at ages twenty-four and younger.

10. Frederick S. Crum, "The Decadence of the Native American Stock: A Statistical Study of Genealogical Records," *American Statistical Association Journal* 14 (1916–17), 214–22. See also Robert V. Wells, *Revolutions in Their Lives: A Demographic Perspective on the History of Americans, Their Fami-lies, and Their Society* (Westport, Conn.: Greenwood Press, 1982), p. 92.

11. Frank W. Notestein, "The Decreasing Size of Families from 1890 to 1910," *Quarterly Bulletin of the Millbank Memorial Fund* 9 (1931), 181–88. Fass, *The Damned and the Beautiful*, pp. 60–64, cites several studies showing considerable decline in the number of siblings in college students' families in the 1920s compared with the number of siblings in their parents' families. See Ray Ervin Baker and Edward Allsworth Ross, *Changes in the Size of American Families in One Generation*, University of Wisconsin Studies in the Social Sci-ences and History, No. 10 (Madison: University of Wisconsin, 1924); S. J. Holmes, "The Size of College Families," *Journal of Heredity* 15 (1924), 407–15; and Amy Hewes, "A Study of Families in Three Generations," *Journal of the Association of College Alumnae* 13 (1920), 5–9.

12. Wells, *Revolutions in Their Lives*, p. 92; U. S. Bureau of the Census, *Statistical Abstract of the United States, 1986* (Washington, D.C.: Govern-ment Printing Office, 1985), p. 56; Donald J. Bogue, *The Population of the United States* (Glencoe, Ill.: The Free Press, 1959), p. 299. Because national fertility statistics were not collected until the twentieth century, birthrates in the nineteenth century have to be estimated from various regional and special surveys, which have been challenged and revised by several demographers and historians. Nevertheless, the downward trend is indisputable, and the propor-tionate change over the century is large indeed.

13. Rudy Ray Seward, *The American Family: A Demographic History* (Beverly Hills, Calif.: Sage Publications, 1978), p. 73; Bogue, *The Population of the United States*, p. 258.

14. Seward, *The American Family*, p. 79; U. S. Bureau of the Census, *His-torical Statistics of the United States: From Colonial Times to the Present* (Washington, D.C.: Government Printing Office, 1975), p. 42.

15. William I. Thomas and Florian Znaniecki, *The Polish Peasant in Eu-rope and America*, ed. and abr. Eli Zaretsky (Urbana and Chicago: University of Illinois Press, 1984), pp. 143–56.

16. See Kathy Peiss, *Cheap Amusements: Working Women and Leisure in Turn-of-the-Century New York* (Philadelphia: Temple University Press, 1986).

17. Ellen K. Rothman, *Hands and Hearts: A History of Courtship in America* (Cambridge: Harvard University Press, 1987), pp. 222–23, 289–90.

18. The Providence data were generated for previous studies, and the Omaha data were collected from Douglas County, Nebraska, marriage records deposited at the Nebraska State Archives, Lincoln, Nebraska. See Howard P. Chudacoff, "Newlyweds and Family Extension: The First Stage of the Family Cycle in Providence, Rhode Island, 1864–1865 and 1879–1880," in Tamara K. Hareven and Maris Vinovskis, eds., *Family and Population in Nineteenth-Century America* (Princeton: Princeton University Press, 1978), pp. 179–205, and Howard P. Chudacoff, "The Life Course of Women: Age and Age Consciousness, 1865–1915," *Journal of Family History* 5 (Autumn 1980), 274–92.

19. Among peer-type marriages, in which two or fewer years separated husband's and wife's ages, husbands were older than their wives about twice as often as wives were older than their husbands. In only a tiny number of marriages were wives six or more years older than their husbands.

20. Gillis, *Youth and History*, pp. 21, 47; Greven, *Four Generations*, pp. 222–23, 272–73; Mary P. Ryan, *Cradle of the Middle Class: The Family in Oneida County, New York, 1790–1865* (Cambridge, England: Cambridge University Press, 1981), pp. 71–75.

21. "What I Did With My Two Daughters," *Ladies Home Journal* 25 (March 1908), 10.

22. U. S. Office of Education, *Biennial Survey of Education in the United States, 1955–56* (Washington, D.C.: Government Printing Office, 1956), table 16, p. 30.

23. Luther Halsey Gulick, "The Policy of the Open Door," *Pratt Institute Monthly* 10 (June 1902), 220; Gulick, "Activities of the Boys' Branch of the P.S.A.L. of New York City," *The Playground Association of America Proceedings* 2 (1908), 412.

24. See Fass, *The Damned and the Beautiful*, pp. 88–89, and James E. West, "Youth Outside of Home and School," in *White House Conference on Child Health and Protection: Addresses and Abstracts of Committee Reports* (New York: The Century Company, 1931), pp. 247–74.

25. This point is made with particular force by Fass, *The Damned and the Beautiful*, pp. 121, 129–36, 211–12. See also R. H. Edwards, J. M. Artman, and Galen M. Fisher, *Undergraduates: A Study of Morale in Twenty-Three American Colleges and Universities* (Garden City and New York: Doubleday, Doran, 1928), pp. 5–25.

26. Daniel Santanello, "Brown University: Pioneer in the Introduction of Intercollegiate Hockey in the United States" (unpublished seminar paper, Brown University, 1980), pp. 4–5.

27. Eugene S. Richards, "Athletic Sports at Yale," *Outing* 6 (July 1885), 453.

28. Arthur Twining Hadley, "Wealth and Democracy in American Col-

leges," *Harper's Monthly* 93 (August 1906), 452. See also Edwards, Artman, and Fisher, *Undergraduates*, pp. 128–46.

29. John Addison Porter, "College Fraternities," *The Century* 36 (1888), 749–60; Frederick Rudolph, *The American College and University* (New York: Alfred A. Knopf, 1962), pp. 144–48; Fass, *The Damned and the Beautiful*, p. 142.

30. P. F. Piper, "College Fraternities," *Cosmopolitan Magazine* 22 (1897), 646.

31. Fass, *The Damned and the Beautiful*, p. 143. See also William Clyde Devane, *Higher Education in Twentieth Century America* (Cambridge: Harvard University Press, 1965), pp. 14–23, and C. H. Frerark, *A College Career and the American Fraternity System* (Lincoln: University of Nebraska Press, 1935), p. 9.

32. Fass, *The Damned and the Beautiful*, pp. 143–44.

33. Quoted in Edwards, Artman, and Fisher, *Undergraduates*, p. 59.

34. Ibid., p. 62.

35. Fass points out that the college peer society in the 1920s exerted a radicalizing force by cultivating and sanctioning somewhat countercultural values in such areas of behavior as work and consumer habits, sexuality, political attitudes, and personal choice. I concur that fraternities and sororities could indeed promote social change in this manner; here, I am simply emphasizing the immediate power and effects of peer influence. See Fass, *The Damned and the Beautiful*, pp. 141–49, 192, 226.

36. Fass, *The Damned and the Beautiful*, pp. 192–98; Edwards, Artman, and Fisher, *Undergraduates*, pp. 182–89.

37. *Report of the Faculty-Staff on the Distribution of Students' Time at the University of Chicago* (Chicago: University of Chicago, 1925), cited in Fass, *The Damned and the Beautiful*, p. 173; see also p. 422, n. 7.

38. See, for example, Carl Bridenbaugh, *Cities in Revolt: Urban Life in America, 1743–1776* (New York: Knopf, 1955), pp. 307–9; Gary B. Nash, *The Urban Crucible: Social Change, Political Consciousness, and the Origins of the American Revolution* (Cambridge: Harvard University Press, 1979), pp. 293–300; and Joel Tyler Headley, *The Great Riots of New York, 1712–1873* (1873; reprint, Indianapolis and New York: The Bobbs-Merrill Company, 1970), pp. 152–59.

39. Headley, *The Great Riots*, p. 131.

40. Kett, *Rites of Passage*, p. 89.

41. Although there were distinct ethnic, class, racial, and gender differences in these patterns, the trend was similar for all groups. For an empirical analysis, see Michael B. Katz, *The People of Hamilton, Canada West: Family and Class in a Mid-Nineteenth Century City* (Cambridge: Harvard University Press, 1975), pp. 256–92, 307–8.

42. Frederick M. Thrasher, *The Gang: A Study of 1,313 Gangs in Chicago* (Chicago: University of Chicago Press, 1927), pp. 74–76.

43. Furfey, *The Gang Age*, p. 137.

44. J. Adams Puffer, *The Boy and His Gang* (Boston: Houghton Mifflin, 1912), pp. 16, 18.

45. Verses quoted in Duncan Emrich, *Folklore on the American Land* (Boston: Little, Brown, 1972), pp. 217ff.

46. Edgar M. Robinson, "Age Grouping of Younger Association Members," *Association Boys* 1 (1902), 34–35; "Retaining the Interest of the Older Scout," *Scouting* 6 (January 15, 1918), 13, cited in David I. Macleod, *Building Character in the American Boy: The Boy Scouts, YMCA, and Their Forerunners, 1870–1920* (Madison: University of Wisconsin Press, 1983), pp. 282, 292.

47. See Collette Hyman, "The Young Women's Christian Association and the Women's City Missionary Society: Models of Feminine Behavior, 1863–1920" (unpublished honors thesis, American Civilization Program, Brown University, 1979), pp. 52–53; Macleod, *Building Character*, pp. 295–98.

48. George E. Bevans, *How Workingmen Spend Their Time* (New York: Columbia University, 1913), pp. 27, 31, 33, 35; Peiss, *Cheap Amusements*, pp. 6–7, 56–57; Roy Rosenzweig, *Eight Hours for What We Will: Workers and Leisure in an Industrial City* (Cambridge, England: Cambridge University Press, 1983), p. 188.

49. Peiss, *Cheap Amusements*, p. 89.

50. Peiss, *Cheap Amusements*, p. 88; Lewis Erenberg, *Steppin' Out: New York Night Life and the Transformation of American Culture* (Westport, Conn.: Greenwood Press, 1981), pp. 156–57.

51. Katherine Anthony, *Mothers Who Must Earn*, West Side Studies, vol. 2, pt. 2 (New York: Russell Sage Foundation, 1914), p. 189.

52. See Peiss, *Cheap Amusements*; Leslie Woodcock Tentler, *Wage-Earning Women: Industrial Work and Family Life in the United States, 1900–1930* (New York: Oxford University Press, 1979); Alice Kessler-Harris, *Out to Work: A History of Wage-Earning Women in the United States* (New York: Oxford University Press, 1982); Susan Estabrook Kennedy, *If All We Did Was to Weep at Home: A History of White Working-Class Women in America* (Bloomington: Indiana University Press, 1979); and Miriam Cohen, "Italian-American Women in New York City, 1900–1950: Work and School," in Milton Cantor and Bruce Laurie, eds., *Class, Sex, and the Woman Worker* (Westport, Conn.: Greenwood Press, 1977), pp. 120–43.

53. See Peiss, *Cheap Amusements*, and Judith Smith, *Family Connections: A History of Italian and Jewish Immigrant Lives in Providence, Rhode Island, 1900–1940* (Albany: State University of New York Press, 1985).

54. YWCA, *First Report of the Commission on Household Employment* (Los Angeles, May 5–11, 1915), p. 19, quoted in Kessler-Harris, *Out to Work*, p. 136. See also David M. Katzman, *Seven Days a Week: Women and Domestic Service in Industrializing America* (New York: Oxford University Press, 1978).

55. Hyman, "The Young Women's Christian Association," pp. 45, 87.

56. Margaret E. Sangster, *Winsome Womanhood* (New York: Fleming H. Revell, 1900), p. 189.

57. Walter Camp, "You Pass Your Physical Zenith Between 31 and 35," *American Magazine* 87 (March 1919), 31–33.

58. E. A. Ross, "The Conflict of Age," *Scientia* 46 (1929), 346–522.

59. Quoted in Bernice Hunt and Morton Hunt, *Prime Time: A Guide to the Pleasures and Opportunities of the New Middle Age* (New York: Stein and Day, 1974), p. 19.

60. U.S. Bureau of the Census, *Historical Statistics of the United States from Colonial Times to 1970* (Washington, D.C.: Government Printing Office, 1975), p. 21.

61. Ben Lindsey and Wainright Evans, *The Companionate Marriage* (New York: Boni and Liveright, 1927), pp. 3–5.

62. Walter E. Pitkin, *Life Begins at Forty* (New York: McGraw-Hill, 1932), pp. 5–7, 11–12.

63. Ibid., p. 114.

64. Sophie Tucker, *Some of These Days* (Garden City, N.Y.: Country Life Press, 1945), p. 95.

65. Granville Stanley Hall, *Senescence: The Last Half of Life* (New York: D. Appleton, 1922), p. vii.

66. Lee Walling Squires, *Old Age Dependency in the United States* (New York: Macmillan, 1912), pp. 28–29.

67. See James T. Patterson, *The Dread Disease: Cancer and Modern American Culture* (Cambridge: Harvard University Press, 1987), p. 79.

68. Louis Faugeres Bishop, "The Relation of Old Age to Disease, with Illustrative Cases," *The American Journal of Nursing* 9, no. 9 (June 1904), 679.

69. For a full and sensitive discussion of these issues, see Carole Haber, *Beyond Sixty-Five: The Dilemma of Old Age in America's Past* (Cambridge, England: Cambridge University Press, 1983), chaps. 2, 4. See also, W. Andrew Achenbaum, *Old Age in the New Land: The American Experience Since 1790* (Baltimore: The Johns Hopkins University Press, 1978), esp. chap. 4, and David Hackett Fischer, *Growing Old in America* (New York: Oxford University Press, 1977), esp. chap. 4.

70. Haber, *Beyond Sixty-Five*, p. 84.

71. Achenbaum, *Old Age in the New Land*, pp. 80–81.

72. Haber, *Beyond Sixty-Five*, pp. 92–93.

73. Ibid., p. 93.

74. *Charities and the Commons* 17, no. 15 (February 1907), 875.

75. Haber, *Beyond Sixty-Five*, pp. 108–11; Achenbaum, *Old Age in the New Land*, pp. 48–49; William Graebner, *A History of Retirement: The Meaning and Function of an American Institution, 1885–1978* (New Haven, Conn.: Yale University Press, 1980), pp. 11–19, 53.

76. Achenbaum, *Old Age in the New Land*, pp. 48–49. During the nineteenth century, the federal government did provide pensions for military veterans, but they were considered rewards for loyal service, not old-age assistance. In addition, Civil War pensions were provided for diseased and disabled

soldiers, as well as for widows, but age criteria were not involved. See Haber, *Beyond Sixty-Five*, pp. 110–11.

77. Abraham Epstein, *The Problem of Old Age Pensions in Industry* (Harrisburg, Pa.: Pennsylvania Old Age Commission, 1926), pp. 115–16. See also Epstein, *Facing Old Age: A Study of Old Age Dependency in the United States and Old Age Pensions* (New York: Knopf, 1922), pp. 141–89.

78. Epstein, *Facing Old Age*, p. 162; Haber, *Beyond Sixty-Five*, p. 121.

79. Haber, *Beyond Sixty-Five*, pp. 122–23.

80. Ibid., p. 119.

81. Quoted in Abraham Epstein, *The Challenge of the Aged* (New York: Macy-Masius: The Vanguard Press, 1928), pp. 268–69.

82. Ibid., pp. 262–91.

83. Achenbaum, *Old Age in the New Land*, p. 50.

84. Haber, *Beyond Sixty-Five*, p. 124.

85. For an example of such humanitarian concern, see Epstein, *The Challenge of the Aged*, chaps. 1–6.

86. Haber, *Beyond Sixty-Five*, chap. 5. Achenbaum, *Old Age in the New Land*, pp. 119–20, argues, somewhat differently from Haber and myself, that some physicians believed that in spite of pathological degeneration, diseases of old age could be "cured." But evidence suggests that most doctors assumed that, at best, senile deterioration could be arrested and seldom reversed.

87. I. L. Nascher, "Geriatrics," *New York Medical Journal* 90, no. 8 (August 1909), 358.

88. Ibid., pp. 358–59.

89. Nascher, "Importance of Geriatrics," *Journal of the American Medical Association* 62 (1917), 2249. See also Nascher, "Geriatrics," p. 358.

90. Epstein, *The Challenge of the Aged*, pp. 259–62.

91. Graebner, *A History of Retirement*, pp. 80, 180–88.

92. See Graebner, *A History of Retirement*, pp. 181–214, and Achenbaum, *Old Age in the New Land*, pp. 127–38.

93. Wilbur J. Cohen, *Retirement Policies under Social Security: A Legislative History of Retirement Ages, the Retirement Test, and Disability Benefits* (Berkeley and Los Angeles: University of California Press, 1957), pp. 17–20. Cohen, in a chapter titled "How Was 65 Selected as the Retirement Age?" used information obtained from Murray Latimore, an authority on industrial pension systems and a leading figure on the CES.

94. Ibid., p. 20.

95. Henry Seidel Canby, "Life in the Nineties: Home and Parents," *Harper's* 169 (1934), 271.

96. William F. Ogburn, with the assistance of Clark Tibbitts, "The Family and Its Functions," in *Recent Social Trends in the United States: Report of the President's Research Committee on Social Trends* (New York: McGraw-Hill, 1933), p. 663.

97. Ibid., pp. 698–700.

98. Warren S. Thompson and P. K. Whelpton, "The Population of the Nation," in *Recent Social Trends in the United States*, pp. 26, 34–35.

CHAPTER 6

1. James J. Fuld, *The Book of World Famous Music*, rev. ed. (New York: Crown Publishers, 1966), pp. 266–68.

2. *New York Times*, August 15, 1934, p. 19.

3. Fuld, *The Book of World Famous Music*, p. 268.

4. *American Magazine* 88 (December 1919), 143.

5. Ibid., pp. 143–44.

6. Ibid., pp. 144–45.

7. See, for example, Ella Gilbert Ives, *The Evolution of a Teacher* (Boston, New York, and Chicago: The Pilgrim Press, 1915); Amelia Gera Mason, *Memoirs of a Friend* (Chicago: Lawrence C. Woodward, 1918); Martha Seymour Coman, *Memories of Martha Seymour Coman* (Boston: The Fort Hill Press, 1913); and Anne Ellis, *The Life of an Ordinary Woman* (Boston: Houghton Mifflin, 1929).

8. Leah Morton (pseud. for Elizabeth Gertrude Stern), *I Am a Woman and a Jew* (New York: J. H. Sears, 1926), p. 3.

9. Mabel Osgood Wright, *My New York* (New York: Macmillan, 1926), p. 171.

10. H. B. Mayer, "The Fallacy of the Elder Brother," *Living Age* 263 (December 11, 1909), 663–70.

11. Wright, *My New York*, p. 229.

12. Ibid., p. 242.

13. Wanda Gág, *Growing Pains: Diaries and Drawings for the Years 1908–1917* (New York: Coward-McCann, 1940), p. 225.

14. Ibid., p. 230.

15. Ibid., p. 226.

16. Ibid.

17. Ibid., pp. 458–59.

18. "Puppy Love Among Boys and Girls," *Ladies Home Journal* 26 (September 1909), 44.

19. "What They Said When I Became Engaged," *Ladies Home Journal* 25 (February 1908), 24.

20. Irene Dale (pseud.), *Diary of a Night Club Hostess* (Girard, Kans.: Haldeman-Julius, 1929), p. 3.

21. Ernest R. Groves and Gladys Hoagland Groves, *Wholesome Marriage* (Boston: Houghton Mifflin, 1927), pp. 59–60.

22. Anon., *How Can I Get Married? A Woman Bares Her Soul. Vividly and Dramatically She Tells the Story of Her Heart-stirring Experiences in Her Search for a Husband* (New York: MacFadden Publications, 1927), esp. pp. xii and 203–4. See also An Old Maid, "Why I Am Glad—and Why Sorry—I Never Married," *American Magazine* 88 (November 1919), 27, 164.

23. "My Young Men," *Living Age* 256 (February 15, 1908), 437–39.

24. Ellis Parker Butler, "Poor Old Ellis Parker Butler Is 50 This Month," *American Magazine* 88 (December 1919), 39, 220–23. Butler expanded his reflections into a full-length popular book, which he published the next year under the title *How It Feels To Be Fifty* (Boston and New York: Houghton Mifflin, 1920).

25. Advertisement in *American Magazine* 87 (January 1919), 64.

26. William Bruce Hart, "Young at Seventy-Eight," *American Magazine* 88 (October 1919), 64–65.

27. Walt Mason, "I Refuse to Grow Old," *American Magazine* 88 (September 1919), 66–67, 185–87.

28. Isaac H. Lionberger, *The Felicities of Sixty* (Boston: The Club of Odd Fellows, 1922), pp. 18–20.

29. Mary M. H. Vorse, *Autobiography of an Elderly Woman* (New York and Boston: Houghton Mifflin, 1911), p. 234.

30. Forrest F. Dryden, "The Kind of Human Beings Who Live Longest," *American Magazine* 88 (August 1919), 26–27, 162–66.

31. Clarence Budington Kelland, "Scattergood Borrows a Grandmother," *American Magazine* 88 (December 1919), 20–23, 85–98. Another amusing yet illustrative popular perspective on age-graded norms and senescence comes from a folkloric bawdy poem, apparently current in the 1910s. I discovered the anonymously authored poem, "Sad But True," in a file at the Kinsey Institute for Research in Sex, Gender, and Reproduction, in Bloomington, Indiana:

> From 20 to 30 if a man lives right,
> It's once in the morning and once at night.
> From 30 to 40 if he still lives right,
> He cuts out the morning or else at night.
> From 40 to 50 it's now and then,
> From 50 to 60 it's God knows when.
> From 60 to 70 if he still is inclined,
> Don't let them kid you, it's still on his mind.
> With women it's different, it's morning or night,
> Regardless whether they live wrong or right.
> Age cuts no figure. They are always inclined.
> Nothing to get ready, not even their mind.
> So after all is said and done,
> A man of 60 has completed his run.
> The woman of sixty, if figures don't lie,
> Can take the old root till her time comes to die.

32. Margaret Sangster, *Winsome Womanhood: Familiar Talks on Life and Conduct* (New York: Fleming H. Revell, 1900), p. 133.

33. Birthdays were uncommon in primitive and non-Western cultures as well. According to a survey taken a half century ago by British anthropologist Ernest C. Crawley, "no record is kept of birth or age" among Congo and other African tribes, and American Indian tribes such as the Hupas and Omahas

refused to keep a reckoning of age even when they had the ability to do so. Though the Chinese observed birthdays, especially from age fifteen onward, and had special celebrations on certain birthdays such as the fiftieth and sixty-first, he noted that the Japanese made New Year's Day the universal birthday, collapsing all personal observances into a common celebratory event. See Ernest C. Crawley, *Oath, Curse, and Blessing* (London: Watts, 1934), pp. 141–47.

34. Ralph Linton and Adelin Linton, *The Lore of Birthdays* (New York: H. Schuman, 1952), p. x.

35. Ibid., pp. 13–26; Linda Rannells Lewis, *Birthdays* (Boston: Little, Brown, 1976), p. 15.

36. Linton and Linton, *The Lore of Birthdays*, p. 53. Name day is not the day of baptism but rather the saint's sacred day. Thus, it is less personal than a birthday.

37. William I. Thomas and Florian Znaniecki, *The Polish Peasant in Europe and America*, ed. and abr. Eli Zaretsky (Urbana and Chicago: University of Illinois Press, 1984), p. 176.

38. Lewis, *Birthdays*, pp. 48–49; Linton and Linton, *The Lore of Birthdays*, p. 25.

39. Lewis, *Birthdays*, pp. 81–82.

40. Quoted in Lewis, *Birthdays*, pp. 94–95.

41. Robert J. Myers, *Celebration: The Complete Book of American Holidays* (Garden City, N.Y.: Doubleday, 1972), pp. 63–69.

42. Ibid., pp. 43–44.

43. Lemuel Shattuck, *Report to the Commissioner of the City Council Appointed to Obtain the Census of Boston for the Year 1845* (Boston: J. H. Eastburn, City Printer, 1846), appendix, p. 2.

44. John E. Keller, ed., *Anna Morrison Reed, 1849–1921* (Lafayette, Calif.: John E. Keller, 1979), p. 48.

45. Ibid., p. 94.

46. Mary Custis Lee deButts, ed., *Growing Up in the 1850s: The Journal of Agnes Lee* (Chapel Hill: University of North Carolina Press, 1984), p. 37.

47. Flo V. Menninger, *Days of My Life: Memories of a Kansas Mother and Teacher* (New York: Richard R. Smith, 1939), p. 28.

48. Lottie A. Spikes, *Memories* (Columbus, Ga.: Gilbert Printing Company, 1910).

49. Carl N. Degler, *At Odds: Women and the Family in America from the Revolution to the Present* (New York: Oxford University Press, 1980), p. 71; Lewis, *Birthdays*, p. 47; Linton and Linton, *The Lore of Birthdays*, p. 25.

50. Wright, *My New York*, pp. 135–37. Elizabeth Marbury, who grew up in Oyster Bay, New York, next door to Theodore Roosevelt, remembered a childhood birthday party attended by "my little friends in the neighborhood," at which large amounts of strawberries were served—a very luxurious treat. See Marbury, *My Crystal Ball* (New York: Boni and Liveright, 1923), p. 9.

51. Lewis, *Birthdays*, p. 19.

52. See, for example, allusion to parties in Robert W. de Forest and Lawrence Veiller, eds., *The Tenement House Problem*, vol. 1 (New York: Macmillan, 1903), p. 342, and reference to birthday cakes in Margaret Jones Bolsterli, ed., *Vinegar Pie and Chicken Bread: A Woman's Diary of Life in the Rural South, 1890–1891* (Fayetteville: University of Arkansas Press, 1982), p. 47.

53. Marion Vallat Emrich and George Korson, *The Child's Book of Folklore* (New York: Dial Press, 1947), pp. 98–99.

54. Gág, *Growing Pains*, pp. 10, 12, 26, 30, 49, 369.

55. Barbara Moench Florence, ed., *Lella Secor: A Diary in Letters, 1915–1922* (New York: Burt Franklin, 1978).

56. Quoted in Lewis, *Birthdays*, p. 159.

57. Alice Weston Smith, *Letters to Her Friends and Selections from Her Note-Books* (Boston: Addison C. Getschell and Son, n.d.), p. 71.

58. Dale, *Diary of a Night Club Hostess*, p. 17.

59. Gág, *Growing Pains*, p. 105.

60. Ibid., pp. 141–42.

61. Ibid., p. 436.

62. Gloria T. Hull, ed., *Give Us Each Day: The Diary of Alice Dunbar-Nelson* (New York: W. W. Norton, 1984), p. 77.

63. Ibid., pp. 184, 246, 325, 377.

64. Anne Foner, "Age Stratification and the Changing Family," in John Demos and Sarane Spence Boocock, eds., *Turning Points: Historical and Sociological Essays on the Family*, in *American Journal of Sociology* 84, supplement (Chicago: University of Chicago Press, 1978), pp. 340–43; Thomas P. Monahan, *The Pattern of Age at Marriage in the United States* (Philadelphia: Stephenson Brothers, 1951), p. 37; Stephen Kern, *The Culture of Time and Space, 1880–1918* (Cambridge: Harvard University Press, 1983), pp. 36–37, 63–64.

65. This card, as are most of the others cited in this section, is found in the collections archived at the Hallmark Card Company, Kansas City, Missouri. Some cards have been numbered for archival retrieval; others, such as this one, have not. Where possible, I have documented cards using the numbers assigned by Hallmark archivists.

66. Ernest Dudley Chase, *The Romance of Greeting Cards* (Cambridge, Mass.: University Press, 1927), p. 6.

67. George Buday, *The History of the Christmas Card* (London: Rockliff Publishing, 1954), p. 278.

68. Hallmark Historical Collections, archive #3784 and archive #4401. See also Chase, *The Romance of Greeting Cards*, p. 19.

69. *The Era of Hallmark Cards, Inc.* (Kansas City: privately printed for the Hallmark Card Company, 1960).

70. A systematic analysis of the exact frequency of occurrence of this phrase was not possible, but almost every card printed by the Prang Company and archived in the Hallmark Antique Card Collection contained the expression "Many happy returns."

71. Chase, *The Romance of Greeting Cards*, p. 121.

72. Hallmark Historical Collections, unnumbered.
73. Chase, *The Romance of Greeting Cards*, p. 123.
74. Hallmark Historical Collections, unnumbered.
75. Hallmark Historical Collections, unnumbered.
76. Hallmark Historical Collections, unnumbered.
77. For example, "A Birthday Greeting to You in the 80s" read, in part:

> May this birthday in the eighties
> Bring you hours of deep content
> As you look back in thought today
> On pleasant years you've spent.

(Hallmark Historical Collections, plate #GR7162, stock #25B252-8.)
78. Hallmark Historical Collections, stock #25B226-9.
79. Hallmark Historical Collections, unnumbered.
80. Chase, *The Romance of Greeting Cards*, p. 129.

## CHAPTER 7

1. "Just One Girl," words by Karl Kennett, music by Lyn Udall (New York: Witmark and Sons, 1898). Most song lyric sources used in this chapter are from the popular sheet music collection found in the Harris Collection of the John Hay Library, Brown University, Providence, Rhode Island.

2. Definitions adapted from Martin W. Laforse and James A. Drake, *Popular Culture and American Life: Selected Topics in the Study of American Popular Culture* (Chicago: Nelson-Hall, 1981), p. viii, and from Herbert J. Gans, *Popular Culture and High Culture* (New York: Basic Books, 1974), pp. 10–15.

3. Irwin Stambler, *Encyclopedia of Popular Music* (New York: St. Martin's Press, 1965), pp. xii–xiii; Sigmund Spaeth, "Foreword," in David Ewen, ed., *American Popular Songs from the Revolutionary War to the Present* (New York: Random House, 1966), pp. vi–viii.

4. Marian Klankin, *Old Sheet Music: A Pictorial History* (New York: Hawthorn Books, 1975), pp. 1–10.

5. See Lester S. Levy, *Grace Notes in American History: Popular Sheet Music From 1820 to 1900* (Norman: University of Oklahoma Press, 1967), pp. 3, 58, 74–77, 165–69.

6. Michael R. Turner, *The Parlour Song Book: A Casquet of Vocal Gems* (New York: The Viking Press, 1972), p. 2.

7. "An Old Man Who Would Be Young," words and music by James M. Maeder (Philadelphia: Krotschmer and Nunns, 1833).

8. "When I Am Old," words and music by Charles Hess (Philadelphia: A. Fiot, 1851).

9. "When You and I Grow Old," words by Emily A. Warden, music by E. Linwood (Philadelphia: W. R. Smith, 1867); "When You and I Are Old," words and music by Harry Percy (New York and Boston: C. H. Ditson, 1872).

10. See W. Andrew Achenbaum, *Old Age in the New Land: The American*

*Experience Since 1790* (Baltimore: The Johns Hopkins University Press, 1978), chap. 3, and Carole Haber, *Beyond Sixty-Five: The Dilemma of Old Age in America's Past* (Cambridge, England: Cambridge University Press, 1983), chaps. 2–3.

11. "When You and I Were Young, Maggie," words by George W. Johnson, music by James A. Butterfield (Chicago: J. A. Butterfield, 1866).

12. "The Old Folks," words and music by T. H. Hinton (Syracuse, N.Y.: Clemons and Redington, 1867).

13. "Old Folks Love Song," words and music by M. W. Hackelton (Chicago: Root and Cady, 1869).

14. "Silver Threads Among the Gold," words by Eben E. Rexford, music by H. P. Danks (New York: Charles W. Harris, 1873).

15. See, for example, "You Are Always Young To Me," words by George Cooper, music by H. P. Danks (New York: Charles W. Harris, 1874), which includes the verse:

> Down the hill of life we stray,
> Soon will come the parting day;
> O'er the river dark and lone,
> We shall meet again, my own;

and "When You and I Were Young," words and music by J. Ford (Philadelphia: F. A. North, 1875), with its verse:

> 'Tis true the hopes we cherished then
> Have vanished with the past,
> And scenes we gazed with pleasure on
> Were all too bright to last,
> Yet live tonight, in memory,
> The songs we gaily sung
> In that dear home of other years
> When you and I were young.

16. "The Old Maid," words and music by Sep Winner (Philadelphia: Lee and Walker, 1860).

17. Robert C. Toll, *On with the Show: The First Century of Show Business in America* (New York: Oxford University Press, 1976), pp. 171–206, 265–94; Gunther Barth, *City People: The Rise of Modern City Culture in Nineteenth Century America* (New York: Oxford University Press, 1980), pp. 192–228.

18. Robert C. Toll, *The Entertainment Machine: American Show Business in the Twentieth Century* (New York: Oxford University Press, 1982), pp. 100–103.

19. "Where Did You Get That Hat?" words and music by Joseph J. Sullivan (New York: Frank Harding, 1888).

20. It is possible to conclude, of course, that the songwriter was not expressing scheduling norms at all but rather was using a handy rhyming convention; "tarried" rhymes with "married." But I believe there is deeper signif-

icance to both the choice of a rhyming word and the use of an explicit age. The term *tarry* was used in songs before the 1880s chiefly in reference to delayed physical movement, not to postponing a life-course event. In addition, as the first section of this chapter has noted, early popular songs almost never speci-fied explicit ages. Thus, these apparently simple lyrics signaled some important social changes.

21. "When You Were Sweet Sixteen," words and music by James Thornton (New York: M. Witmark and Sons, 1898).

22. "Feather Queen," words and music by Mabel McKinley (New York: Leo Feist, 1905); "When I Was Twenty-One and You Were Sweet Sixteen," words by Harry Williams, music by Egbert Van Alstyne (New York and De-troit: Jerome H. Remick, 1911); "When You Were Six and I Was Eight," words by A. M. Grimaldi, music by B. L. Henri (Detroit: Grant Publishing Company, 1915); "When I Was Twenty-One," words and music by Harry Lauder (New York: T. B. Harms and Francis, Day, and Hunter, 1918).

23. "Old Before His Time," words by Sidney Rosenfeld, music by Ludwig Englander (New York: T. B. Harms, 1894).

24. "Old Maid Blues," words by Web Maddox, music by David W. Guion (New York: T. B. Harms and Francis, Day, and Hunter, 1918). Unmarried women of advanced years received further scorn in this period. One of Irving Berlin's early compositions, "The Old Maid's Ball" (New York: Waterson, Berlin, and Snyder, 1913), summarized the negative images in its chorus:

> There were old maids short and tall,
> Dancing 'round the hall.
> One who knew us drew up to us,
> She was older than St. Louis,
> Miss Melinda Rand,
> Led the female band and
> When they played "Here Comes the Bride,"
> Four old maids sat down and cried,
> Someone hollered, "There's a man outside,"
> And broke up the Old Maid's Ball.

25. Grimaldi and Henri, "When You Were Six and I Was Eight."

26. "The Days When We Were Young," words and music by Charles P. Weston (Brooklyn: Charles B. Weston, 1912).

27. "When You're Five Times Sweet Sixteen," words by Jack Mahoney, music by George L. Cobb (New York: Leo Feist, 1916).

28. David Hackett Fischer, *Growing Old in America* (New York: Oxford University Press, 1977), chaps 3, 4; Achenbaum, *Old Age in the New Land*, chaps. 5, 6; Haber, *Beyond Sixty-Five*, chaps. 2, 3, 6.

29. Fischer, *Growing Old in America*, p. 155.

30. "When Grandma Sings the Songs She Loved at the End of a Perfect Day," words by Bartley Costello, music by Robert A. Keiser (New York: Sha-piro, Bernstein, 1916).

31. "For Sale—A Baby," words and music by Charles K. Harris (New York: Charles K. Harris, 1903).

32. "The Little Lost Child," words by Edward B. Marks, music by Joseph W. Stern (New York: Joseph W. Stern, 1894). For more details about this song, see Margaret Bradford Boni, ed., *The Fireside Book of Favorite American Songs* (New York: Simon and Schuster, 1952), pp. 48–51, and David Ewen, ed., *American Popular Songs from the Revolutionary War to the Present* (New York: Random House, 1966), pp. 227–28.

33. "Youth Is Life's Time of May," words by Henry C. Watson, music by Vincent Wallace (New York: William Hall and Sons, 1893).

34. "Toyland," words by Glen MacDonough, music by Victor Herbert (New York: M. Witmark and Sons, 1903).

35. Toll, *The Entertainment Machine*, pp. 103–15.

36. Ibid., p. 114.

37. "When You and I Were Seventeen," words by Gus Kahn, music by Charles Rosoff (New York: Irving Berlin Music Publishers, 1924).

38. "Young and Healthy," words by Al Dubin, music by Harry Warren (New York: M. Witmark and Sons, 1932).

39. "Keep Young and Beautiful," words by Al Dubin, music by Harry Warren (New York: M. Witmark and Sons, 1933).

40. "When You're Over Sixty and You Feel Like Sweet Sixteen," words and music by Little Jack Little, Dave Oppenheim, and Ira Schuster (New York: Olman Music, 1933).

41. "When Hearts Are Young," words by Cyrus Woods, music by Sigmund Romberg (New York: Harms, 1922).

42. "While We're Young," words by Haven Gillespie, music by J. Fred Coots (New York: Harms, 1933); "When I Grow Too Old to Dream," words by Oscar Hammerstein, music by Sigmund Romberg (New York: MGM, 1935).

43. "My Old Man," words by Mort Dixon, music by Harry Woods (New York: Remick Music, 1929).

44. For another example of the new prominence of birthdays in songs, see "Baby's Birthday Party," words and music by Ann Ronald (New York: Famous Music, 1930).

45. "When I First Met Mary," words and music by George A. Little, Joe Verges, and Larry Shay (Chicago: Milton Weil Music, 1927).

46. "When Your Hair Has Turned to Silver," words by Charlie Tobias, music by Peter De Rose (New York: Joe Morris Music, 1930).

47. "Always," words and music by Irving Berlin (New York: Irving Berlin, 1925); "Through the Years," words by Edward Heyman, music by Vincent Youmans (New York: Miller Music and Vincent Youmans, 1931); "September Song," words by Maxwell Anderson, music by Kurt Weill (New York: De Sylva, Brown, and Henderson, 1938).

48. "Little Old Lady," words by Stanley Adams, music by Hoagy Carmichael (New York: Chappell, 1936).

49. See, for example, William Graebner, *A History of Retirement: The Meaning and Function of an American Institution, 1885–1978* (New Haven, Conn.: Yale University Press, 1980).

50. See "Young Love," words and music by Ric Cartey and Carole Joyner (New York: Lowery Music, 1956); "School Days," words and music by Chuck Berry (New York: Arc Music, 1957); and "Sweet Little Sixteen," words and music by Chuck Berry (New York: Arc Music, 1958).

51. "Hello, Young Lovers," words by Oscar Hammerstein II, music by Richard Rodgers (New York: Williamson Music, 1951); "Too Young," words by Sylvia Dee, music by Sid Lippman (New York: Aria Music, 1951); "Young At Heart," words by Carolyn Leigh, music by Johnny Richards (New York: Cherio Corporation and June S. Tune, 1955); "April Love," words by Paul Francis Webster, music by Sammy Fain (New York: Twentieth Century Music, 1957).

52. Toll, *The Entertainment Machine*, p. 121.

53. Ibid., pp. 121–22.

54. Ibid.

## CHAPTER 8

1. Delia T. Lutes, "Why I Don't Tell My Age," *Forum* 47 (April 1937), 244.

2. See *Life* 25 (June 19, 1950), 34, and *Newsweek* 96 (August 11, 1980), 74.

3. John Knowles, "All Split Up," *Seventeen* 25 (May 1966), 184. The very magazine that published Knowles's lament, of course, reinforced the horizontal division he was denouncing.

4. Quoted in Elizabeth Hall, "Acting One's Age: New Rules for Old," *Psychology Today* 13 (April 1980), 66.

5. Ibid., p. 68.

6. For summaries of the early history of developmental psychology, see Don C. Charles, "Historical Antecedents of Life-Span Developmental Psychology," in L. R. Goulet and Paul B. Baltes, eds., *Life-Span Developmental Psychology: Research and Theory* (New York and London: Academic Press, 1970), pp. 24–53; Karl J. Groffman, "Life-Span Developmental Psychology in Europe: Past and Present," in Goulet and Baltes, *Life-Span Developmental Psychology*, pp. 54–68; and Robert J. Havighurst, "History of Developmental Psychology: Socialization and Personality Development through the Life Span," in Paul B. Baltes and K. Warner Schaie, eds., *Life-Span Developmental Psychology: Personality and Socialization* (New York and London: Academic Press, 1973), pp. 4–24.

7. Havighurst, "History of Developmental Psychology," pp. 7–8. See also Groffman, "Life-Span Developmental Psychology in Europe," p. 64; Charlotte Bühler, *Der menschliche Leberslauf als psychologisches Problem* (Leipzig: Hirzel, 1933); and Bühler, "Genetic Aspects of the Self," *Annals of the New York Academy of Science* 96 (1962), 730–64.

8. I have chosen to omit a wide range of age-related issues deriving from

the psychoanalytic theories of individuals such as Freud, Piaget, and Gesell, because to include them would extend and complicate the book unnecessarily. Moreover, the work of these individuals, while leading to some general theories, has emphasized individual case studies or models of maturity that assume stability, rather than age-related change, in adulthood. See, for example, Inge M. Ohammer, "Social Learning Theory as a Framework for the Study of Adult Personality Development," in Baltes and Schaie, *Life-Span Developmental Psychology*, p. 254.

9. See Erik H. Erikson, *Childhood and Society* (New York: Norton, 1950); Erikson, "Identity and the Life Cycle," *Psychological Issues* 1 (1959); and Robert J. Havighurst, *Developmental Tasks and Education*, rev. ed. (New York: David McKay, 1952).

10. Glen H. Elder, Jr., *Children of the Great Depression: Social Change in Life Course Experience* (Chicago: University of Chicago Press, 1974). See also Reuben Hill, *Family Development in Three Generations* (Cambridge, Mass.: Schenkman, 1970).

11. Quoted in "When Age Doesn't Matter," *Newsweek* 96 (August 11, 1980), 74. See also Orville G. Brin, Jr., and Jerome Kagan, *Constancy and Change in Human Development* (Cambridge: Harvard University Press, 1980), and Harvey Peskin and Norman Livson, "Uses of the Past in Adult Psychological Health," in Dorothy Eichorn et al., eds., *Present and Past in Middle Life* (New York: Academic Press, 1981), pp. 154–81.

12. White House Conference on Child Health and Protection (1930), Report of the Committee on Growth and Development, *Growth and Development of the Child, Part IV: Appraisement of the Child* (New York: Century, 1932), pp. 18, 36.

13. Myrna L. Lewis, "The History of Female Sexuality in the United States," in Martha Kirkpatrick, ed., *Women's Sexual Development* (New York and London: Plenum Books, 1980), p. 28.

14. Alfred C. Kinsey, Wardell B. Pomeroy, and Clyde E. Martin, *Sexual Behavior in the Human Male* (Philadelphia: W. B. Saunders, 1948), pp. 218–19.

15. See ibid., p. 172, and Kinsey et al., *Sexual Behavior in the Human Female* (Philadelphia: W. B. Saunders, 1953), pp. 286–87, 298–99.

16. Lester David, "How To Tell a Woman's Age," *Science Digest* 35 (March 1954), 80–82. See also Harvey C. Lehman, " 'Intellectual' versus 'Physical' Peak Performance: The Age Factor," *Scientific Monthly* 61 (August 1945), 127–37.

17. N. J. Berrill, "How Old Are You Really?" *Science Digest* 35 (May 1954), 7–12. See also C. J. Foster, "How Old Are You?" *Ladies Home Journal* 59 (April 1942), 102–3; M. Gumpert, "What Is a Man's Best Age?" *New York Times Magazine* (October 22, 1944), 18ff.; and G. Lawton, "What Do You Mean, Old?" *American Home* 44 (June 1950), 23.

18. William de B. MacNider, "Age, Change, and the Adapted Life," *Science* 99 (May 26, 1944), 118. More recently, of course, experience and research

have demonstrated that it is an oversimplification to point to aging as the key cause of cancer. See James T. Patterson, *The Dread Disease: Cancer and Modern American Culture* (Cambridge: Harvard University Press, 1987), pp. 56–57.

19. A good summary of these changes, taken from longitudinal surveys in Oakland and Berkeley, California, is Leona M. Bayer, Dorothy Whissell-Buechy, and Marjorie P. Honzik, "Health in the Middle Years," in Eichorn et al., *Present and Past in Middle Life*, pp. 55–88.

20. See, for example, Paul C. Glick, "Updating the Life Cycle of the Family," *Journal of Marriage and the Family* 39 (February 1977), 5–13; Marvin B. Sussman, "The Family Life of Old People," in Robert H. Binstock and Ethel Shanas, eds., *Handbook of Aging and the Social Sciences* (New York: Van Nostrand Reinhold, 1976), pp. 218–43; and Howard P. Chudacoff and Tamara K. Hareven, "From Empty Nest to Family Dissolution: Life Course Transitions into Old Age," *Journal of Family History* 4 (Spring 1979), 69–83.

21. Barbara Fried, "The Middle-Age Crisis," *McCalls'* 94 (March 1967), 88–89. See also Gail Sheehy, *Passages: Predictable Crises of Adult Life* (New York: E. P. Dutton, 1974), esp. chaps. 2 and 21.

22. Daniel J. Levinson et al., *The Seasons of a Man's Life* (New York: Knopf, 1978), esp. pp. 34–35; Sheehy, *Passages*, chaps. 2, 22; Don A. Schanche, "What Happens Emotionally and Physically When a Man Reaches 40," *Today's Health* 51 (March 1973), 40–43. Quotation is from "Best Years of Our Lives?" *Newsweek* 71 (February 19, 1968), 88.

23. Lewis M. Terman, *The Measurement of Intelligence* (Boston: Houghton Mifflin, 1916); E. A. Doll, "The Average Mental Age of Adults," *Journal of Applied Psychology* 3 (1919), 317–28; Edward L. Thorndike, "On the Improvement in Intelligence Scores from 14 to 18," *Journal of Educational Psychology* 14 (1923), 513–16.

24. N. E. Jones and H. S. Conrad, "The Growth and Decline of Intelligence: A Study of a Homogeneous Group Between Ages 10 and 60," *Geriatric Psychology Monographs* 13 (1933), 225–98. See also D. Wechsler, *The Measurement of Adult Intelligence* (Baltimore: Williams and Wilkins, 1939).

25. Dorothy N. Eichorn, Jane V. Hunt, and Marjorie P. Honzik, "Experience, Personality, and IQ: Adolescence to Middle Age," in Eichorn et al., *Present and Past in Middle Life*, pp. 89–116.

26. Paul B. Baltes and K. Warner Schaie, "Aging and IQ: The Myth of the Twilight Years," *Psychology Today* 7 (May 1974), 35–40.

27. Ibid., pp. 37–38.

28. Harvey Levenstein, *Revolution at the Table: The Transformation of the American Diet* (New York: Oxford University Press, 1988), p. 162.

29. Bernice L. Neugarten, "Age Groups in American Society and the Rise of the Young Old," *Annals of the American Academy of Political and Social Science* 415 (September 1974), 187–99.

30. Several counteracting forces, of course, have intruded upon these accomplishments and expectations. Since 1920, automobile accidents and the

rise in the incidence of cancer have brought death to all age groups, including those saved by medical advances from formerly fatal diseases. Also, at this writing, the epidemic of Acquired Immune Deficiency Syndrome (AIDS) is threatening age groups from newborns through adulthood, though it remains to be seen whether dire predictions of catastrophic death rates will prove accurate.

31. Jody Gaylin, "The Age Gap Is Narrowing," *Psychology Today* 9 (April 1976), 9.

32. John Modell, Frank Furstenburg, and Theodore Hershberg, "Social Change and Transitions to Adulthood in Historical Perspective," *Journal of Family History* 1 (1976), 7–32; Peter Uhlenberg, "Cohort Variations in Family Life Cycle Experiences of U.S. Females," *Journal of Marriage and the Family* 36 (1974), 284–92; Peter Uhlenberg, "Changing Configurations of the Life Course," in Tamara K. Hareven, ed., *Transitions: The Family and Life Course in Historical Perspective* (New York: Academic Press, 1978), pp. 65–98.

33. Landon Y. Jones, *Great Expectations: America and the Baby Boom Generation* (New York: Random House, 1980), pp. 310–12.

34. Of course, the magazine articles and television programs in question were also a response to women's liberation, careerism (especially the two-career marriage), and general affluence, but these other social trends also could be linked to the huge expansion of higher education and professional training demanded by, and granted to, the baby boom generation.

35. Herbert J. Gans, *The Levittowners: Ways of Life and Politics in a New Suburban Community* (New York: Vintage Books, 1967), p. 22.

36. Gwendolyn Wright, *Building the Dream: A Social History of Housing in America* (Cambridge: MIT Press, 1981), pp. 256–60.

37. Allyson Sherman Grossman, "Women in the Labor Force: The Early Years," *Monthly Labor Review* 98 (November 1975), 3–9.

38. Deborah Pisetzner Klein, "Women in the Labor Force: The Middle Years," *Monthly Labor Review* 98 (November 1975), 10–16.

39. *Statistical Abstract of the United States, 1987* (Washington, D.C.: Government Printing Office, 1986), p. 376.

40. Beverly Johnson McEaddy, "Women in the Labor Force: The Later Years," *Monthly Labor Review* 98 (November 1975), 17–24.

41. A measured approach to these issues can be found in Janice G. Stroud, "Women's Careers: Work, Family, and Personality," in Eichorn et al., *Present and Past in Middle Life*, pp. 356–92.

42. See, for example, Harold L. Wilensky, "Orderly Careers and Social Participation," *American Sociological Review* 26 (June 1961), 521–39; Wilensky, "The Moonlighter: A Product of Relative Deprivation," *Industrial Relations* 3 (October 1963), 102–24; Glen H. Elder, Jr., "Occupational Mobility, Life Patterns, and Personality," *Journal of Health and Social Behavior* 10 (1969), 308–23; and M. L. Kolm and C. Schooler, "Occupational Experience and Psychological Functioning: An Assessment of Reciprocal Effects," *American Sociological Review* 38 (February 1973), 97–118.

43. John A. Clausen, "Men's Occupational Careers in Middle Years," in Eichorn et al., *Present and Past in Middle Life*, pp. 321–55. See also C. Tansky and R. Dubin, "Career Anchorage: Managerial Mobility Aspirations," *American Sociological Review* 30 (September 1965), 725–35.

44. *Statistical Abstract of the United States, 1987*, p. 137.

45. Ibid., pp. 64, 80, 137, 139.

46. Ibid., p. 63. It should be emphasized that these patterns pertain to *married* women. At the same time that age at first birth for married women was rising, rates of teenage pregnancy and illegitimate births also were rising, especially among black women. Thus, I would not claim that the trend was linear and homogeneous. Nevertheless, the general statistics, though they can be deceiving, do mark a change, if only for large numbers of middle-class whites.

47. "How Old Is Old?" *Business Week* (September 1, 1945), 104–6.

48. Reported in *Science* 105 (January 3, 1947), 9.

49. These publications are far too numerous to list here. For a selected list of those published in the 1950s and early 1960s, see National Association of Manufacturers, *Report on Employment of Mature Workers* (New York: National Association of Manufacturers, 1960), pp. 33–36.

50. Recently, historians have engaged in debate over the reasons for the decline in the labor force participation rate of older workers after World War II. Originally, historians, economists, and gerontologists had assumed that low demand—that is, employer decisions not to hire older workers because of their age—explained the decline. But Brian Gratton, in his article, "The Labor Force Participation of Older Men, 1890–1950," *Journal of Social History* 20 (Summer 1987), 689–710, has argued that the explanation lies rather in decrease in supply, caused by voluntary withdrawal from the labor force of older workers whose incomes, through pensions, social security, savings, and the like, enabled them to live comfortably enough without employment.

51. National Council on the Aging, "The Employment Position of Older Workers in the United States: A Collection of Facts," in *Age Discrimination in Employment: Hearings Before the Subcommittee on Labor of the Committee on Labor and Public Welfare, United States Senate* (Washington, D.C.: Government Printing Office, 1967), pp. 162–65.

52. *Age Discrimination in Employment: Hearings*, pp. 119–44, 233–34.

53. The text of this order has been published in the legislative history *The Civil Rights Act of 1964: What It Means to Employers, Businessmen, Unions, Employees, Minority Groups* (Washington, D.C.: BNA Incorporated, 1964), p. 379.

54. *The Older American Worker: Age Discrimination in Employment*, Report of the Secretary of Labor to the Congress under Section 715 of the Civil Rights Act of 1964 (June 1965), p. 5.

55. Ibid., pp. 6–8, 16.

56. Ibid., pp. 21–25.

57. Of the thirty-eight American commercial airlines in 1967, fourteen, in-

cluding TWA, the second largest, and American, the fourth largest, had age ceilings. See *Age Discrimination in Employment: Hearings . . .* , pp. 229–31.

58. Julia E. Stone, "Age Discrimination in Employment Act: A Review of Recent Changes," *Monthly Labor Review* 103 (March 1980), 32–36. The 1978 amendments exempted tenured faculty employed by institutions of higher learning; that is, colleges and universities were allowed to retain mandatory retirement at age sixty-five for five years in order to open up more positions for younger faculty, especially women and minorities, and to save money by replacing high-salaried older employees with lower-salaried younger faculty. The 1986 amendment allowed colleges and universities to retain compulsory retirement of faculty at age seventy until at least the end of 1993.

59. "Constitutional Amendment to Reduce the Voting Age to 18," *Hearings Before Subcommittee No. 1 of the Committee on the Judiciary*, U.S. House of Representatives, October 20, 1943 (Washington, D.C.: Government Printing Office, 1943), p. 4.

60. Ibid., p. 10.

61. "Lowering the Voting Age to 18," *Hearings Before the Subcommittee on Constitutional Amendments of the Committee on the Judiciary*, U.S. Senate, March 10, 1970 (Washington, D.C.: Government Printing Office, 1970), pp. 222–33. A sharp expression of age and generational conflict emerged early in the Senate committee hearings when Senator Marlow Cook of Kentucky voiced apprehension that the proposed amendment would not pass out of the House Judiciary Committee, which New York Representative Emmanuel Celler, then nearly eighty years old, had been chairing. Celler had been frustrating the amendment since Representative Jennings Randolph had first introduced it in 1943. Cook complained, "I think one of these days we should look to the problem that we face in America, and that is that medical science is seeing to it that people are growing older and older and older, and maintaining a major proportion of the voting rights in this country, and I think those of us who represent the middle of the age spectrum . . . find ourselves in need of some help sometimes and I think that help may well come from the political vitality of the 18-, 19-, and 20-year-old voter." See ibid., pp. 13–14.

62. *Statistical Abstract of the United States, 1987*, pp. 14–16.

63. See "The Graying of America," *Newsweek* 89 (February 28, 1977), 50ff.

64. David Hackett Fischer, *Growing Old in America* (New York: Oxford University Press, 1977), pp. 35, 179–81.

65. W. Andrew Achenbaum, *Shades of Gray: Old Age, American Values, and Federal Policies Since 1920* (Boston: Little, Brown, 1983), pp. 50–51.

66. Ibid., p. 69.

67. Ibid., pp. 95–96; Fischer, *Growing Old in America*, p. 187; W. Andrew Achenbaum, *Old Age in the New Land: The American Experience Since 1790* (Baltimore: The Johns Hopkins University Press, 1978), p. 146.

68. Achenbaum, *Shades of Gray*, p. 117.

69. *Statistical Abstract of the United States 1987*, pp. 93, 98. The latter

figure, however, constitutes only about 5 percent of the country's total elderly population.

70. Barbara Isenberg, "Senior Power: Aging in America," *The Nation* 216 (May 14, 1973), 626–28; Frances Fitzgerald, "A Reporter at Large: Sun City Center," *New Yorker* 59 (April 25, 1983), 54–109; "The Old in the Country of the Young," *Time* 96 (August 3, 1970), 49–50.

71. Isenberg, "Senior Power," p. 628.

72. Neugarten, "Age Groups in American Society," pp. 187–99.

## CONCLUSION

1. Desmond Morris, *The Book of Ages* (New York: The Viking Press, 1983).

2. For a discussion of issues pertaining to need and public policy, see Bernice Neugarten, ed., *Age or Need? Public Policies for Older People* (Beverly Hills, Calif.: Sage Publications, 1982).

3. See Martin Kohli, "The World We Forget: A Historical Review of the Life Course," in Victor W. Marshall, ed., *Later Life: The Social Psychology of Aging* (Beverly Hills, Calif.: Sage Publications, 1986), pp. 271–303.

4. See John Modell, Frank F. Furstenberg, Jr., and Theodore Hershberg, "Social Change and Transitions to Adulthood in Historical Perspective," *Journal of Family History* 1 (1976), 7–32, and G. O. Hagestad and Bernice L. Neugarten, "Age and the Life Course," in R. H. Binstock and Ethel Shanas, eds., *Handbook of Aging and the Social Sciences*, 2d ed. (New York: Van Nostrand Reinhold, 1985), pp. 35–61.

5. Kohli, "The World We Forget," p. 288.

6. W. Andrew Achenbaum, *Shades of Gray: Old Age, American Values, and Federal Policies Since 1920* (Boston: Little, Brown, 1983), pp. 148–49.

7. See, for example, Herbert Gans, *Popular Culture and High Culture: An Analysis and Evaluation of Taste* (New York: Basic Books, 1974), p. 45.

8. Paul Hanley Furfey, *The Gang Age: A Study of the Preadolescent Boy and His Recreational Needs* (New York: Macmillan, 1928), p. 139.

9. Much of this discussion is based upon cogent arguments presented in Peter H. Schuck, "The Graying of Civil Rights Law: The Age Discrimination Act of 1975," *Yale Law Journal* 89 (November 1974), 27–93.

10. Glen H. Elder, Jr., *Children of the Great Depression: Social Change in Life Course Experience* (Chicago: University of Chicago Press, 1974).

11. The term *mass longevity* was coined by David W. Plath in *Long Engagements: Maturity in Modern Japan* (Stanford, Calif.: Stanford University Press, 1980), pp. 1–2.

12. Daniel Callahan, *Setting Limits: Medical Goals in an Aging Society* (New York: Simon and Schuster, 1987).

13. *New York Times*, October 14, 1987.

14. See Leonard D. Cain, "Political Factors in the Emerging Legal Age Status of the Elderly," *Annals of the American Academy of Political and Social Science* 415 (September 1974), p. 72.

# INDEX

Achenbaum, W. Andrew, 54, 110, 113, 154
Adams, William Taylor (Oliver Optic), 47
Adler, Felix, 88–89
Administration on Aging, 180
adolescence and adolescents, 45–46, 61, 67, 68, 70–72, 76, 85–86, 92, 98–99, 109, 118–19, 149, 151, 161, 168
advertising, 123–24, 125
advice literature, 20–24, 50–51, 144
age discrimination. *See* discrimination, age
Age Discrimination Act (ADA) of 1975, 180
Age Discrimination in Employment Act (ADEA) of 1967, 175–76, 178, 180
age of consent, 85–86
ageism, 182, 186–87
Alcott, William A., 23–24
American Association for Old Age Security, 113
American Association of Retired Persons (AARP), 179–80, 182
"American Bandstand," 156
American Geriatric Society, 179
*American Magazine*, 118
American Society for the Prevention of Cruelty to Animals (ASPCA), 43–44
Ariès, Philippe, 29
autograph books, 103–4
Ayers, Leonard, 69–70

baby boom, 154, 158, 167–71, 173
Baltes, Paul B., 167
Bancroft, Jessie Hubbell, 74–75, 77, 78
Banner, Lois, 58–59
Barnard, Henry, 32, 34, 35
Bergh, Henry, 43–44
Berlin, Irving, 151, 153
Billard, Charles Michel, 42
Binet, Alfred, 79–80
Binet-Simon Intelligence Test, 80
birthday cards, 132–37

birthdays, 25, 26, 117–18, 126–32, 152
birthrates, 11–12, 55, 93–95, 171–72
Boas, Franz, 79
Bowditch, Henry, 45
Boy Scouts of America, 104
Boys' Brigades, 105
Brown, I. F., 46–47
Bühler, Charlotte, 160–62
Bunker, Frank Forest, 71
bureaucratization, 35–36, 78
Burlend, Rebecca, 25–26
Bushnell, Horace, 27
Butler, Ellis Parker, 123
Butler, Nicholas Murray, 61, 63
Byrd, William, 25

Calahan, Daniel, 188–89
Camp, Walter, 107
Cattell, J. McKeon, 79
Charcot, Jean Martin, 79
child development, 9–10, 41–45, 52–53, 61, 67–72, 73–77, 78–82, 82–85, 87–89, 144, 148, 159–60, 161
childhood: definition of, 9–10, 144; in popular music, 148–50
children: birth order of, 12; status of, 11–13, 43–44
Civil Rights Act of 1964, 175, 180
Clausen, John A., 171
climacteric, 54, 56, 109
Cohen, Wilbur, 116
colleges and universities, 16, 60, 99–102, 167, 171
Comenius, John Amos, 30–31
commercialized leisure, 105–6
Cone, Thomas, 45
Conrad, H. S., 166
Cremin, Lawrence, 15, 16
Curtis, Henry, 76

Danzinger, Sheldon, 189
Day, Charles William, 20
death rates, 11, 13–14, 110, 168
Demos, John, 24

Dewey, John, 66, 82
discrimination, age, 158, 173–78, 180, 186–89
diseases: of childhood, 52–53; of middle age, 166; of old age, 55–58, 168, 181, 188
drinking age, 173, 178
Dunbar-Nelson, Alice, 132

"The Ed Sullivan Show," 156
Eddy, Daniel, 22
Edson, Cyrus, 51
Eggleston, Edward, 40
Elder, Glen, Jr., 163, 187
"elimination," in schools, 67–71
Eliot, Charles W., 60, 61
Emerson, Ralph Waldo, 25
Erikson, Erik, 161
etiquette manuals. See advice literature
Evanson, Richard T., 43
Executive Order 11141 (1964), 175

family, age organization of, 10–14, 93–98, 167–68
Fass, Paula, 102
Fischer, David Hackett, 24, 148, 153–54
Forty Plus clubs, 173
fraternities and sororities, 16, 100–101, 105
Freiberg, Albert, 89
Freud, Sigmund, 161, 164
Furfey, Paul Hanley, 92, 103, 186

Gág, Wanda, 120–22, 130–31, 131–32
Galton, Sir Francis, 79, 160
games and play, 16, 17, 74–77
gangs, 92, 102–3, 186
geriatrics, 114–15, 147
Gerontological Society, 179
Gerry, Elbridge T., 44
Gesell, Arnold, 66
Gray Panthers, 179
Gulick, Luther Halsey, 73–74, 76, 78, 85, 89, 99

Haber, Carole, 54, 56, 57, 110, 112, 113, 154
Hadley, Arthur T., 100
Hall, G. Stanley, 22, 66–69, 71, 73, 75, 76, 78, 80, 85, 88, 92, 109, 160

Hall, Joyce Clyde, 134
Hallmark Cards, Inc., 134–37
"Happy Birthday to You," 117–18
Harper, William Rainey, 68
Harris, William T., 36
Hart, William Bruce, 124
Havighurst, Robert J., 161
Hawes, Joel, 21–22
Hill, David J., 63
Hill, Jessica M., 117
Hill, Mildred J., 117
Hill, Patty Smith, 117
Holt, L. Emmet, 52–53
Hoover, Herbert, 116
hospitals: for children, 43; treatment of older people in, 58

infant schools, 33, 34, 36
Institute on Aging of the National Institutes of Health, 181
intelligence quotient (IQ), 81–82, 160, 166–67

Jacobi, Abraham, 44, 45, 84–85, 89, 114
James, John A., 22
Jefferson, Thomas, 57, 128
Johnson, George Ellsworth, 76–77, 78
Johnson, Lyndon B., 175, 180
Jones, N. E., 166
jukeboxes, 151, 156
Junior Chamber of Commerce, 107
juvenile courts, 84–85, 189

Kelland, Clarence Budington, 125
Kett, Joseph, 16, 37, 71
Kinsey, Alfred C., 164
Klumpp, Theodore G., 173–74
Kohli, Martin, 184

law: age discrimination in employment, 172–76, 188; child labor, 17, 19, 77, 87–91; custody, 82–84; marriage age, 10, 17, 85–86; school attendance, 79, 148; voting, 173, 176–78
Lee, Agnes, 26, 129
Lincoln, Abraham, 128
Lindsey, Benjamin B., 84–85, 108
Lionberger, Isaac, 125
Lockwood, Belva, 63
Lovejoy, Owen, 89

MacFadden, Bernarr, 123
Macleod, David, 46, 71
MacNider, William de, 165
magazines, children's, 47–48
Mann, Horace, 31, 35, 37
marriage: age at, 95–97, 122–23, 168, 169, 171–72; age norms for, 20, 22–23, 50–51, 122–23, 145, 146–47, 171–72
Mather, Increase, 24
Maunsell, Henry, 43
Maxwell, William H., 69
Mead, Margaret, 177
Medicare, 181, 189
medicine: practice of, and old age, 55–59, 110, 114–15, 188–89; practice of before 1850, 31, 41–45. *See also* geriatrics; pediatrics
Meigs, John Forsythe, 43
Malancthon, Philip, 30
Menninger, Flo, 63, 129
mental testing, 66, 78–82, 166–67
Mercier, Charles, 57
middle age, 24, 107–9, 118, 123, 152, 164–66, 169, 170, 173, 176
monitorial system of education, 32, 34, 35
Morris, Desmond, 183
Mott, Frank Luther, 47
music, popular, 138–56

Nascher, I. L., 114–15
National Child Labor Committee (NCLC), 88, 89
National Council of Senior Citizens, 179
National Education Association (NEA), 60, 61, 68
National Retired Teachers Association (NRTA), 179
Neugarten, Bernice, 157, 163
Newcomb, Harvey, 21

Ogburn, William F., 116
old age, 24–25, 53–59, 107–8, 109–16, 118, 119, 124–26, 141–43, 144, 147–48, 151–52, 155, 158, 169–70, 176, 178–82, 187–89
old-age homes, 58, 110–11, 167, 180
Older Americans Act of 1965, 180

Omaha, Nebraska, marriage patterns in, 96–97
organizations: for adults, 106–7; for youths, 16–17, 45–47, 99, 102–3, 104–5

pediatrics, 30, 40–44, 51–53, 148
peer groups, 7, 15, 71, 72, 73–74, 75, 76, 77–78, 91, 92–116, 119, 120, 126, 131, 150, 151, 155–56, 158, 167–68, 186
Pepper, Claude, 188
Pestalozzi, Johann Heinrich, 31–32, 33, 42
Philbrick, John D., 35–36
phonograph, 150, 155, 156
physical development, 23–24, 75–78
physical training, 75–78, 107, 148
Pitkin, Walter, 108–9
Playground Association of America, 76
playgrounds, 76, 78, 148
poverty relief, age restrictions in, 17–18, 189
Prang, Louis, and Co., 133
preadolescence, 67
Preyer, Wilhelm, 66, 160
Providence, Rhode Island, marriage patterns in, 96–97
psychology, theories of development, 23, 56–58, 66–67, 78–82, 109, 158, 159–63
Public School Athletic League (PSAL), 74, 78, 99
Puffer, J. Adams, 103
Puritans, 15, 24, 27

Quetelet, Adolphe, 160

radio, 151, 156
Read, Anne Morrison, 26
Reagan, Ronald, 181
Reed, Anna, 129
religion, 15, 24, 27, 38–40, 68–69
"retardation," in schools, 69–71
retirement and pensions, 19, 55, 111, 112–13, 115–16, 154, 158, 169, 172–73, 174–76, 179, 180–81, 188, 189
retirement communities, 167, 180–81
Robinson, Edgar M., 104
Roosevelt, Franklin D., 115

Ross, E. A., 107
Rousseau, Jean-Jacques, 31
rural communities, 17, 25

Sangster, Margaret, 126
Schaie, K. Warner, 167
scheduling, 49–64, 144, 146–47
schools: elementary, 34–37, 59–62, 68, 72, 98; graded common, 34–38, 144; high, 37, 60–62, 68, 71, 72, 98–99; junior high, 70–71, 98–99, 148
Scott, James Foster, 54–55
Secor, Lella Faye, 131
senescence and senility, 56–58, 109–10
sexual behavior, 86–87, 164
Shakespeare, William, 10, 57
Shattuck, Lemuel, 129
Shearer, William, 62
Simon, Theodore, 79–80
Smith, Alice Weston, 131
Smith, Samuel Harrison, 32–33
Smolensky, Eugene, 189
social security, 115–16, 154, 173, 174, 176, 179
Society for the Prevention of Cruelty to Children (SPCC), 44
Spearman, Charles Edward, 79
Spencer, Anna Garland, 86–87
Spikes, Lottie A., 129–30
sports, 6, 16, 73, 74, 78, 99, 100
Stanford-Binet Intelligence Test, 80–81
Starr, Louis, 52
Stern, William, 80
Stowe, Calvin, 31
Strayer, George Dayton, 70
suburbs, 167, 169
Sunday schools, 38–40, 68–69

Taylor, Frederick W., 39
television, 156, 177
Terman, Lewis M., 66, 80–82, 88, 166

textbooks, school, 37–48
Thomas, William I., 95
Thompson, Warren S., 116
Thoreau, Henry David, 25
Thorndike, E. L., 160
Thrasher, Frederick, 103
time, meanings of, 49–50
Tin Pan Alley, 145, 148, 151, 155, 156
Titcomb, Timothy, 23
Townsend, Dr. Francis, 179
Tucker, Sophie, 109

United States Bureau of the Census, 65, 70

vaudeville, 144–45
Vietnam War, 159, 173, 177
Vincent, John H., 40
Vorse, Mary, 125
voting age, 173, 176–78

Washington, George, 128
Watson, James B., 160
Whelpton, P. K., 116
Willard, Frances, 50, 51
Wise, Daniel, 22
witches, 24
Witmer, Lightner, 70
Woolley, Celia Parker, 59
work and workplace, 15, 18, 77, 106, 111, 169–71, 173–76
Wright, Mabel Osgood, 120, 130
Wundt, Wilhelm Max, 79

Young Men's Christian Association (YMCA), 17, 46–47, 73, 78, 104
Young Women's Christian Association (YWCA), 104, 107

Znaniecki, Florian, 95